RUTHANNE CUNNINGHAM

IT'S NOT JUST A SONG

THE ULTIMATE GUIDE TO WRITING HIT SONGS AND NAVIGATING THE MUSIC INDUSTRY

Dedicated to my two girls, Mommy loves you

CONTENTS

05	Introduction
22	Chapter 1: The 10,000 Hours
26	Chapter 2: Songwriter Speed Dating
48	Chapter 3: Top 10 'Rules' of Hitmaking
76	Chapter 4: Breaking the Rules: 'The Exceptions'
88	[Interlude 1] Songwriter Stories
95	Chapter 5: The Psychology of a Writing Room
118	Chapter 6: The Art of Staying Inspired
131	[Interlude 2] Songwriter Stories
139	Chapter 7: Production
162	[Interlude 3] Producer / Songwriter Stories
172	Chapter 8: Sampling
192	Chapter 9: The Boys' Club
206	[Interlude 4] Songwriter Stories
212	Chapter 10: Bad Deals vs Good Deals
236	Chapter 11: How Do We Get Paid? Music Royalties Explained
247	[Interlude 5] Songwriter Stories
253	Chapter 12: The Best Piece of Advice I Ever Got...
258	Chapter 13: What's Next? 10 Steps to Success
264	Chapter 14: Inspirational Quotes
267	Glossary

RuthAnne at Abbey Road

INTRODUCTION

"I do a lot of music composition, but I need Bono to finish the song, so we complement each other; we don't ever cancel each other out. It's addictive. We shine brighter working together than we ever could on our own, and I think that's why the band is still together, as much as the friendships are sort of the same... meaning, the friendships are real, and they work."

THE EDGE (U2)

Scan this code to listen to the songs featured in the book.

Where do I begin? For starters, this is not an autobiography, although I'm that long-winded I could write a whole book on JUST my story. Instead I'll edit this intro down to just give you a snippet of my journey. Before I get into all the knowledge and wisdom I've learned along the way about being a songwriter and forging a successful career in the music industry, I feel it's important to tell you a bit of my story. I want you to have full context around how I got here and why I am writing this book, and I want you to feel safe in my hands and know that everything I'm talking about is coming from my lived experiences.

There are a lot of books out there that talk about how to write a song, but just like the title says, it really is 'not JUST a song'. Now don't get me wrong, the song is a massive piece, your talent is a massive piece, being a great songwriter is a massive piece, but I've met some of the most talented people who don't know or were never shown how to actually make it in the music industry, how to navigate the business side. Talent isn't always enough… There are so many factors that go into making a successful long-lasting career in music. And there's a lot that needs to align for a song to be a hit.

RuthAnne singing at karaoke aged 7

Where I started

I've been singing and writing songs since I was 7 years old, a proud, wee Irish girl from a very small house in Dublin City suburbs, a working-middle-class background. We didn't have much money, but I never even knew that until I was older; to me I had everything I needed. Our house was full of song, singing, dancing, laughter, imaginative play. My parents played guitar and piano and sang in church every Sunday and music echoed in every room in our house. My dad air-guitaring to Led Zeppelin and Phil Lynott, my mum baking in the kitchen humming along to Garth Brooks. Music was the soundtrack in our house. The great storytellers were always playing – Carole King, Leonard Cohen, James Taylor, Aretha Franklin – and I was hooked on their every word. My mum will tell you that it was on my Christening day as I was put to bed, a classic Irish sing-song began and the whole neighbourhood was singing all night long in my garden, me fast asleep by the window, the music like a lullaby to my ears. My mum is convinced something happened that night, music was pumped into my veins like the air I breathe, and my fate was set. My first words were also sung... I sang the theme tune to *The Snowman* – 'Walking in the Air' – as my dad flew me around in his arms.

A wee Irish girl

I was in church choir from when I was 4 years old. Usually the joining age was 6 or 7 but I would sit in church belting out the songs from the pews, so they had no choice but to let me join early! This is where I learned song structure; we were handed lyric sheets with verse, pre-chorus, and every week there was choir practice and then mass on Sunday. This is where I had my first solo, an exciting day that I don't remember of course but my parents do. I sang 'This little light of mine, I'm gonna let it shine'. I was so tiny I think people clapped just in awe of my size and confidence at that age, and most of all I just loved music and singing. In fact, my parents said I sang everywhere we went. There're plenty of stories of me standing on tables and chairs in our local pub, McDonalds and Burger King, singing at the top of my lungs for anyone who would listen.

RuthAnne singing, aged 7

I also spent many years in a local Irish stage school, The Billie Barry Stage School, and I lived for it! Dancing and singing on theatre stages all around Ireland, it really gave me amazing experiences of performing, auditions, rehearsals, how to be professional, and the training I got there was the most amazing foundation for the music industry I could've possibly had.

Songwriting start

Songwriting followed from 7 years old. I started by re-wording existing songs for my mum and dad's birthdays and Mother's Day, replacing lyrics with simple cuteness: 'I love my mum, you're the best dad', etc. From there I wrote my first song called 'He Lied to Me' which was three lines sung over and over getting louder each time... My mum's first reaction was, 'That's great, but who lied to you?' This was swiftly followed by my first proper full song called, 'Baby I Need You' (*I didn't say it was a good song btw... but a song nonetheless*). It was simple, direct, and I had no idea who I was talking about at 7 years old, but it became a hit around the neighbourhood... as in my local friendship group. We would sing it all day and all night. My parents were never pushy but just nicely encouraging, saying things like, 'That's so good. Well done, can you write another one?' They were always so interested, they listened to every song I wrote from start to finish and always encouraged me to keep writing.

To say I became a professional songwriter at 17 years old always feels weird to me because I had written over 600 songs by the time I was 17. I had been singing since I could talk and recording myself from age 10 with my dad's mic and an old 2-track tape recorder he gave me, singing Mariah Carey riffs over and over until I got them perfect, teaching myself how to harmonise. I'd been playing the piano since I was 12 and started making beats out of loop CDs I got for free in cereal boxes aged 13. By 14 I had formed my own girl band (my four best friends) and by 15 we were in recording studios all over Dublin, trying to make it to the top. So to me, it was just always what I did, professional or not, it was my passion, my obsession, my everything. It was what I was meant to do and there was really nothing else I was good at. Singing and songwriting, that was me and still is.

Technically speaking, I never made a dime from songwriting until I became a professional songwriter at 17 years old. So I've now been twenty years in the music industry professionally, which is WILD!! I feel so old saying that but it's the truth. Am I the biggest songwriter in the world? No, not even close, but am I a successful songwriter? I would say, hell yes! And I would say that proudly because I've worked very hard for every bit of success and forged a long-term career doing what I love. I've also admittedly been in the right place at the right time – by fate or by the choices I made that led me to those places and opportunities. Either way, I've had lucky breaks and I've had to make my own luck and work incredibly hard.

RuthAnne singing, aged 10

I've also nearly quit every year since I started. But I haven't given up yet. I've fought for my spot, I've cried, I've laughed, I've travelled the world. I've been in every type of writing room and writing scenario you can think of, and I've worked with some of the greatest artists and writers and producers of all time. I've met incredible people along the way, gone through best times and hard times, highest of highs of success and lowest of lows of failure. I've been rich, been broker than broke and then rich again. Had hits, had no hits and had hits again. Been traumatised, been fulfilled, made mistakes and learned a lot of lessons.

This music industry is one hell of a ride. Truly, it's a rollercoaster but one that you just keep riding over and over because if you love music as much as I do you just can't help it. The music business may be your biggest love and your biggest heartbreak. Just like a partner who keeps breaking your heart over and over and never values you the way they should, but you keep coming back because it's the making of the art, the music, that has always been the most important thing. It is my true love, and I simply couldn't live without it.

Jacob's Song Contest

It's 2004, I'm 17 years old and I've just won Ireland's biggest songwriting competition – the under 20s 2fm/Jacob's Song Contest – with a song called 'Battleground' that I'd written and produced myself and performed with my girl group Dolce Vita (the name clearly needed work!!!). The late, great Irish broadcaster Gerry Ryan presented us with the award at a venue called Vicar Street in Dublin and we performed the song live in front of a crowd including our families, and it was the best night!! As the songwriter, I won €10,000-worth of Yamaha equipment, which was EVERYTHING!!

And I have my dad to thank as he submitted the demo to the competition without me even knowing, but that was my dad, always looking for every opportunity for me, staying up late printing my demo CD's with the latest picture of the band on the cover, driving me to and from any and every audition, every recording studio session. He and my mum believed in me so much and supported me from the get-go. They knew that I wanted to be in music and despite having no money they really did everything they could with what they had to support my dreams to make this my career. I owe everything I am and everything I achieved to them and their unwavering belief in me.

RuthAnne with her girlband 'Dolce Vita', aged 14

Naively, I'd felt ready to be discovered at 15 years old and wanted to leave school, but my mum wanted me to do my final school exams so that I always had my education to fall back on if need be. So I made music my passion alongside my education, wrote a lot of lyrics during school classes and would even sneak to the music room in school when I should've been studying, to play and sing my songs. Some teachers would even come in to listen to my latest tracks. Everyone knew music was what I would pursue, and my parents, teachers and friends couldn't have been more supportive of my dreams.

From my bedroom to Hollywood

Something I'm going to talk about more as we go is 'preparation meeting opportunity'. My first big break was definitely one of those moments. In a way, I had been preparing for it my whole life up until that point. Even though I was so young when the luck came knocking, I took it with both hands, with no fear, grabbed hold tightly and ran with it.

RuthAnne and Andrew Haas writing in LA

I think back to that day in 2004. I had just flown to LA with an Irish manager and his family the day after sitting my final school exam. It was my first time flying to America and my first time away from my family and friends. I was a very young 17 year old and arrived in Hollywood with all the innocence and confidence in the world. My manager at the time had assured my parents I had all the talent it takes to 'make it' and he would make sure I was well looked after, get me a record deal and develop me as an artist. He had an apartment in west Hollywood and an American business partner and was all set up over there. He also managed two other artist/writer/producers, Danny and Mark, who would go on to become The Script. At the time they were in LA writing and producing, and they spent a lot of time developing me as well, which I'm very grateful for. I was so young, naive and sheltered and they really were my first co-writing sessions. I'd never written with anyone before, so co-writing was brand new to me. I learned so much from them about co-writing and they were like mentors.

The big break

My manager had worked with legendary songwriter Billy Steinberg, who had written songs like 'True Colours' and 'Like a Virgin' among tonnes of other big worldwide hits. As we walked into his house, a grand piano stood right in front of me with Grammy Awards on top of it that he had won. I knew this moment was important. I sat and played a new song I'd written, and he loved it and invited me to come back to write with him and his co-writer

Josh Alexander to write some songs for my artist project. I was so excited to have writers at his level writing with me for my album. It was all very surreal.

Billy Steinberg, RuthAnne and Josh Alexander at the ASCAP Pop Awards 2007

I didn't know that walking into the studio that day with Billy and Josh would give me the biggest break of my career and change my life forever, but it did. That day we wrote two songs. One was called 'Kinky' and the other was called 'Too Little Too Late' – which was really Josh's story to his ex. As I recorded them both, there was something about 'Too Little Too Late' that just instantly made me think of a young American artist called JoJo. She'd had a hit called 'Get Out (Leave)' and it felt like 'Too Little Too Late' was the sequel to that song. I didn't say that on the day but as I was singing it, I was thinking of her and channelling her in a way, I think.

Now, the interesting part of this story is that her A&R eventually heard it and it became her song. It didn't get cut by JoJo until about a year later, and it took two years from when we wrote it to when it was released. So, I was 19 years old when it came out. And from then everything just went from zero to 100. It became a huge, huge global hit. I remember hearing it on the radio for the first time in a yellow cab in New York City. It was such a special moment and, honestly, I've heard it on the radio in so many countries and the feeling never gets old. I won my first ASCAP Songwriters Pop Award for that song, and I have so much gratitude for Billy and Josh giving me that opportunity, having me in the room with them that day and giving a young songwriter a chance and a big, big first break.

RuthAnne with Jojo and The Stereotypes

The College of Professional Songwriting

I had somehow gotten in the door in a big way with a big hit. Every major publisher wanted to sign me off the back of the success of 'Too Little Too Late' and I signed my first publishing deal at 19 years old. I received more money than I knew what to do with, and I spent the next few years writing all over the world. I call these years 'The College of Professional Songwriting' because that is what it felt like. The truth is, I had no clue what I was doing. I was thrust into a very adult world of songwriting, and I didn't know how it worked at all, — the etiquette, or how to navigate the music world. I was constantly in rooms with new people every day all around the world from London, Miami, New York, Florida, Nashville, Oslo, Copenhagen, LA, and I often travelled alone so it was quite a lonely time. I missed my friends and family a lot, and in LA I couldn't drive or drink as I was under 21, so socially it was lonely too.

I was enjoying the writing sessions, but I always found it strange being put in a room to write for an artist who wasn't actually there. I had grown up thinking artists wrote their own music, so to learn that this wasn't always the case was new to me. I was also still finding my feet collaborating and co-writing and learning so many different processes of writing and different dynamics of rooms, but because I'd been part of this massive hit I felt a lot of pressure and expectation to do it again. I definitely felt a lot of imposter syndrome and anxiety around that time.

However, at the same time I was so grateful to be in these huge rooms with big producers and writers and I learned so, so, so, so much during those years. I gained a huge amount of experience and took something from each writing session I was in. Over those years I had lots of songs released with more artists and some were hits in different countries, but nothing was quite as big as the JoJo song. I learned very quickly that this kind of global success with a song wouldn't happen every day.

You're only as good as your last hit

What a saying… It haunted me from the moment I had my first hit at 19. Was it luck? Was it a fluke? Could I have another global hit? Did I know what the feck I was doing? No, not a clue. I was just going into rooms and writing songs and doing the absolute best I could. As I look back now, I know those years after the JoJo hit were the years of learning the ropes of the music industry whilst also getting more experienced and more skilled at the craft of songwriting, especially co-writing. I decided instead of just going back and forth to LA it was time to move there. I lived there from 2012 for eight years, and it was that decision that led to the next global hits I would have – 'Work Bitch' with Britney Spears, 'In the Name of Love' with Martin Garrix/Bebe Rexha and 'Slow Hands' with Niall Horan.

These stand-out songs are among many others that were released during the time I lived in LA and I sometimes forget just how massive they were in their own way. 'In the Name of Love' has over a billion streams and is triple platinum; 'Slow Hands' reached No. 1 on the USA Pop Airplay chart, the Dance chart and the Hot AC chart and is also triple platinum. I don't often think of these songs and the stats because I'm always moving forward and onto the next song, but in writing them down for this book it really hits me that I'm just a middle-class girl from a small town in Ireland. How did I end up here? Songs I've co-written have amassed over 11 billion streams… gold and platinum all over the world. It's all a bit insane!

When I think of me aged 7, writing my first song, to where I've come it's pretty unbelievable and I realise I'm giving you a very concise version here of a much longer story. It's not been all hits, hits, hits – it was a lot of hard work, a lot of determination, a lot of rejection, a lot of 'no's, and years in between of countless writing sessions… Then a lot of luck, stars aligning and being in the right place at the right time, fighting to be in rooms, writing 99% of some songs, writing 5 to 10% of others, contributing and giving my absolute best in every room I was in.

'Work Bitch'

I'll never forget the phone call I got sitting in my apartment in Beverly Hills. I had written a song called 'Fingers to the Sky' with my friend Anthony a few months before and out of the blue he called me and said, 'Hey, remember that song we wrote a few months ago? So I'm working with Will.I.AM and I put the parts we wrote into this song he's working on, and I wanted to play you it.' He said, 'Guess who's singing it?' He played it down the phone and immediately I screamed, 'Is that Britney Spears?!?' and he said in her iconic turn of phrase, 'It's Britney, bitch!!! This is her comeback song and it's coming out in four days!' I screamed and ran around the apartment. I could not believe it! *The* Britney Spears, who I had been a fan of since I was 13 years old. Her 'I'm a Slave 4 U' choreography is still my party piece.

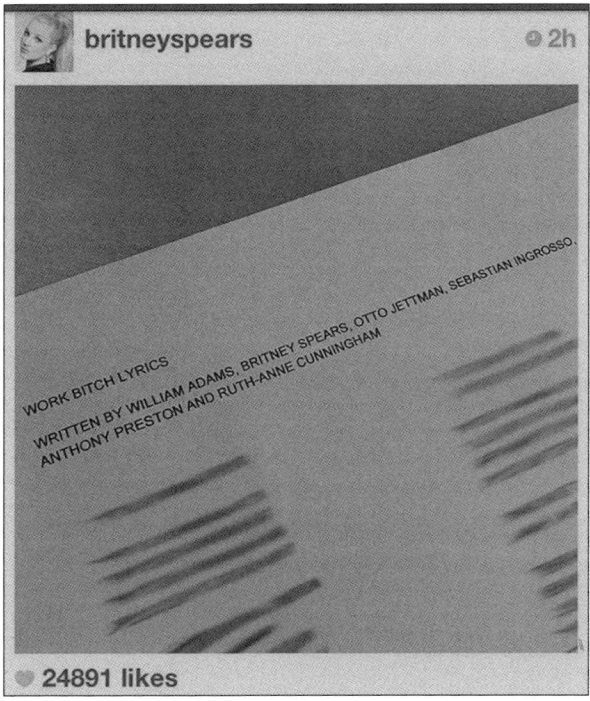

The Britney Spears tweet

Two days later she tweeted a snippet of 'Work Bitch' lyrics and there was my name... and my phone started blowing up. 'Britney Spears has just tweeted your name', 'Britney Spears knows your name?' 'Britney Spears is releasing a song you wrote on?' The song came out two days later and went to No. 1 all over the world. It became a big cultural moment, and I knew the song had really made it when we got it synced in *South Park* – they changed the lyrics to, 'you better work out slut' and it was hilarious. I still get memes of the song, and in gym classes I go to the song blasts and I just chuckle to myself that I'm a part of this track that is used in workout classes worldwide. I remember taking my friends to her Las Vegas residency show and everywhere was 'Work Bitch' merch, hats, bags (of course I bought some and of course when my friends told the shop that I co-wrote the song they didn't believe it, lol). Britney opened the show with the song, and it was just the best feeling, looking around seeing people singing along and jumping up and down: a real 'pinch me' moment. It still feels surreal being a teeny tiny part of a pop princess's music history.

Dan Wilson, RuthAnne and John Legend

Grammy nominated? Twice?

It was summer in LA and my management at the time also managed John Legend, and he was making a Christmas album. I remember voice-noting my best friend Jenni 'Ordinary People' on piano non-stop as a teen (and I'm just a girl from Dublin, like, how is this happening?!) but of course when I got there, I put my professional songwriting hat on and tried to keep the fan girl inside me from jumping out. He was sitting at the piano, and we only had a few hours before he had to go. He was lovely, a real gent. He had a melody idea, and I had a title idea, 'There's No Place Like Home' inspired by *The Wizard of Oz*... but with 'at Christmas Time' to add the festive spirit for his Christmas album.

Minutes later, we're sitting together by the piano singing back and forth and sometimes I felt like I was at my own personal John Legend concert. His voice is smooth like butter and the song felt like it was writing itself. He went into the booth, sang it down and it made it onto the album *A Legendary Christmas*, produced by Raphael Sadiq, another massive inspiration of mine. The album went on to be nominated for Best Traditional Pop Album at the 2020 Grammy Awards. We didn't win, but to be a part of a Grammy-nominated album was a dream come true.

It happened once again in 2022, this time with the iconic Diana Ross. Grammy nominations came knocking for a song I co-wrote at an all-female writing camp, 'SheWrites', with

Autumn Rowe, Violet Skies and Charlie McClean called 'I Still Believe' on her album *Thank You* – nominated in the same category. Again, we didn't win, but maybe by the time this book comes out I'll have won a Grammy. It's still on my goal list and what I've learned is it's never too late. I'll be writing songs until I'm old and grey, so I'll keep taking my shot.

To be a Grammy-nominated songwriter still blows my mind. And I don't say these things to big myself up but more to give you some background into my career so you can know I'm speaking to you as someone who is still a creative working every day in the industry. I'm 38 now and still here, still writing, still singing, still navigating this crazy business the best I can. Still in love with making music.

Every creative is an artist

Someone once said to me, 'Songwriters are the artist's ugly best friend, you know the way in movies you have the lead girl, the star and her ugly best friend, that's what songwriters are and that's how they're also treated.' It really stuck with me. I've been a performer, a singer for my whole life, and I would always describe myself as a songwriter and an artist. The industry has always told me, 'You are JUST a songwriter.' But every songwriter I've ever met is an artist. It's just in what capacity. Some songwriters don't like performing or being front and centre, some are born performers, whilst some songwriters thrive behind the scenes, yet they are still artists.

Some songwriters I meet are absolute superstars, stars that no one has ever heard of but have all the same traits as the artists we know and love and have more talent than anyone will ever really know or get to see on the world stages. I am a songwriter and an artist, and, for me, one can't thrive without the other. Creative fulfilment is so important to me and it's how I get the best out of myself. Singing is my safe place and it's not about who is listening. I don't think anyone should get to decide what you are or are not – you and only you can decide that.

Someone in the industry once looked at me and said, 'Here's the problem, you're not pretty enough to be a popstar like J.Lo or Beyoncé and you're not fat enough or quirky enough looking to be a rockstar like Beth Ditto or Amy Winehouse, you're cute but cute doesn't sell, sure you're so talented but talent isn't enough.' Those words broke my heart into pieces. Crazy how words can be so powerful and so damaging. That conversation held me back from fully pursuing being an artist for a long time, but then in 2017 I thought to myself, why would I let anyone tell me what I am or who I am or put a ceiling on what I can do or achieve? So I thought feck it, I'm gonna make an album, an album I wanna make. Sure, I'm not Adele but that doesn't make me any less of an artist than her.

The truth is I've achieved things as an artist that I never thought I would: I toured with one of my idols, Alanis Morrisette, with Hozier and X-Ambassadors, played festivals all over the world, played my own headline shows and have had so many amazing syncs of my artists' songs that have led to people discovering my music. I've had a huge impact on people's lives and soundtracks to their moments and that's what art should do. I've never been in this for fame, because to me fame is fleeting. I love to sing; I'll sing for two people in a pub or thousands of people at a festival. Music is how I connect. It's a connection that has brought so much light and love to my life. It's my gift. Everyone has gifts and once you find yours it becomes your purpose, your contribution, your power. Music is also my therapy, it's how I process things, accept things and let things go. I write a song about it and it's healing to me.

I've always said if you want money and fame, those are not the right reasons to pursue a career in music. It has to be your love of it first because that is what will carry you through. If it's purely money and fame you're after, this may not be the book for you. But keep reading – it might just give you a different perspective that will unlock something creative inside of you and be the key or missing link you were looking for.

RuthAnne & X-Ambassadors

A perfect storm

Back in the day, if a record label thought a song was a hit, more often than not that song would be successful. There were considerably fewer songs being released back then. Currently, there are over 100,000 songs released every day. Think about that number... that's 700,000 songs a week. Which is 2.8 million songs every month! These days more than ever it is not JUST the song that makes a hit.

One Republic's frontman and Grammy-winning hit songwriter/producer Ryan Tedder calls it 'the perfect storm' and Grammy-winning songwriter/producer Julian Bunetta calls it 'unlocking the five-point combination code of the perfect timing, the right artist, the momentum that artist is having, if the song speaks to the culture at the time, all of that plus the stars aligning. Would 'Thriller' have been a hit if Michael Jackson didn't sing it and have that famous music video with the iconic dance alongside it?'

Songs need that perfect storm in order to have a huge global impact. The song is still of course the most important piece of the puzzle, it still has to be world class, but it's also about what is built around it. Songwriters today need to be smarter and more strategic with how they spend their time and also accept that there are a lot of things not in their control.

Some things will be left completely up to chance, like someone unexpectedly hearing your song from walking past the door of a meeting that they're not even in and popping their head round and saying, 'I want that song for my artist.' This is how Avicii's manager heard my song 'All You Need Is Love', which he then took to Avicii (and this is how I ended up with a song with Avicii which I co-wrote and sang). Or the session you were meant to have that day gets cancelled, leading you into a different room which leads you to writing a song that will go on to be a hit… My point is that whilst there are a lot of things in the music business that you can't control, the one thing you can be in control of is making the best song possible wherever and whenever you write.

The house always wins… but you can learn to play the game

It's important to acknowledge that this is the music business, and in a lot of ways it is a game. As ever, those who know how to play the game the best usually win the best! Sometimes, as a creative you can feel as though you are playing the lottery, gambling in Vegas, and as the saying goes, 'the house always wins' and in the music business the house really does always win. BUT the creatives who not only can write the best songs but know how to play their cards right and play the game well can win alongside the house. If you can't beat 'em join 'em, right? It's not for the faint-hearted. You've got to have thick skin; be ready to hear a lot of no's among fewer yes's and be ready to go on the rollercoaster of a lifetime, and when the business gets you down, channel all your frustrations into the music.

At all times make good art. Good, right? So good I have 'Make Good Art' tattooed on me, and it's my motto at all times.

Being a professional songwriter

I've been in every type of writing session you can think of. Thousands of sessions, thousands of collaborations, and I have learned so much from each and every one. I've watched the very best in action, been mentored, been inspired, been anxious, been blown away by talent in the room, been a part of the most magical writing rooms and the hardest writing rooms. Every session has helped me get better at the craft of songwriting.

NOTE TO SELF

Being a professional songwriter means that no day is ever the same. Each day brings something new. It's the unknown; the career path is never stable, the highs are addictive, and the lows are more often than not. But the music and the love of creating keeps you in the game and in this game, you only get what you give.

RuthAnne performing on Jimmy Kimmel

Why I'm writing this book

I'm writing the book I wish I'd had. I knew how to write a song, but I had no idea what being a day in, day out professional songwriter/creative entailed. And I always wonder if I'd had more of an insight going in would I have been more successful? I was very young and naive coming into this industry. There was just so much that I knew absolutely nothing about. I really had to experience and live it to learn, and I guess I want to spread the word on what I've learned to help other creatives.

There is nothing without the song. Songwriters are the foundation upon which the entire music industry is built. Without songwriters, there is just silence. Songwriters are the foundation. Producers are the backbone. Producers bring the songs to life – without producers there would be no music. Artists are the messenger, the vehicle the song is channelled through. Without artists to deliver these messages the songs stay on hard drives, never heard by the world. Each of these roles are vital to the music industry and whichever role you are, or strive to be, having knowledge and insight in your back pocket to go along with you on your creative journey will be so valuable.

There is so much more to being successful in this industry than talent alone and this is a book to help creatives navigate this crazy music industry world, to get the best out of themselves and write the best songs possible. I want to help you find the best teams, understand how the industry works and be able to forge long-standing careers in music.

I interviewed a bunch of very talented and successful songwriters/producers and artists for this book, and I've also included quotes from some other songwriter/producers as I want you to hear not only my perspective but also hear from the best in the business. You'll hear their stories, their wisdom, insights and journey and I hope it will inspire creatives out there, because we need you!

With all that said… Here's everything and anything I've learned along the way: all the secrets, all the tips of the trade; how to write hits and navigate the music industry, forging a long-lasting career in music.

CHAPTER 1

THE 10,000 HOURS

"When you switch on the dirty tap, dirty brown water is going to flow out for a substantial amount of time, then clean water will start to flow out, and now and again you might still get a bit of dirty water, but it will always go clean. When I started writing I got the bad songs out of me, and in the beginning you will write a lot of bad songs. My songs were terrible, my raps were awful, but the more and more you write and the more you experience, the songs get better and better and then you'll be on a streak. And now and again you'll write a bad song, but then you've got that song out of you and you can move on to more good songs."

ED SHEERAN

"Anyone who wants to be a songwriter should listen to as much folk music as they can, study the form and structure of stuff that has been around for 100 years."

BOB DYLAN

The '10,000 hours' rule is a concept that an author called Malcom Gladwell wrote about first in his 2008 book, *Outliers, the Story of Success* (a great book, by the way). Throughout the book he consistently refers to the '10,000 hours' rule, which is that the key to achieving true expertise in any skill is simply a matter of practising, in the correct way, for at least 10,000 hours and then you can be successful at it. He talks about how this concept helped The Beatles become household names due to the vast amount of shows they performed live between 1960–1964 (over 1,200 gigs), so they basically accumulated more than 10,000 hours by gigging non-stop.

Let's not get too focused on the exact number of hours, but more the principal of what this concept is saying. Practise, practise, practise, put the work in or, as the New Radicals song says, 'You only get what you give'. The first piece of advice I always give aspiring new songwriters is to write a song every day. Hone the skill and craft of songwriting.

> *I know everyone talks about the 10,000 hours thing, but I think that's kind of real. I think regardless of how you land in this industry, whether you start literally from the bottom or you come in and get signed straight away you still have to do those 10,000 hours one way or another.* **Plested**

Throughout my career I've lived by this motto:

Preparation + Opportunity = Success

The more practice you do of your skill, the more prepared you are for when that lucky door of opportunity comes knocking, and a lot of the time in music luck and opportunity have a big part to play.

In my own journey I had already written about 600 songs between the ages of 7 and 17 years old. Put that on top of writing hundreds of songs a year since then as a professional songwriter means I have definitely completed the 10,000 hours and more in my time. I really do agree with this concept when it comes to creating music – being a songwriter, a producer, or a singer. I believe with songwriting in particular that it's a muscle that needs to be worked out, practised and dedicated and committed to, to really hone the skill and craft.

Sometimes even things from your childhood are all a part of honing your skills and you might not have known it at the time. Piano lessons, messing around with a mic and a keyboard, voice lessons, teaching yourself an instrument by ear. Downloading free loops and playing around with them. Every little moment like that counts. Hit songwriter Dan Wilson recalls being in the car with his mum and brother singing:

> *Our mom would teach us harmony parts in the car and then we'd try to sing in harmony. I had been also taking piano lessons – my piano teacher taught me the circle of fifths and key signatures and the relationships between the major and the relative minor – and that was really, really priming for songwriting. Then our parents gave us a guitar to share. The first thing we did with this guitar was when we were about 11 or 13. My brother's idea was 'I'll*

write a song first and when I'm done you'll write a song.' I loved his song and I really was bummed about my song cos I could tell it wasn't as good. My brother and I got accustomed to writing songs together, teaching each other how to do it, reverse engineering Beatles songs.
Dan Wilson

Being a student of song

Part of the 10,000 hours is not only writing songs but truly becoming a student of song. Having a vast knowledge of songs and music is all part of perfecting your own skills. And this really helps keep your creative flow going. Deconstructing songs from the ground up, analysing every part of them, from the melodies to the lyrics to the production, every beat, every string line, every element of song. I've studied songs ever since I can remember because I truly believe it helps with your own craft of songwriting.

I think there are different parts of 10,000 hours. There's the actual craft, the niche craft of being a songwriter or being a mixer, but then there's the general [craft]. There's almost like a pre-10,000 hours that has to happen where your brain is paying attention to the nuances of the thing when you're a child growing up. You know, kids that play basketball and go into the NBA, they don't say, 'What's this sport? I wanna go play this sport that I've never watched or never paid attention to.' That doesn't happen. They've been watching and studying it from afar before they ever get on the court. So it's like a precursor to the 10,000 hours, when there's no intention behind it but you're writing lyrics or writing poetry or learning the guitar. Then I think the 10,000 hours starts when you make a commitment to being great at this thing with more of an adult brain.

But the hard 10,000 hours is when you're competing against people. You could play guitar from the time you're 10 years old to the time you're 40 years old and have so many hours, but that doesn't mean that they are constructive hours with intention and focus. I think that 10,000 hours means with intention and focus and purpose. In high school I was playing drums, kind of making beats, kind of being in a rock band. It wasn't until I got my first publishing deal at 19 years old that the 10,000 hours really started.

I think it's learning the craft of what it means to be a songwriter – how to write a song structure, rhyme scheme, production, what it means to be a producer – and my first successes didn't really come till I was 29, 30 years old, so that's ten years of those hours.
Julian Bunetta

The songwriting muscle

When I was a teenager, 12 to 15 years old, I was writing almost every day, even if they weren't full songs, verse/choruses, etc. I was so obsessed with songwriting, and even though none of those songs ever saw the light of day, other than my parents replaying them over and over with pride, probably wondering what they were about (TV shows I was watching mainly inspired my teenage catalogue and general teen angst), it was what I did without anyone asking me to or expecting me to, no pressure, no expectation. I almost couldn't help it.

I had a little 4-track recorder that I would do the drum track on, then I'd do the bass, then I'd do the guitar. I just loved creating, so that was obviously a big part of my journey. And then when I moved to LA, I met a great crew who had sort of already established themselves a bit in the industry, and I started working with them. In this business, you can't do it alone – you need mentors, and you need to learn and put in those 10,000 hours. **John Ryan**

As I got older and started writing professionally and got published, I was doing a lot of sessions all around the world, co-writing in many rooms, so in those earlier years I was constantly working-out what I call the 'songwriting muscle'. I also had spurts where I would write for myself every day; 'song diaries' is what I called it. Some were more finished than others, but it brought me back to writing just for myself. Sometimes, after collaborating, you need a burst of just you. Often these spurts really helped me creatively to get out whatever was inside me that doesn't always get the chance to come out when you're in rooms full of writers.

Just like an athlete who trains the muscles in their body to run faster or jump higher, or a vocalist who trains their vocal cords to sing higher, hold notes longer, I believe the songwriting muscle can be trained. Of course it's creative and it's always going to be creative, but I believe the more you write songs in the beginning the better you get at writing songs long-term. Once you've worked that songwriting muscle and know what gets the best out of you as a writer, the more it can become quality over quantity, whether you're at home in your bedroom writing by yourself or collaborating with other people.

For the few songs I've had released that were big songs, there are thousands of songs that have never seen the light of day. I was known as the guy who came to New York and LA and just outworked everybody. So it's hard work. It doesn't just happen quickly. You have to put in the work. **Toby Gad**

I think for new writers, like in this day and age, just be good at everything. Like try your hardest. There's no excuse for you to not be playing an instrument. There's no excuse for you to not be recording your own vocals. Especially because it's so difficult to get in the rooms with people at the beginning. So we have this luxury now of the internet so there's literally constant inspiration and free guitar/piano lessons. So work hard and be a beast on guitar or be a beast at singing and/or be a beast at cutting vocals and make your own songs 100 percenters so that you're ready. And it will be weird and hard and it'll take a minute to adapt to a songwriting room, but you can't deny skill. And skill doesn't happen overnight. Like, you know, it takes time. It's a muscle that you need to work out. **Ali Tamposi**

CHAPTER 2

SONGWRITER SPEED DATING

"When you first start out, people think this is super easy and you find your crew super quick. But you've really got to go through songwriter boot camp to find your people."

JULIA MICHAELS

"Obviously writing with John [Lennon] was the ultimate collaboration. I think we were both very lucky to find each other, because we played perfectly off each other... I think we wrote just short of 300 songs together. And I look back on it now in some kind of wonder, because we never had a dry session. Every time we got together and sat down we would always come up with a song."

PAUL McCARTNEY

FIND YOUR TEAMS

One of the most important things in your life as a songwriter is finding your teams in a process I like to call 'Songwriter Speed Dating'. Every writer goes through this in their career. It's all about getting out there and exploring different writing dynamics and scenarios and finding that magic connection. The Bernie Taupin to your Elton John. And often, just like in their case, you'll stumble upon your greatest collaborator by chance and/or fate. If you don't put yourself out there, you'll be missing a vital step.

Bernie and Elton were both trying to make it in the music industry. Bernie had submitted song lyrics to a publisher and Elton met with this said publisher, played him some songs and that publisher handed him Bernie's lyrics and said, 'Try write to these.' Both were unsigned and both unpublished, so this moment was life-changing. Elton went home and the first lyric of Bernie's he put the music/melody to was 'Your Song'. Imagine that!! This started the collaboration of a lifetime that would last the test of time.

Of course it won't happen with everyone like that. Just like with any relationship you must kiss a few frogs to meet your prince, or in music terms you must have written some bad songs to get the great songs. Doing these rounds of writing with new and different people is so important to learn what you like or don't like; what works for you and what doesn't work for you. Through this process you'll find the people you write the best songs with and the teams of writers/producers you want to continue writing with.

NOTE TO SELF

Put yourself out there. Writing by yourself in your room with countless songs on your laptop that no one hears is not going to help you find your best collaborators.

Get out into the world and collaborate, I promise it'll make you a better writer.

What is the magic chemistry?

Just like with any friendship or relationship, it's that magic chemistry, that connection, that lightening in a bottle that you can't quite describe... It's meeting a writer/producer for the first time and just instantly connecting on a level where creating feels effortless and easy and even when/if you stumble into the mud you know how to get the best out of each other in all scenarios. It's the yin and yang, the salt to the pepper, the fish to the sea.

This can be a creative who is the total opposite to you in a lot of ways but is the perfect other half to your songwriting/production. The strengths to your creative weaknesses and vice versa. When you write together it's like writing with a friend. You can be honest with each other, the ego is out the door and you're both serving the song and know when the song has been served to its fullest. It's important to know when you have found this as you won't find it every day, so hold on to these collaborators.

Keep writing with your best teams

Now, even when you do find these magic connections that doesn't mean you'll write a hit song every day. But that's why it's important to keep writing together. The more you have a special music connection/collaboration the more likely you are to get a great song. Even on the days when you don't, you at least know you'll have a good day, or if you're having a bad day these collaborators are people who will help you through or they'll take a breather with you and meet you where you are. You may also find throughout your career you build a few writing teams or lots that you work well with.

I can't stress enough how important these music relationships are to your career and your soul as a songwriter. Keep working with these collaborators and watch the great songs come.

Where to find collaborators

In today's world, there are so many ways you can find potential collaborators. Social media, for all my gripes with it, can really be an amazing way to connect with other writers, producers and artists. Now I'm not saying if you message Adele or Diplo that they'll even see it or respond, but what have you got to lose? Take your shot and you never know.

I'm also talking more about writers and producers who are up and coming like you might be. People who are at the same level can be great to get in with because then you can rise up to the top together or learn something from each other. Seek out open mic nights, industry events or workshops. Take every opportunity to network and be around other creative people. You just never know who you will meet that could lead to the collaboration you've been waiting for.

Some collaborators won't end up being the one, but they could lead you to the one, so stay open-minded and try people out. Don't ever be afraid to reach out or upload some of your music online, because you never know who's looking or listening. And as Lady Gaga once famously said, 'There can be 100 people in a room and all you need is one person to believe in you.'

NOTE TO SELF

You don't need 100 collaborators, you only need one, and that one can lead to great songs and more collaborators and more opportunities.

THE QUALITIES OF A GOOD COLLABORATOR

Chemistry ★ The chemistry between collaborators is such a huge important thing. It's also something that you can't predict beforehand, and you can't force. It's something that just happens when you get in a room together.

I think the chemistry of the way you communicate back and forth in a room when you're not writing is important. All of the people I've had success with I've been able to hang out with all day and laugh and have a lot of fun and then joy emerges from there because you start talking to each other truthfully and you're disarmed and someone says something that resonates that's really truthful, and you're, like 'wow that just hit me hard let's write about that.' So I found that my best collaborative people are the ones that like to hang out and we're actually friends. **Julian Bunetta**

Makes you feel comfortable ★ I always say that the people I write the best music with are the people who I feel the most comfortable with. Comfortability leads to confidence, where you feel you can say silly ideas – whacky, quirky thoughts that could actually be a hit idea. The people who make you feel comfortable and confident in your creativity and where you feel free to explore your creativity to the fullest is so important.

Being around people who can laugh at themselves and not take themselves too seriously, and also being able to say if an idea is shit and we can laugh about it. **Kamille**

A great collaborator makes the room feel safe and brings out the best in everyone. **Steph Jones**

Being creatively flexible ★ There are only so many times creatives can hear the word 'NO' without shutting down completely. A good collaborator is open and willing to try. My favourite phrase is 'let's try it'. Even if I think it's not gonna work, sometimes I'm pleasantly surprised. I'm able to admit how wrong I was and that it does in fact work and works so well it stays in the song. Or, in the trying sometimes you hear it back and you all know in the room it isn't working, but often the trying really helps everyone feel heard and listened to which makes for good and productive collaboration.

My favourite collaborators are equal parts open-minded and opinionated, love to tell honest stories, and aren't afraid to have bad ideas. If everyone in the room is afraid to say something stupid, nothing will ever get written, and in my personal experience, I have to say so many wrong lyrics to find the right ones, so I love writers who just go for it. **Amy Allen**

Emotional intelligence, adaptability, openness, having a strong point of view without ego, and genuinely just loving music! **Steph Jones**

A good listener ★ Sometimes my favourite collaborators are just the best listeners. They are listening to everything, taking it all in and jumping on what they hear that's great.

Also, knowing just when to step back and listen and not jump in. It's such a necessary skill for a creative to have. Listen and you'll hear the magic.

The ability to listen is really important because ultimately it should just be the best idea wins. **Ilsey Juber**

Timing is so important during a writing session, like knowing when to come in with your idea and knowing when to not say your idea. Say there's two writers working on a verse thing and I have another idea. I'm gonna wait and let them work out their verse and then, in like an hour once the dust settles, I'll say, 'Hey, what if that verse was a quarter note to the left. I was hearing it on a different downbeat.' I won't be like, 'No, I hear it differently' straight away because you have to let ideas unfold before you start editing them. The wrong timing can kill the room. **John Ryan**

Complements your strengths and weaknesses ★ I always say a lot of the best collaborators are opposites — just like in relationships, opposites attract. For me personally, I'm not the fastest or best with chords, so I love working with collaborators who are amazing musicians. Sometimes I can hear the chords and direct them to it, or they just hear what I'm singing and play exactly what's in my head. Some days you'll be in a session where someone is on fire with lyrics and you'll be on fire with melody and that's why it works, or vice versa. If there are too many people in the room doing the same thing it can be harder to get on the same page and you can creatively clash. Find the collaborators who can fill the gaps in your creative brain that day and it'll be a creative match made in heaven.

My favourite spot is when I've got a brilliant musician/producer and they can play any chord in that scenario. That's when it's just pure joy. **Amy Wadge**

I love it when I find a wordsmith that's fast at writing lyrics cos they're channelling just like me. It's like a fast really satisfying game of tennis. **Lauren Christy**

Easy to work with ★ I personally love collaborators who are easy to work with — the process is always fun, enjoyable and a good time is had by all, no matter the outcome. The less stress the more success.

I would say what's most comfortable for me is getting to the session and talking for a long time and getting inspired just from the conversation, asking people what's going on with them and remembering things that sound like lyrics or song ideas. It's very much about connecting with people, and whether or not we get a song from there I still feel like the day was a success to me. It's almost more important to me that everyone in the room feels good and comfortable. I would rather everyone leave the session without a song but being like 'I loved spending time with Emily.' That's the number one priority, because if we have that, then they'll wanna work with me again and we'll get the song at some point. **Emily Warren**

Encouraging ★ I think every creative will agree that encouragement in a session is so vital. Supporting each other's flow and getting in the zone with each other and following the vibe can really make a difference.

> *Believing in an idea is really important. I get inspired if someone has an idea for a song and their excitement and belief inspires me to say, 'Let's explore that.' Because maybe there's something under that hood that I didn't see or didn't understand, and then it gets the motor going and I get to do what I do. All I need is one little spark and then I go, go, go.* **John Ryan**

Sharing the same goal and vision ★ It's important that creatively everyone is on the same page in a writing session, so there's not one person writing a ballad and another thinking it's an 80s upbeat pop song. Understanding the vision and goal for the song you're collaborating on is important and being willing to sometimes go with someone else's vision. Or they can follow your vision instead of fighting it.

> *The best session I have had was when I worked with Justin Vernon, Bon Iver. It was just so magical and special, and he writes in exactly the same way that I write. And to find somebody like that where we're just basically sitting there interpreting what each other is doing was really special.* **Ilsey Juber**

> *Melodies can come to me quickly, but lyrics definitely take time. I'm so down to sit into the middle of the night getting the lyric just right, and it's fun to find people who are down to do that too.* **Emily Warren**

> *I look for collaborators who are willing to dare to do something different and who have that fire in their eyes of 'let's create something that's never been heard before.'* **Ed Drewett**

Mutual respect ★ The foundation of any good collaboration is mutual respect – if you don't have that you'll run into problems from the get-go. Having respect for each other's expertise and talent and knowing each other's strengths and how they can contribute to the success of the song/project is vital. Treat everyone with respect and you'll see the collaborations flourish.

> *Have the smallest ego you can. You can't be continuously successful and do what we do with too big of an ego. You've got to put yourself aside for the greater good of the song.* **John Ryan**

> *When people walk into a room with ego and feel like they need to make it their idea you miss the magic sometimes. When you just want what's best for the song and not what's best for yourself then you get the best result.* **Ilsey Juber**

> *I always think you need to do everything to serve the song and leave the ego at the door because if you're not serving the song then there's no point.* **Amy Wadge**

Good communication ★ Developing a rapport, mutual understanding and strong collaboration takes great communication. The more you communicate, the more you will find the hit song ideas and nip any looming conflicts in the bud.

Trust ★ Building trust as collaborators is so valuable, knowing that you will each deliver in the roles you play, and trust helps to build a strong and lasting collaboration.

> *To get the best song we need a room of vulnerability, a room of trust, a room of warmth and a room of feeling like we can say 100% what we want and not feel judged.* **Autumn Rowe**

> *People need to communicate, it can be a bit speed datey when you first write with someone like 'we've never met but open your heart and tell me everything' … so make everyone comfortable and be humble and not overbearing.* **Jamie Hartman**

Managing conflict ★ Give feedback or criticism in a constructive, respectful way, understanding your collaborator and how to manage debates or conflicts in the right way, and knowing how to resolve issues respectfully and fairly for the good of your collaboration. Don't be afraid to be transparent and have the hard conversations respectfully.

Building your core team ★ I interviewed some of my favourite writers/producers for this book and they all said the same thing about how important it is to build a core team around you and how it really helped with their success. It really can make or break a career.

I always say this ship is yours to sail but you need co-captains sitting right there beside you to help you steer the ship, keep it afloat and to be your anchor when you need it. Over the years, especially starting my professional songwriting career at 17, I definitely had some great teams and some not-so-great teams around me. And you really get to know the difference, trust me. I want to share with you what I've learned when it comes to building that core team. Managers, publishers, lawyers really do have your life in their hands. They can add so much value to your career and they can also really help elevate you to the levels you need to be at.

> *My manager Gabz Landman has truly changed my life in so many ways and so many times. She's believed in me since the day we met even before I had any real success and over the years our friendship and work relationship has just gotten stronger and stronger. I think because songwriting is such a vulnerable profession, it's been really impactful for me to have someone in my corner who unwaveringly believes in me and who I know I can trust to the Nth degree.* **Amy Allen**

> *Both my manager and publisher took me on when I had nothing, literally nothing, going on. They saw something in me. I don't know what they saw but something, and we've grown together, which is amazing. Zach, my manager, I think he's the best manager ever. And part of why he's the best is because I come at things from such an emotional place and he comes from such a logical place, so when we debate, we're both kinda right and we both take on each other's thoughts. And where we end up somewhere in the middle is always such a cool, special place. I love talking to him about stuff and both of us care so much about being fair and making sure we treat people how I wanna be treated.* **Emily Warren**

I want to give you a good insight into what to look for when building your core team. These music business relationships are key and often you'll speak to your team more than friends and family, so it's really got to be thought out and not about just going with the first person you meet or being so flattered that someone wants to manage you or publish you that you overlook the red flags. (I did that in the past and, boy, I learned some tough lessons from rushing into management deals.) Take your time – it's better to be self-managed for a period whilst you find the right fit than be managed by a bad manager.

I now always advise a few months' 'dating' period where you get to properly know each other and trial how you would work together without any contracts signed. The last thing you want to do is get stuck in a binding contract with someone who you don't actually vibe with or like after a few months. In Chapter 10, I go into all the ins and outs of music contracts, but for now let's talk about the foundations of building your core team.

Remember that everyone who wants to manage you or publish you or sign you in any capacity is always going to promise you the world. What you need to work out before jumping in headfirst with the first manager who says the words, 'I'll get you a Grammy' is can they actually deliver? Can they add value to what you're doing and help to elevate your career? Expectations are important in these music partnerships; talking through each other's expectations as you start working together will help set the tone for a healthy working relationship from the get-go.

WHAT IS A MUSIC MANAGER?

A music manager is a person who manages all the business aspects of a songwriter/producer/artist's career.

The qualities of a great music manager ★ Great managers need to be experienced, creative and ready to hustle. They have a key job behind the scenes to take care of everything and anything related to the business of their client. Your manager acts as a buffer between you as the creative and the rest of the music industry. They speak on your behalf and should protect your best interests at all times so that you can focus on being creative whilst they handle your business. It is a vital partnership for your career and here are the main qualities I believe you should look for in a manager.

> *My manager, Fran, she's everything for me. She's utterly phenomenal and she is the perfect blend of what I need in a manager, and everyone respects her. She travels with me, and she just always makes me feel like anything is possible. She's like, 'If you want to do it, we'll make it happen.' I've got it wrong before with management and having the right manager is so important and I only got it right when I met Fran.* **Amy Wadge**

Communication skills ★ Being a good communicator is a vital quality. Managers need to be able to do this effectively and consistently with everyone involved in your business, conveying your needs and wants whilst also being flexible and transparent. Keeping you in the loop, updating you, catching up and making sure you are being heard and listened to, and communicating together often to keep a good flow going and always moving the needle forward towards your goals.

Well connected ★ Not just name-dropping but actually having the right connections to elevate your career or get you better opportunities and in front of the right people to help you get to the next level. Remember that it's then your job to deliver in those scenarios; managers can only help to get you through the door but then it's you in those rooms. The right connections can add so much weight and value to your business – that excellent network to pull from to get you bigger and better opportunities you wouldn't be able to get yourself.

Experienced ★ Has the knowledge and experience of how to make it in music and understands fully how the industry works, all of its complexities and ins and outs. Can use their prior experience to know how to handle situations that may arise in the most effective ways.

Organised ★ Managers are often multi-tasking and handling many aspects of your career along with other careers that they manage. This requires great organisation and attention to detail and really having it all together for each of their clients.

Calm in a crisis ★ I don't know about you, but I can certainly spiral in a crisis. Having a manager who can step in, stay calm but in control and help fix whatever needs to be fixed or advise you on what to do, whilst calming you down in the process and relieving the stress that comes with this career is so valuable.

Critical thinking ★ This quality is important for long-term goals, decision-making and advising on which opportunities are best. Having a good strategy on the why and the potential outcome and what to prioritise is crucial to support the long-term success of a creative's career.

> *It needs to be someone you can have important conversations with. This is about navigating the music industry, so you need to be strategising. It's the manager and publisher getting to know what gets the best out of you and what's working for you and what's not working.*
> *Julian Bunetta*

Negotiation skills ★ A very important aspect of a manager's job is negotiating deals on your behalf, and excellent negotiation skills can make the difference between a good deal or bad deal.

Financially responsible ★ Managers who know how to handle finances responsibly and are not reckless with budgets and business spending understand that when you make money, they make money and do not take advantage of that.

Reactive and resourceful ★ The music business is forever changing and evolving, and a good manager adapts, pivots and doesn't get phased by any challenges or roadblocks in their way, and will make the best of it and get the best for you in any scenario.

People skills ★ It's so important that you have a manager that has a good reputation and is respected and liked in the industry. Someone who's not going around burning bridges and taking your reputation with them. They represent you and so it's vital they have great people skills.

Trustworthy ★ Trust is so important. You have to go with your gut and put your full trust in someone to essentially run your life for you, speak on your behalf, entrust them with your name and reputation. Take note of how they conduct other business relationships and believe who they are when they show you.

A good human being ★ Anyone who is representing you should possess a lot of the same morals and values as you because they represent you in the industry. A good human being is liked by people and is accessible, approachable, nice to work with and have dealings with. They are someone you feel is your friend, supports you and makes your whole team feel closer.

> *I've had the same managers for the last thirteen years. They're like my family at this point. We don't even see each other as having a manager-and-client relationship anymore. I think you need people that you can just be completely honest and open with, people that will tell you the truth no matter what. People who will humble you when you're getting too ahead of yourself and also elevate you when you don't believe in yourself. I think those things are crucial.* **Kamille**

Will do the ground work ★ When a manager wants to manage you, they have to be willing to jump into the trenches with you and meet you where you are at in your career, having their ear to the ground with the business as you focus on the creative side. Doing the groundwork and networking, making it so you can fully concentrate on the art. Handling all aspects of the business side of things, whether that's booking flights, taxis, hotels, running your calendar, sending your music around, doing the emails, or finding you the rest of your team to help elevate your career, coming to your shows so they are on the ground networking whilst you're on the stage, meeting with A&Rs to make sure they are aware of you and what you're doing, checking in, pushing you forward for the opportunities, finding you extra revenue wherever and however they can.

> *My manager/brother Damon has been absolutely crucial because my natural tendency is to stay in the studio and work and I'm not great at answering emails or phone calls, so without having my brother running the business and having his team out there putting my name out in the world, trying to drum up business, trying to get me in the room with people, I wouldn't have as many opportunities.* **Julian Bunetta**

Firm but fair in business ★ No one wants a manager to be a pushover or be overeager to please or accept the first offer. And no one wants a manager who goes in too heavy-handed and kills the deal instantly. A balance in business deals is preferable. A manager who knows how to get what you want without destroying the business relationships. Being firm but always fair is the best foot forward for a long term career.

Passionate about what you do ★ Your manager should love your music, love what you do and genuinely want you to succeed. They should have a sincere passion for their job and be willing to go above and beyond for their creatives because they understand this is your life and you go above and beyond creatively every day. When you win, they win too and they will do anything to ensure you thrive because they believe in you.

> *My managers were instrumental in making me feel like I was able to do what I did, and they believed in me. This is such an isolated profession and sometimes you just need someone to tell you that what you did is really good.* **Simon Aldred**

> *My managers at Crush [management] have always viewed me as an artist, and even when I'm writing for other people, I'm still an artist in that respect. They have the sensitivity to know that's it's not a nine to five for me and they give me the freedom to feel like I can be myself and not have to do things that I'm not comfortable doing. They've always been so supportive.* **Ilsey Juber**

> *My manager tenaciously believes in me as an artist. Even when I'm going through my doubts, he's there looking out for me and thinks my best work is still ahead of me.* **Dan Wilson**

Knows how to get the best from you ★ Your manager should always listen and get to know what way you like to work, what gets the best out of you creatively and even how to approach you with business things to always protect your creativity. Once they know what gets the best from you, they can utilise that and help to get you in the best creative scenarios.

> *Damon is my sounding board – when the session's over I call him and we discuss the day. Maybe he'll push back and give me a new thought about this or that, and that helps me work through my problems and my struggles with him there as my mirror.* **Julian Bunetta**

HOW TO FIND A MUSIC MANAGER

One of the main questions I get asked by young songwriters is, 'How do I find a manager?' And honestly, there's no one direct way. There are so many managers out there and it's all about finding the right one for you, and that can take some time. You could meet your future manager through another creative you work with. Or a manager may hear your music online and reach out or see you playing live somewhere and approach you. You may get introduced by a mutual friend or meet at a music industry event, or you may already be friends from school or college. I guess my main advice on finding a manager is get yourself and your music out there, be a part of the music community, go to events, play live gigs, put music online, email management companies about your music, attend writing sessions with the other creatives, because you just never know when that introduction will happen that could change your life. Even if you end up meeting with a manager who isn't looking to take on more clients, still meet with them and pick their brain on who they might be able to connect you with that makes sense for what you're looking for.

My manager, Hannan, and I, we went to school together. We were friends and when we got into music it just felt natural for him to manage me. And the good thing about that is he knows me without me having to say anything. If I'm tired or overworked he just knows and he'll say, 'Let's give it a week, just relax and take some time off.' The wins are ten times better because I get to win with him, and, honestly, because we came up together we both learn at a similar rate. He's learning about the business side and I'm learning about the creative side. I think it's so important to have someone on your side who is willing to learn and not always be right. **Plested**

A manager is your co-captain, sitting in the passenger seat right beside you, in the trenches with you; when you win, they win. This can be a lifelong relationship so it's someone you could honestly think of as family. It's not a decision to make lightly. Make sure you spend time getting to know a potential manager before you make your final decision.

WHAT IS A MUSIC PUBLISHER?

A music publisher works closely with songwriters and composers, licensing and administering copyrights for their writers' musical works. A music publisher helps songwriters reach record labels and artists whilst collecting and distributing royalties to their clients.

The qualities of a great music publisher ★ A great music publisher can really elevate your career, introducing your work to bigger and better modes of exposure and getting you into the rooms with the right collaborators and bringing in opportunities that you might not be able to get yourself. They are a vital component of your core team and they really can help massively in building careers. Sometimes when it comes to publishing deals, we focus on the advances offered but forget to also focus on the key person who will be your day-to-day music publisher. This key person is so important to get right. I've put together a list of qualities that I feel a music publisher should have for you to make the most of the relationship and really elevate your career.

I think it's important to have a good relationship with a publisher where you like each other, otherwise they're not gonna be thinking about you. I always try to nurture my publisher relationship and make sure they're my friends. **Kamille**

Music contacts ★ Your publisher really needs to have great music contacts and connections within the industry. They need to be able to get to executives that you can't reach. Networking, being on the ground and having good relationships are important.

Recognising great songs ★ Of course music is subjective, but music publishers have a good ear for when a special song comes in, and that is so important. Hearing a song and knowing where it can fit, who to send it to and ultimately how to help it get to the right home can make all the difference. Having a good idea of what genres and trends are happening and what songs can fit into those trends or break those trends to stand out is vital.

Knowing your catalogue ★ One of the most important things a publisher can do for you is to know your music. They must listen to your songs and really know your catalogue. I always say this because if there's a brief that comes in or they're in a meeting and they know your music so well, then they can capitalise on that moment and play the right song or send the right song and, boom, you have a song cut. They live with your music, listening a lot more times than once. I was once signed to a publisher at one of the major publishing companies, who will remain nameless, he had 40 songwriters on his roster, which is an insanely huge number. I often wondered how he could possibly keep track and know everyone's catalogue. And he barely knew mine – I constantly had to remind him of songs I'd written, re-send the same songs over and over, and he often wouldn't respond to me when I did send songs. It felt very unproductive and was very deflating for me as a songwriter. If a publisher wants to sign you, make sure they are a fan of what you do and will listen to your songs and know them very well.

Time to devote to your business ★ Knowing what artists and labels are looking for song-wise, researching new artists that might be good for you to get in the room with, pitching your songs in meetings and always looking for opportunities for you is so valuable. Making those vital connections with collaborators that might turn into hit songs shows they're fully investing in the business of their writers.

Promotes your songs ★ There are a lot of gatekeepers in this business and your publisher shouldn't be one of them. Pitching your songs where appropriate and promoting your songs to potential homes is such an important role to play and not being shy about it – shooting their shot because you never know what song will connect with who they are playing it to.

Know how to get the best from you ★ A good publisher will get to know you and how you like to work. They want the best from you and knowing how to get the best songs will make for a great publisher/creative relationship from the get-go. Every creative is different and works in different ways. Some want their diary full of writing sessions every day, some prefer quality over quantity. A publisher will adapt and work around how their creative likes to create.

Level-headed amidst creative ebbs and flows ★ Having consistent meetings and catch-ups with a creative is vital for a music publisher. Creatives can go through ups and downs with the nature of the music business, and a publisher who can meet their creative and encourage and support them will always help the creative to flourish and not feel the constant pressure of 'writing a hit'.

Knowing the dynamics to put the right people in the right rooms ★ Your publisher should always try to put you in rooms that will get you the best results. Understanding the dynamics of a writing room and making sure it is a room where you can deliver and flourish and help you make fruitful creative collaborations will add so much value.

RuthAnne, Ali Tamposi, Donna Caseine, Golnar Khosrowshahi – Reservoir Publishing

Understanding song licensing and publishing agreements ★ A good publisher will always issue the appropriate license: recording licenses, synch licenses, print licenses, sub-publishing licenses, and also register your songs correctly.

Persistence ★ Having a publisher who is persistent and understands that one day you send a song to an A&R it just might be the wrong day the wrong time. If you believe in a song, you never give up on a song. You find another moment maybe six months later and you send the song again... and all of a sudden, the A&R likes it and has a home for it. This has happened many times in history — a song doesn't get any bites and then two years later you send it out again and, boom, everybody wants it. A great song is a great song always, sometimes it just takes a second to find it a home. Good publishers know this and don't give up.

> *My first publisher was instrumental in hooking me up with lots of artists, including Sam Smith and Rag'n'Bone Man. Right at the start when I didn't have any contacts or any way in, she was really there, meeting with the A&Rs every morning and really hands-on. She went above and beyond for me.* **Simon Aldred**

> *What I'm looking for as a publisher now is how much can you do on your own? Like, how much can you do, you know, on the days where there aren't sessions happening? And also looking at if you have that business sensibility where you are looking for new artists to collaborate with, reaching out to and putting in that work, it's just such a bonus. That'll get you a long way if you can be the core crew of a new artist that has a lot of potential and is growing. You have things to keep you occupied and inspired.* **Ali Tamposi**

I asked my own publisher, the legendary Donna Caseine, what as a publisher makes her want to sign a writer.

> *I'm just a fan of music and I like to sign creatives whose music I just love and am a fan of. I love delving into a writer's songs and hearing their style and lyrics and melodies and I'm drawn to songs and music where I can't always predict where it goes, where it does something different and unique. I never give up on a great song, as a publisher I may not get a bite straight away on a song that I pitch but that doesn't mean the song is not strong. Sometimes it's timing, sometimes the A&R doesn't hear the strength in it or doesn't have the right artist for it yet and then one day six months later it's a different story, so never give up on a great song.* **Donna Caseine**

A good music publisher believes in you, knows your music, listens to your songs, gives constructive feedback and will always be pitching you and your music for the best opportunities to elevate your career. Do not underestimate the role of a good music publisher. Find a key person who will root for you and give your songs the best chance at success.

Now that we know what to look for in your core team let's get back to you...

YOUR NAME IS EVERYTHING

One of the most valuable assets in the music business along with your talent is your name. So many connections and opportunities in this industry are through word of mouth. It's vital that your name is respected and carries a good reputation with it because it could make the difference of whether or not you get asked to be in the rooms that can lead you to write life-changing songs or not.

How to create a good name ★ It's really the easiest thing to create a good name in the industry. It's being a nice person — kind, reliable, talented, fun to be around, having integrity and easy to work with. Being able to deliver when the pressure's on and bring a nice vibe to the writing room. It's important that people want you in their writing rooms because not every session will result in a hit song, BUT if the people you're writing with enjoy themselves regardless, enjoy the process of writing with you, then they'll want to do it again and again, therefore increasing the likelihood of getting that great song. It's all about opening the doors, and having a good name means the doors will open so much faster. Then you can walk in, be your fabulous self and wow them with your talent.

Don't burn bridges with people ★ You've got to be in this for the long game not the short game. Burning bridges is the quickest way to stifle your career. I'm not saying not to stand up for yourself or be shafted but there is always a way to handle conflict. Handling yourself appropriately, respectfully and fairly will lead to mutual respect and understanding with collaborators and lead to healthy working relationships that will last. If you burn bridges with people on the way up, then I promise you there will be nobody there for you on the way down, and nobody just stays at the top in this business. It is a constant rollercoaster, up and down and round and round, so making sure you have good relationships to take that ride with you is imperative. Sometimes you may lose touch with a collaborator for a few years, but you never know when you might bump into each other again or be working on the same project again, and having solid relationships should last forever even if your business together has paused. Being able to pick right back up again where you left off is crucial. It's also important that when your name is brought up and you're not there, that people speak highly and respectfully of you. The fewer people you've annoyed, the less likely your name will be dragged through the mud. Everybody talks in this business... A good thing to remember.

> *I need them to walk around town saying that they wrote their best song with me. And so I'm constantly making sure that even if I have to write all the lyrics and melodies that it's something that is special to them.* **Ross Golan**

Don't only focus on the big people ★ Throughout my time I've seen new writers or young artists come into the industry and I've learned to never count anybody out. Even if I'm not sure they have what it takes, or may not have the songs or the right team around them at that point, I've learned that anything is possible in this business, and you should never just count somebody out. All this being said, don't just focus on the big people, treat everyone you meet or work with in music on the same playing field and keep your name good with all. You don't wanna be that writer who treats the new kids badly and the big dogs like kings. Everyone deserves equal kindness, respect and humanity, and in a genuine way too. People can sniff out a climber or a hustler or an agenda. Be genuine, and that will stand you in good stead for your whole career. People want to help people who are good people. They will root for you, they want you to win. Remember, you want longevity not a quick hit.

RuthAnne on stage with Niall Horan | credit: Christian Tierney

How to handle music industry conflicts ★ My biggest advice is don't hide behind your management or lawyers. Be a good communicator and be able to have hard conversations when you need to. If a song deal is going awry and management and lawyers are hitting a wall it's important to know when to step in and talk to your collaborators. And most importantly, play fair. I try to always play fair — I look at the situation and attempt to see things from everybody's side and ultimately what is fairest in each scenario, and then have a transparent, respectful, calm adult conversation about it. Often it is in miscommunication or no communication that most conflicts happen. It can be hard to confront these things head-on, but it can also be important for your name. Remember, everyone speaking on your behalf is representing your name. Ultimately everything comes back to you and your name, and if someone is mishandling the situation, they won't get the backlash of that but you will. It's important that whoever is representing you and your name operates in a way that coincides with your morals, values and how you handle conflict, and don't be afraid to step in and take the lead when necessary. I have found the more personable and transparent and communicative I am with the people I work with in the industry, the more respected I am and the closer my business relationships are.

Your name really is everything. Everywhere you go remember that and carry it with you and watch the word of mouth spread in your favour and the opportunities flow in. The universe will work in your favour because you are a good person with the talent to top it all off and a good reputation that is respected, loved and admired.

The A-list room (is your room) ★ When I was writing with Niall Horan for his first and second album a lot of writers were sending me songs or asking me, 'How can I get in the room with Niall?' and it's a question I get asked if I'm in with any big writer, big producer or big artist. It's really the number-one question: 'How do I get in bigger and better rooms… The A-list rooms?'

There's just no way every big artist would ever be able to get in with every single creative out there. It's physically impossible. But I've come to believe that the 'A-list room' can really be any room that you are in. And with that mindset I feel you can really take over the world. Great songs are written every day in rooms with not always a big songwriter or big producer in them and then when that song becomes a huge worldwide smash – guess what… That little unknown writer or little unknown artist becomes the room everyone wishes and wants to be in.

Go where the love is for what you do, and you can't go wrong ★ Take Finneas and Billie Eilish. Finneas had been a songwriter/producer for a while in the industry, he did the rounds, he wrote with a lot of people. I'm sure he was trying to find ways, like we all do, into the bigger rooms. But he very smartly focused his time and energy into a project he believed in, a project he could develop from the ground up: his little sister and insanely talented artist/songwriter, Billie Eilish. He told her 'I'm gonna help you become the biggest popstar in the world' because he could see it from the early days when no one knew who they were. The industry was ticking on not knowing that in Finneas's bedroom the two of them were creating what would become Grammy-winning, Oscar-winning, massive worldwide hit songs that an entire generation would fall in love with and feel spoken to and sing along to at the top of their lungs every chance they get. They uploaded 'Ocean Eyes' to the internet and it went viral, kicking off both their careers. So when people ask me 'How do I get in the rooms?' my first piece of advice is, 'Look around you, look at your own network, or get out there and find your network, your community, find peers who you connect with and make great music with and rise together. Make your room THE room, and utilise all the resources you can – your instruments, your laptop, the internet – and find your collaborators.'

Finneas created his own A-list room from his bedroom; no big budgets, no fancy recording studio, just him and Billie forming their own world, their own A-list room that now everybody wants to be a part of. Finneas won Grammy Producer of the Year in 2020 and is highly sought after. There are hundreds of creatives out there who have done the same thing. They found collaborators they believed in and wrote great songs with, and the rest is history.

Of course, being in with a big artist on paper means you have more of a chance of the songs being cut and released, but do not be deflated if you haven't reached those levels yet. There are other ways to make that happen... And what if the next biggest thing walks into your writing room but you just don't know it yet. Steph Jones has been writing with Sabrina Carpenter for years from when she was a brand-new artist and had not had her breakthrough, and she continued to believe in her over the years, and now she has had her biggest success with her, co-writing the global smash single 'Espresso'.

> *We met around ten years ago through being set up in a session, and I could immediately see how special she was – both as an artist and as a person. She's always had this incredible work ethic and such a clear vision for herself. Watching her evolve and have this massive breakthrough has been so cool to see, and I couldn't be more excited to see her celebrated the way she deserves!* **Steph Jones**

Steph Jones & Sabrina Carpenter

'SONGS I WROTE WITH AMY'

During my interview with Grammy-winning singer/songwriter Amy Wadge, she told me that Ed Sheeran was actually the first artist she wrote with as a songwriter, before he was 'the' Ed Sheeran of course. She had been an artist for years but then decided to pivot to songwriting.

I signed a really small deal at BDR music, was eight months pregnant, and I just said, 'Send anyone you have, I just wanna write songs.' My daughter was born in January and the first person they sent to write with me was Ed [Sheeran], when he was 17.

I think I was the second songwriter Ed had been put in with and he was the first artist I'd been put in with to write professionally and I think what connected us was that I still did gigs here and there to make money and he was doing the exact same. We were both living that early musician/artist lifestyle, which bonded us. We wrote nine songs in two days and *Songs I Wrote With Amy* – one of the EPs he went on to release – is those songs we wrote when we first met. I didn't know at the time – it was about a year later he said, 'Oh, I'm gonna put those songs out as an EP called *Songs I Wrote With Amy*.' That was how my songwriting career started. And it took about seven years from meeting/writing with Ed where I was knocking at the door of the industry to let me in. And it wasn't until I wrote 'Thinking Out Loud' with Ed when I was 37 years old that everything changed.

Why her story is so important is that Amy had no idea that she was in fact in the biggest room she could've been in at the time. She wrote with an artist at 17 who was gonna become one of the biggest in the world.

I went on to ask her, 'So this 17-year-old new artist in front of you who would go on to be arguably one of the biggest and best songwriter/artists of this generation, if not the best, the unknown Ed Sheeran, did you know he was special?'

She said:

I did... I knew... I had this shed in the garden and I kept running back into the house to my husband and saying, 'OMG, this kid, this kid is unbelievable.' Of course I could never have known how big he was going to be, but I remember Ed saying to me that he had been told to stop his loop pedal and dye his hair or he wouldn't make it. I do remember saying to him, 'I bet my house that you're gonna be someone.' I did have a really strong feeling.
Amy Wadge

NOTE TO SELF

You don't have to be in the biggest rooms to make your room big. You as a creative have the power to create music that people will want to be a part of. Write music that has an impact and you will see the doors fly open and everybody wanting to be a part of what you have created.

CASE STUDY

'Thinking Out Loud' – Ed Sheeran
Written by: Amy Wadge, Ed Sheeran

> When we wrote 'Thinking Out Loud' I had just gone to Ed's for the weekend, just to hang and for him to play me *Multiply*, his new album at the time, which was finished, so I wasn't there to write with him, we were just hanging out. We basically stayed up for two days, catching up and chatting. He went to take a shower and I picked up a guitar and started singing the opening lines of the song – God knows where it came from – I guess I was channelling what we had been speaking about. He shouted down from the shower, 'What's that?' I said, 'I don't know.' And he started singing 'take me into your loving arms...' And then we went to dinner with his parents and came back and finished it. He recorded it just on his phone and he kept saying, 'Woah, this song, this song.' I drove away the next day, thinking, 'Yeah, we wrote a good song, I dunno...' He messaged me that night saying he had cut the song, and then he messaged me a week later saying it was on the album, and then messaged me the following week saying it was gonna be a single, and then it was just mental. I didn't know it was a hit, I just didn't know.

I asked her if she thinks it was one of those 'lightning in the bottle' moments, of having that collaborative bond already, the talking, the hanging out, those deep conversations the comfortableness that you were friends who had written many times before that led to the moment of this song.

She said,

> Yeah, I do. It was a moment where we were going through similar things – my mother-in-law was dying, and Ed had just lost his grandfather. That's what we had been talking about, what it is to love someone for your whole life and the reason why it stops at 70, cos that's where Alzheimer's and other health things can come in, and that's definitely where the song was floating in the air.

Everything they were talking about bled into the lyrics naturally and magically. They went on to win a Grammy for the song.

Amy Wadge & Ed Sheeran

Make your room the A-list room.

Make the best music possible and the people will come to you.

Trust the process.

CHAPTER 3

THE TOP 10 'RULES' OF HITMAKING

"It's incredibly important to me that you remember a song right after the first or second time you hear it. That something sticks to you, something that makes you feel 'I need to hear that song again', that's fundamental. Something you want again. And again."

MAX MARTIN

"Often the simplest song is the hardest to write."

PATTI SMITH

"I can have chords all day long, I can play any chord in the book but unless I'm going, '75, I'm still alive ain't nothing but jive', unless I have great lyrics, great melodies, what do you got? What are we talking about? Where are you going with this? What does it mean? Why do I want to listen to this song again?"

JOHN SHANKS

Now it's time to get into the nitty gritty. The real secrets behind the sauce. The foundations and layers that make up a hit song. People have always asked me, 'Can anyone write a song?' and my response is, 'Of course; but the real question is can you write a GREAT song? Can you write a HIT song? Can you write a song that can connect with people all around the world?' If you want to know how hit songs are written and what makes the difference read this chapter over and over and take notes.

These hitmaking 'rules' are more like principles or tips that can encourage creative opportunities in your songwriting, giving you all the power to make *your* songs stand out from the rest. It's very important to highlight that there is no single magic formula for writing a hit song; if there was, we'd all be doing it, but there's no 'one size fits all' in music. Even songwriters who have had lots of hits have also had songs flop, however some have a better hit rate than others.

Music is subjective but there are certain methods, tools and tricks of the trade that can help your hit rate and turn a good song into a big song that millions of people worldwide will connect to and will sing at the top of their lungs (a feeling like no other!). Music trends are always changing and evolving, so some tips that will appeal to masses some years may not appeal to masses other years, and as a songwriter you've got to be evolving and growing and learning all the time whilst also implementing your strengths where you can. You've got to keep an ear and eye on culture, communities and moments.

It's also worth noting that I have never sat and studied a list of songwriting rules, but I did become a student of song — by listening and listening and listening, I found certain patterns that I started naturally applying through time and experience. I created my own list of hit-making tips from all that I've seen, heard and picked up from writing with the biggest and best songwriters in the world. I don't advise that you ever approach writing so clinically that you lose the heart of it, but there is also a craft and skill to it.

A SONGWRITER'S DNA

The real secret is that these 'rules' are so embedded in many songwriters' brains it has become part of their songwriting DNA — so much so that they don't even know they're using them. It becomes a natural instinct and thus makes the difference between a good songwriter and a hit songwriter.

The more you know the 'rules', the more you won't even have to think about them anymore and you'll be comfortable with knowing which ones to apply in each song. You'll gain more and more confidence knowing what's best for each song, and we must always serve the song. There will also be times when breaking all the rules is actually what's best for the track, and we'll explore what I call 'The Exceptions' in the next chapter.

There is no specific order to these tips because the inspiration for a hit song can vary from chords on a guitar, a title idea, a melody on a voice note, a synth pad, etc. You never quite know what each writing session will bring, but what *you* can bring is this songwriter tool kit, so when the spark happens, you can take that magic and mix it with this knowledge and craft it into a hit song.

THE TOP 10 'RULES' OF HITMAKING

1. A great **title** and **concept**
2. Hooks, hooks and more **HOOKS**
3. **Sing-along-ability**
4. **Rhyming and phonetics** are *eh-vuh-ree-thing*
5. **Unique simplicity**
6. Start each section **differently**
7. **Trim the fat**
8. **Craft 'n' graft**
9. Make me **feel** something…
10. **Repetition**, repetition, repetition

Now, let's break these down one by one…

1. A GREAT TITLE AND CONCEPT

THE TITLE:

I always go into sessions with a bunch of title ideas because often a great title can spark the concept, or at least get everyone talking and break the ice. The title is your bottom line, it's the sum-up line that everything in the lyric is centred around and builds up to. It's the pay-off line and fundamentally of huge importance in hit songwriting.

When I first start writing a song I usually write the title first. **Justin Tranter**

Phrases ★ Listen out for famous phrases or a clever twist on a well-known phrase, slogans, movie titles, book titles or even something unique a friend says to you or something you're hearing people around you say a lot. A good example of this is Shania Twain's 'Man! I feel like a woman!' What an excellent, attention-grabbing, unique turn of phrase, a catchy title and now a classic hit.

Listen ★ Be a good listener: observe and lean into conversations because great titles can land on your lap from anywhere at any time, and write them down as soon as they come. Your title should grab the listener and should be easily identified in the song. Try to stay away from generic titles like 'I Love You' or 'You Broke My Heart' because they just won't stand out, especially not in today's crowded market. Titles like 'Blinding Lights', 'Havana', 'Rolling in the Deep', and 'Shape of You' are stand-out, interesting and unique.

Recycle ★ Recycle titles because you can't copyright or own them, so if you bring a title into a session and write a song and the titles are great but everything else is average, keep the title in your back pocket to use again for a brand-new song another time.

Talk ★ Conversations between the creatives in the room can always lead to titles, so if you're stuck, go for a coffee or lunch, start talking and the title will find you.

Stuck? Keep digging! ★ What happens if you start a song without a title and as you go on the title is not becoming apparent, or you finish the song and don't know what to call it? Then you're missing a vital step, go back and keep digging until you find it!

Title reuse ★ Bonus points for getting your title in the verse as well as the chorus, or extra places throughout the song. This must be done in a clever way where the listener doesn't get bored but instead it serves as a familiar anchor for the song. Max Martin is the king of this as demonstrated in his Backstreet Boys hit song, 'I Want It That Way'.

Another example of this is from the incomparable artist Billie Eilish. In her song 'Ocean Eyes' the title is repeated multiple times. We never tire of hearing that beautiful lyric as it is placed so essentially and frequently, bringing us back to the bottom line each time.

> **Verse:**
> I've been watching you for some time, can't stop staring at those ocean eyes
> Burning cities and Napalm skies, fifteen flares inside those ocean eyes
>
> **Chorus:**
> No fair, you really know how to make me cry when you gimme those ocean eyes
> I'm scared, I've never fallen from quite this high, fallin' into your ocean eyes
> Those ocean eyes

As demonstrated in those two examples, the listener should know the title of the song without you having to tell them. They should be able to pick it out easily, which means it needs to be repeated throughout the song, or it needs to be the pay-off line either at the start or end of the chorus.

THE CONCEPT:

Tell it ★ Songwriters are storytellers; find your story and tell it.

Spin it ★ There are many ways you can spin a title; discuss the ways and choose the best way for your concept.

> *You have to know what you mean to say.* **Peter Bunetta**

Believe in it ★ If you don't know what you're writing about then neither will your listener. It's okay if the listener interprets the story or lyric in their own way or if it takes on a different meaning for the listener, but you still must be clear on your story and what you want to say so that it's not confusing for the listener.

Relate to it ★ Be fearless and open with your ideas; real conversations bring out real and relatable concepts. I always start writing sessions with a chat — call it the Irish in me but there's nothing I love more than getting to know people or catching up over a cup of tea and a biscuit. I find that through the talking, the concept unveils itself and even if the concept isn't something you are currently going through, I usually just tap into the most relatable situation I've been in that I can pull from to meet the other person's story. The song then becomes a fusion of our collective experiences. A top tip — in hit songwriting, try to find concepts that are the most universally relatable — there's a good reason why break-up songs are ever-popular and always a winner…

Twist it ★ You can stay in the moment, or you can have the story twist and turn, just make sure the story is never too complicated to digest in three minutes and make sure the twist is the pay-off line in the chorus. Songs are like time capsules; they don't need to always have a fairy-tale ending or a resolve. You have three minutes to sum up a feeling and it's important to stick with that feeling to the end. So, when you're coming up with concepts be very clear on what feeling you are trying to evoke for yourself and for the listener.

> *My writing process revolves around a single talking point. I've found the only times I've walked away without a song are the times that didn't start with a good concept. You can sing melodies for hours but what are you saying? What are we saying before any melody comes out of my mouth?* **Ed Drewett**

> *My whole goal is to help the artist say what they're trying to say, so it's a lot of just listening and pulling things out of what they're saying and just helping to shape*

it and mould it. **Ilsey Juber**

I get moved by something and that's where I start. I write it down. Raw emotion. At the height of being caught up in my feelings, or about something going on in my life, I write it down. Then I go back to it, like a method actor. I find that what I've written down about that moment, I can tap right back into it. **Lauren Christy**

2. HOOKS, HOOKS AND MORE HOOKS

The next three rules are linked together so you can't really have one without the other but they're each so crucial they all deserve their own place in the top 10 tips.

What is a hook? ★ By definition, it's something designed to grab your attention, and in songwriting it's the part of the song that simply hooks you in. The chorus: everything is built around the hook and, just like the old saying 'Don't bore us, get to the chorus', the chorus of a song should never take more than one minute to get to. Some hit songs start right off the bat with the chorus, or give a little tease of it (half a chorus or one line of the chorus).

Find your hook ★ The hook is the catchiest part of the song that everyone will want to sing immediately with you and then want to come back to because it's just so infectious.

Many hooks ★ The more hooks in the song the more universal your song will become.

Title in the hook ★ Make sure the title is some part of your hook. As noted above, the title is usually the pay-off line lyrically matched with the pay-off line melodically, and, if so, get it in the song as much as possible. Drill that title in as much as you can. Think about someone listening to a song for the first time — they should be able to pick out the title without you telling them, and if they can't, well, that's the first place you could improve things.

Melody ★ This is the key part of your hook and the key part of how sing-along-able your song is. We've all encountered that person who is like, 'I have no idea what this song is saying but I just love to sing along — I don't even know the words!'

Earworms ★ Your focus should be creating earworm melodies, so after one spin the listener can sing along. It should be instant, catchy and simple, but definitely not boring.

Always ask yourself, can anyone sing your hook? The best singers, the worst singers, even the tone-deaf singers? A universal melody has no bias; it makes everyone want to get involved.

Typically I go on the mic and the melody comes immediately for me, or it doesn't come at all. That's usually a telltale sign that the beat isn't for me, but if I do get a melody I love, then I'll go to my list of millions of song ideas that I have and then I start to piece together what the song's gonna be about from there. **Kamille**

The bottom line: Chorus is king, so find it and let it sit pretty on its throne.

3. SING-ALONG-ABILITY

So, what makes a hook? It's a melody that is easily sing-along-able. Something instant – the perfect ear candy that'll leave you singing it in your head all day long. It's a catchy melody that's irresistible and instantly sounds and feels right.

Hooks and riffs ★ The biggest hit songs always have a chorus hook that you can sing with lyrics that are easy to grab, plus a musical hook that is played on an instrument, for example, the bassline of 'Billie Jean' by Michael Jackson, or the opening guitar riff of Guns 'N' Roses 'Sweet Child O' Mine' that makes everyone do their best air guitar impression along with their best 'Du du du duh-in duh-in'.

And/Or ★ A one-word hook sung over and over that is so catchy you just can't get it out of your head (pun intended).

Kylie Minogue's 'La la la la' hook in 'Can't Get You out of My Head' is so catchy and such an epic earworm that it never gets old. As is Coldplay's rousing 'Oh oh OHH oh oh oh' hook in 'Viva La Vida', so much so that throughout their 2016 Glastonbury headline show the crowd of 150,000 people kept singing that exact hook completely unprompted in between the songs in their set. Now that's what I call a worldwide stadium-sized HOOK!

CASE STUDY

'A Thousand Miles' – Vanessa Carlton
Written by: Vanessa Carlton
Produced by: Ron Fair

When I was working with legendary Grammy-winning writer/producer Ron Fair, he told me the story of how he produced 'A Thousand Miles' for Vanessa Carlton.

> *She had been signed to the label for a while but nothing had come out yet and they were actually thinking of dropping her. They gave me a brown bag of CDs of songs that were never*

going to be released and one of those CDs was of her demos. Jimmy Iovine asked me to listen through, so I had a listen through and there was this one song that was just called 'Interlude', which was really an instrumental, and as I was listening I heard that now famous piano hook 'du di di di' [sings the piano hook from 'A Thousand Miles'] and I immediately knew it was special. I just kept playing it over and over. So I called Jimmy and said, 'There is a smash here, we cannot drop this artist' and I asked Jimmy if I could meet with Vanessa and talk to her about re-recording this song. And so we met and she wrote 'A Thousand Miles' with that hook. And production-wise we set up a basic track session to really articulate the composition to have more impact and make the transitions more powerful. The song starts with the piano hook and after each chorus that piano hook repeats and, boom, it was a No. 1 worldwide gigantic hit. **Ron Fair**

Melody is so powerful in hit songs: it has the power to unite everyone together. Therefore, the structure of melody in a song is important. I think of the melody of a song like a three to four course dinner and the songwriters are the chefs. You don't want to leave people too full or starving, you want to serve just enough so they'll want to come back for more (so they listen to the song over and over). Let's always strive to make it a five-star song experience.

Verse melody: The starter ★ This is usually the lowest part of the song range-wise so that you have somewhere to go.

Pre-chorus: The palate cleanser ★ This is the build-up to the chorus. Usually shorter than the verse, it's the glue that sticks together the verse to the chorus and should always feel like it's leading to the pay-off, which is the…

Chorus: The main course ★ The hook, the sing-along-able main melody of the song.

Post-chorus: The sides to the main ★ The post-hook to drill your title and/or a melody hook played on an instrument/synth.

Bridge and last chorus: Dessert ★ This is usually a brand-new melody and an interesting departure melodically. You can go somewhere totally new here with the melody and/or new chords and really make the melody climax and lead back to the chorus melody to bring it home.

What you might be starting to see as you read on is how these 'rules' are intrinsically linked and when put together really can make all the difference. We've talked about hooks and sing-along-able hooks. So, the real question is 'what makes a hook *hooky*?' There are a few factors. It is of course having earworm melodies like we've spoken about, and it's also the sounds that we choose to put with that melody.

Enter our good friends and never to be underestimated, the power of rhyming and phonetics.

4. RHYMING AND PHONETICS ARE *EH-VUH-REE-THING*

Now what's the last piece of the puzzle that makes a hook even hookier when paired with a melody that is easily sing-along-able? Well, that would be the phonetics of it. If you want to have a hit song that reaches and connects with the most ears globally, that's when phonetics really come into play. It is so important to listen to how each section sounds and make it both enjoyable to listen to and easy on the ear.

What can make a song globally successful is when the sounds of the words in your hook are digestible and have a certain ring to them so that anyone, no matter what language they speak, can still sing along. Hit songwriting is knowing what sounds to use when and how to place the sounds throughout the song. Rhyming makes everything easier to digest. The rhyming and phrasing of these phonetics are all key players in hit songs and it's the exact rhyming, near rhyming and inner rhyming of these phonetic lyrics that glue it altogether. So, let's dig in.

You will notice that in a lot of hit songs with big vocal hooks that they are always on a 'Awwww' sound or an 'Oh' or 'Ahhhh' 'AaaaYy' 'I' sound. It's that nice, big, open sound that really can give a chorus melody a lift: *'We could've had it **ALLLLLLLL**' (**AWWWWLLLL**), 'I came in like a wrecking **BALLLLL**', 'Since you've been **GONNE**' (**GAWHHHHHNNNN**), 'I'm so moving **ON**', 'You shoot me down, but I won't **FALLL** I am **Ti-TAAAAANNN-ni-UMMM**' (**AWHMMMM**)* — all big, round and open vowels. The reason for this is because they are so easy to sing and pleasant on the ear.

In verses you'll hear a lot of '*ee*' or '*ooh*' words. It's also important to note that you need to switch up the phonetics in each section. So if the verses are '*ees*' and '*oohs*' then your chorus should be '*ahhhs, ohs, alls*', etc. and vice versa. It's a good idea to differentiate your sections not only melodically but also phonetically.

The best way to show you how phonetics work in hit songwriting is to break down the lyrics of some big tunes and look at how phonetics are used. Let's use the huge smash hit of a song that is Dua Lipa's 'Levitating'. This song was a huge global success — let me show you just one of the reasons why. The rhyming and phonetics are music to my ears, and the rest of the world who could not get enough of this.

CASE STUDY

'Levitating' – Dua Lipa
Written by: Dua Lipa, Clarence Coffee, Sarah Hudson, Stephen Kozmeniuk

*If you wanna run **away** with **me** I know a gal**axy** and **I** can take you for a **ride**
I had a premo**nition** that we fell into a **rhythm** where the music don't stop for **life**
Glitter in the **sky**, glitter in my **eyes**, **shin**ing just the way you **like**
If you're **feel**ing like you **need** a little bit of com**pany** you met me at the perfect **time***

*You want **me**, I want you you **baby***
*My sugar boo I'm **levitating***
*The Milky **Way** we're **renegading***
Yeah yeah yeah yeah yeah
*I got **you moonlight** you're **my starlight***
*I need **you** all **night***
*Come on dance with **me**, I'm **levitating***
You, moonlight**, you're **my starlight
*I need you **all night***
*Come on dance with **me** I'm **levitating***

This song showcases an amazingly phrased assonance (the similarity in sound between two syllables that are close together, created by the same vowels but different consonants, for example 'back' and 'hat') and rhyming phonetic lyric that weaves between exact rhyme, near rhyme and inner rhyming perfection. Verses focus on 'ayy' and 'ee' sounds and the chorus switches to 'oooh' and 'iiiii'.

Everything falls nicely on the ear where you don't feel overloaded, just phonetically very satisfied.

When writing melodies, a great rule of thumb is to sing the vowels and consonants that feel right and sound right, even if they sound like gibberish, and then find the lyrics that fit the sounds. This is where the websites like rhymezone.com or rhymewave.com become a songwriter's best friend. They show exact rhymes and near rhymes and help speed up the rhyming phonetic lyric process. It's almost like approaching it as a puzzle and you've got to fit the right sounds with the melody. It can take quite the brain power to solve the puzzle of phonetics but the more you get into the swing of doing it, the more it'll become second nature.

5. UNIQUE SIMPLICITY

A hit song is a song that is usually very simple, it's usually something where everyone says, I could have written that. And it's very instant, people want to sing along, and it's very memorable, it's unique, it's not like something out there, it brings something new to the music landscape. **Toby Gad**

When you create a song that is unique and simple you really have hit the jackpot. And when you talk to songwriters this is often the hardest thing to do. Songwriters are empaths – we feel deeply! We have so much to say but simplicity is about **saying the most you can in the fewest words** and finding fresh new ways to say things that may have been said many times before. Hit songs are usually quite simple and that's what the real task is. It's finding the balance between simplicity and uniqueness.

The best practices to achieve this are:

Use **colourful imagery,** catchphrases, expressions, questions and personal statements mixed with conversational lyrics. In hit songwriting it's all about finding the balance. Right now people want to hear authenticity in music, so always think, 'How would I say this in a conversation with someone?' and go from there. Songwriters really have an opportunity here to just tell it like it is and cut to the truth of the matter.

Really great lyricists have a way of saying something in a **unique** and **unexpected** way. When so many songs have been written and so much has already been said, think about ways to say something like no one ever has before. Always sprinkle in some colourful words so that your lyrics aren't too generic.

Make every line count. When writing lyrics, it's good practice to try and write more lyrics than you need – that way you can improve on your initial lines or replace lines as needed.

CASE STUDY

'Rolling in the Deep' – Adele
Written by: Adele Adkins and Paul Epworth

This incredible hit song by Adele is the perfect example of unique simplicity, which is why people belt it out at the top of their lungs the world over.

In 'Rolling in the Deep' the lyrics are quite simple and conversational – 'we could've had it all, you had my heart inside of your hands' – but what makes it different and colourful, whilst also being easy to understand and relate to, is the 'rolling in the deep' line which comes from an urban slang term for 'having someone's back' (roll deep). That one phrase turns a simple concept into something unique and fresh for the listener. This simple lyric paired with the soaring, hooky melody on the chorus, 'we could've had it ALLLLLL, rolling in the deep', makes this song hit all the right notes to create a worldwide smash.

Paul Epworth and Adele at the 54th Annual GRAMMY Awards, photo by Kevin Winter © Getty Images

6. START EACH SECTION DIFFERENTLY

This one is often overlooked or forgotten about, but if you get it right, it can really be a game changer. Make each section of your song start on a different note and a different beat so that it creates just enough variation and doesn't feel too samey or boring.

★ The pre-chorus should never be at the same range melodically as your chorus.

★ The chorus should always feel like an arrival, a payoff and its own moment.

★ The chorus is usually the highest part of the song melodically and range-wise.

A good rule of thumb is to vary the beat that your sections start on. For example, if your verse starts on beat 2, then make sure your chorus starts on beat 1 or vice versa. Let's use one of the biggest hits of 2022, Miley Cyrus's hit song as an example.

CASE STUDY

'Flowers' – Miley Cyrus
Written by: Miley Cyrus, Michael Pollack, Gregory Hein

Verse: Starts on **the note C and starts on the off-beat 3**. The verse is low in range and spacious, really setting the melodic tone and giving the listeners time to digest it.

Pre-chorus: Starts one note higher than the verse starting on the **note D, before beat 1** which gives it a slight lift, and the melodic rhythm picks up some pace, giving it more energy as it builds to a perfect set up of the chorus. They also cleverly use a rising melody of the scale to get to the chorus.

Lyric: *'Re-mem-bered I'*

Chorus: The chorus starts on the **note E**, has the highest range of the song and starts **on beat 2** which again differs from the verse and pre-chorus. What I love about this chorus is also the space in it. Never underestimate the power of space for the listener to digest each line and catch our breath.

'I can buy myself flowers'

(space space)
'Write my name in the sand'

(space space)
'Talk to myself for hours'

(space space)
'Say things you don't understand'

(Space space)

7. TRIM THE FAT

This is one of my own personal favourites and really comes into play after you have your song written. This is when you need to think of yourself as an editor and do what I call 'trim the fat'. I usually approach this by taking the song back down to its rawest form and that's when you find the parts that need trimming. A song stripped back to its rawest form is always the best test of how good it is. Sometimes the drums, strings and synths can create an amazing vibe in the room to the point where it feels good and distracts you from knowing if the topline (melody/lyric) of your song is actually great.

So, grab a guitar or piano and sing it acoustic in the room like that. Trust me – you will know straight away if it's the best it can be.

RuthAnne in the studio

Songs should always work on a guitar or on a piano. If that works, then you can always add a track to it later. But if the song isn't great on the guitar or piano, then the track sometimes can't save it. **Toby Gad**

I think the through line for me has always been, can you sing the song on piano or acoustic guitar and what is it at its core? Then people can take it and run with it and do anything with it. **Ilsey Juber**

Sections will stick out for good or bad reasons, and that's when you start trimming that fat. This is such a useful tool to really craft your song and make sure everything is sitting exactly where it should. I like to imagine a singer in a pub or people sitting around a campfire with guitars jamming an impromptu sing-song. Sing the song and imagine those settings – is the song strong on its own without the bells and whistles? You now know what to do if it's not – trim the fat!

Ask yourself questions like...

★ Is my intro too long?

★ How long is it taking to get to the chorus?

★ Is my post-chorus too long?

★ Halve the second pre-chorus perhaps?

★ Does this song need a bridge or just a breakdown chorus and double chorus to end?

The reason songs get finished is because you've trimmed the fat across the day and kept all the stuff that feels good. **Ed Drewett**

8. CRAFT 'N' GRAFT

Do you ever watch interviews and the artist and/or songwriters say 'the song just came out in like 20 minutes and almost wrote itself'? Okay, so sometimes that really does happen, and there have been tonnes of hits where it really feels magical and other-worldly when it does, BUT more often than not a lot of craft and a lot of graft goes into hit songs – days and/or weeks of really crafting it to get it right. Sometimes you have the perfect chorus but the verse and pre-chorus just aren't quite setting it up right; sometimes you have the hit melody, but the lyrics just aren't fitting right, which is where the crafting and grafting come into songwriting. Some songs need to be crafted, they need discussion, debate, trial and error to really get the best lines with the best melodies. There's a phrase 'try and beat it' that I keep in mind. Or sometimes I call a line 'just a placeholder for now' until the right line sticks. Some people give up way too soon on an idea without fully realising the potential of it and sticking with it just a bit longer, or leaving it for a few days or even a few months and coming back to it with fresh ears. It really is worth it to dig in and not settle for average when you can take a track to a hit song level, especially when you know you have a strong idea going. A song can also be produced so many different ways, and sometimes you'll be on version ten and realise 'wait, the magic was in version one' and go back to that, or sometimes version ten might hit the jackpot and be the magic version. You've got to be willing to go there and experiment and try things. Leonard Cohen famously wrote 80 different verses versions of 'Hallelujah'. The song was crafted over a span of five years before he felt it was ready.

Writing alone, I take weeks. And I'm so, so patient. I go back, I rewrite this thing, that chord's not right, that lyric's not right, that mix isn't right, let's go back. And I don't send it until I'm really proud of it. **Ross Golan**

CASE STUDY

'Teenage Dream' – Katy Perry
Written by: Bonnie McKee, Max Martin, Benjamin Levin, Katy Perry, Łukasz Gottwald

Bonnie McKee famously talked about how much craft and graft went into the writing of the Katy Perry smash hit 'Teenage Dream', with four or five versions being written. At one point Max Martin told her to 'move on, we have other songs to write' but Bonnie knew there was something special in it and she kept going. Some of the chorus lyrics that were tried and tested were, 'You make me feel like I'm born again, all brand new, come on, Peter Pan'. But she knew she could beat those, so she started thinking of her first love and got lyrics like 'you think I'm pretty without any makeup on,' and then had the word 'Teenager', which, because it had too many syllables, she shortened to 'teenage' and added 'dream' on the end and, voila, she had it. She went back to Max with it, and they finished it together. He said to her, 'I wish I could bottle this feeling.' She said, 'What feeling?' He said, 'When you know you've written a hit.' And he was right, the song went on to become a massive hit. But imagine if Bonnie had not spent that extra time crafting it to get it right.

Dig deeper
One of my own songwriting mentors, Julian Bunetta, used to do this exercise when we were writing that I've kept doing ever since, which is to write more verse lyrics than you need. Normally you need two verses, so write four and then you can really see which ones are the strongest lyrics and which to use. Or you might switch the order of them around or put different lines together. He used to say 'I like that verse. Write another one, see if you can beat it.' Or sometimes we'd each write a line and pass the laptop to the next writer and so on until we had a verse. It was a challenge, but it was always worth it.

CASE STUDY

'Where Do Broken Hearts Go' – One Direction
Written by: Julian Bunetta, Teddy Geiger, RuthAnne Cunningham, Ali Tamposi, Harry Styles

When we wrote 'Where Do Broken Hearts Go' for One Direction we originally had all the melodies. First, we each went in the booth and sang melodies down with no words and then we listened back and pieced together the strongest melodies. It was that last part of the chorus melody we were really digging and digging for, what that pay-off lyric would be. We tried a lot of different lyrics and then Julian just said, 'Where do broken hearts go?' We sang it and it felt great. Now, we definitely had debates about whether or not that was the right lyric but after three hours of digging some more we kept coming back to that lyric and that title. That title then gave us our concept and our story, and then the rest of the lyrics were written more easily because we had cracked the code of the title and concept. We put the graft in.

Liam Payne, Louis Tomlinson, Julian Bunetta, John Ryan and Jamie Scott

It can feel at times like mental gymnastics, your brain trying to get all the best pieces lining up together. You've got to be willing to put that graft in and get crafting and make your song the absolute best song it can be.

Nothing is as important as the song. **Max Martin**

9. MAKE ME FEEL SOMETHING

The song should always evoke some kind of emotional or physical reaction and response. Whether that's making someone feel like they want to cry, dance, smile, laugh, kiss, make love... it should always be something.

I look for a feeling that music gives me. I'm always chasing that feeling. **Julian Bunetta**

Depending on your genre there are different ways to create a feeling in your songs with the production sonically, but when it comes to the topline make sure to use a range of emotional, physical and visual lyrics. This will make it very easy for the listener to instantly grasp and form a reaction without them even really thinking about it.

I think it's really important to have some sense of poetry in the lyrics and get to some real emotional truths. **Ilsey Juber**

I love the way that Alex Turner from the Arctic Monkeys writes – he really just like paints a picture describing a scenario where like you walk into a crowded bar and the person you walk with sort of pulls their hand away from you the second they walk in the bar – describing and painting those type of pictures that tell so much about where you're at with a particular person. I just love visual scenarios in that way. It keeps me going and it keeps me excited too when I hear something profound. And I always push for that – keep pushing for something thought-provoking. **Ali Tamposi**

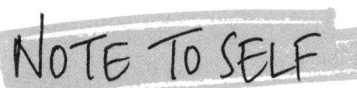

Make your listener feel first and think later.

Let me show you some examples, all taken from hit songs.

Physical lyrics
'I wanna swing from the chandelier'
'Dancing in the dark with you between my arms'
'I'm off the deep end watch as I dive in'
'I keep bleeding love'
'I wanna hold your hand'
'And we'll run for our lives'
'You can stand under my umbrella'

Visual lyrics
'Among the fields of barley'
'Barefoot on the grass'
'I see trees of green, red roses too'
'You're the sunshine in the rain when it's pouring'
'Tears come streaming down your face'
'White lips pale face, breathing in snowflakes'
'Pull the sheets right off the corner of that mattress that you stole'
'Thunder only happens when it's raining'
'Ooooh I'm blinded by the lights, no I can't sleep until I feel your touch'

Emotional lyrics

'I could hold you for a million years, to make you feel my love'
'Only know you love her when you let her go'
'Sometimes it lasts in love but sometimes it hurts instead'
'Nothing compares 2 U'
'I have loved you for a thousand years, I'll love you for a thousand more'

I want a lyric to cut through me emotionally, make me cry. **John Shanks**

I think that my strength in the room is making sure that the song is connected to an emotion and really embodying whatever it is we're talking about and physically putting myself there. It has to be that truth that's connected to that emotion lyrically. I think a very important focus for me in a room is the storytelling component. I've always like gravitated to the Joni's of the world, the Alanis Jagged Little Pill, *those songs to me are nothing without those lyrics and it doesn't always have to be necessarily profound, but there's unique and interesting ways of saying things.* **Ali Tamposi**

10. REPETITION, REPETITION, REPETITION

I'm hoping you have already got this sentiment from all I've said throughout this chapter, but in the spirit of repetition I will say it again and again and again. There're no ifs or buts about it; the key melodies and key lyrics need to be repeated throughout your song and you are missing a huge trick if you have nothing that repeats. If there is too much information, it just won't land and it will overload the listener. You have just three minutes to make the listener not only connect with your song but remember it, and how you make it memorable is through repetition.

I'm going to start by using nursery rhymes as an example – which may puzzle you because these are not exactly pop songs, but let's be honest, they are global hits and sung by children all over the world. When I say the words 'Baby Shark' you know exactly what I'm talking about. For better or for worse that song sticks in the heads of millions daily, playing over and over in households, and there's a reason why. Repetition.

'Baby shark du du du du du, baby shark du du du du du du, baby shark...'

And let's not forget one of the most famous nursery rhymes of all time...

'The wheels on the bus go round and round, round and round, round and round
The wheels on the bus go round and round all day long'

(Using the same melody, it continues...)

> 'The horn on the bus goes beep beep beep, beep beep beep, beep beep beep
> The horn on the bus goes beep beep beep all day long'

I could go through hundreds more songs that all do the same thing. The main point here is to just remember the foundations of nursery rhymes and translate this concept of patterns and repetition into your songwriting.

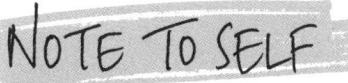

Songwriting is always about finding the balance between repetition and variation, and it's knowing what the key moments are to repeat and when it's time to vary and switch it up. That's something that with experience and practice you will come to find.

When I co-wrote Martin Garrix and Bebe Rexha's 'In The Name Of Love' – which went triple platinum and has now been streamed over 2 billion times (which still blows my mind) – we knew we had such a strong title there and we just wanted to create something anthemic that anyone could sing along to. We use the phrase 'in the name of love' not only as the main hook (repeated over and over) but we also use the title at the end of every verse. We did this very intentionally to reinforce the title and the hook.

> If I told you this was only gonna hurt
> If I warned you that the fire's gonna burn
> Would you walk in, would you let me do it first?
> Do it all in the name of love
> Would you let me lead you even when you're blind
> In the darkness in the middle of the night
> In the silence when there's no one by your side
> Will you call in the name of love?

Hook:
> In the name of love
> Name of love of love

Here's another example of a hit song that uses the title over and over again as the main hook, pairing the title with a melody that repeats over and over again. This song became one of the biggest songs of 2022/23. The simple chorus repeats the title with the same melody.

CASE STUDY

'As It Was' — Harry Styles
Written by: Harry Styles, Kid Harpoon, Tyler Johnson

As it was
As it was
As it was
You know it's not the same

It does a higher melody on the forth line and then back to repeating

As it was
As it was
As it was
You know it's not the same as it was

Then the chorus ends with the title and same melody again, and brings in the musical hook of the song, two hooks in a row… Pop perfection.

Now let's talk about melodic structure which can help you know which parts should repeat and when, because knowing when to use repetition and then some variation to keep your song interesting is very important.

You will notice a lot of songs use an AABA melodic structure in the verses and choruses:

A = first line of your verse melody

A = second line repeats the same melody with new lyrics

B = third line usually changes or varies the melody slightly with new lyrics

A = fourth line goes back to the original melody with new lyrics

A – New melody
A – Repeat that melody
B – Go away from that melody slightly or significantly
A – Come right back to it

You can also use the melodic structure of ABA, AAB, or AAAB, but no matter which one of these it is, the As are repetitive and the Bs are the variations.

A GOOD PLACE TO START

If I'm writing for myself or it's a pitch session, I'll either look into my notes for little lines or ideas I've written down (I usually keep a running list of them, or I just start with chords and see if that inspires something). I try to let my process change and adapt all the time because every session is so different (which is why I love songwriting), so for me it's not really possible to have a one-size-fits-all process. I love how songs can come from so many sorting angles!
Amy Allen

RuthAnne, photo by Jack Newhouse

Sometimes when it comes to writing songs you can get stuck and not know the best place to start. So I have one more mini tip just outside of my top 10. It's not essential but it can be a good place to start, and that is...

The Four Chords of Pop

Chords for a songwriter are the building blocks of a song, just like the alphabet is a building block for our words. We use letters to form words like we use chords to form music. A chord progression is the way the chords are arranged – the order, the sequence, and there are several different chord progressions that work well together and can create the mood and set the tone of the song. Many of you may be familiar with a recent court case involving Ed Sheeran for his song 'Thinking Out Loud'. The case became centred around the chords which were similar to the Marvin Gaye hit 'Let's Get It On'. Ed took the stand to defend his case. Guitar in hand he played a sequence of chords which are in fact the foundations of hundreds and thousands of songs. Not just songs, hit songs (see list below). These are known as the **Four Chords of Pop** and are used across every genre of music.

The origins of this chord sequence date way back to the 18th century, when they were written down as a 'Canon' by the German composer, Pachelbel, and they were most likely used before that too! The fun fact about chords is you can't copyright them, meaning no one actually owns them, much like no one owns the alphabet! Ed Sheeran won his case by proving just that.

There are only so many notes and chords to play and music is made up of all of them. Arguably the most popular chord progression in popular music in any key is:

I – V – vi – IV

(Meaning in simple terms – I is the first chord, V is the fifth chord, vi is the sixth chord and the IV is the fourth chord in any key.)

Let's take C major as an example:

C – G – Am – F
(I) – (V) – (vi) – (IV)

And the rotations of this chord sequence (meaning the same chords in different order):

V – vi – IV – I
= G – Am – F – C

vi – IV – I – V
= Am – F – C – G

IV – I – V – vi
= F – C – G – Am

I'd like to list for you just a tiny handful of the hundreds of massively successful hit songs across all music genres that have used these chord sequences.

'Let It Be' – The Beatles
'Zombie' – The Cranberries
'Someone Like You' – Adele

'Run' – Snow Patrol
'Ghost' – Justin Bieber
'If I Were a Boy' – Beyoncé
'Someone You Loved' – Lewis Capaldi
'No Woman, No Cry' – Bob Marley
'Umbrella' – Rihanna
'Adore You' – Harry Styles
'Thinking Out Loud' – Ed Sheeran
'We Found Love' – Calvin Harris/Rihanna
'Bad Blood' – Taylor Swift
'Don't Stop Believin'' – Journey

And that's just scratching the surface...

Now, plenty of hit songs don't use the Four Chords of Pop so you don't *have* to use them. There are so many options and beautiful chords to use, so don't be afraid to explore and try different chords for different songs, but have the four chords of pop in your bag to whip out if and when you need them.

> *I'm really inspired by chords, just great chords. I'm a sucker for a guitar riff. And I think that's why when I met Andrew Watt, my career took a total 180 in the best way. Because he knew exactly what chords and riffs to play to get that emotion out of me. And it completely woke me up. When he played the 'Let Me Love You' guitar riff that went on to be released by DJ Snake and Justin Bieber a fire reignited in me. And I feel that I write my best when I feel like the spiritual kind of connection that is awakened in me through chords.* **Ali Tamposi**

The biggest songs in the world often use a form of rotating the Four Chords of Pop so it can be a good place to start to keep it simple and get your creative juices flowing.

I know some of you reading this are saying to yourself, 'I can name hit songs that don't have these 'rules/tips'.' Well, that is true, there are lots of hit songs that break all these 'rules' and still become worldwide hits. So, let's talk about them after the 'Espresso' case study.

CASE STUDY

'Espresso' — Sabrina Carpenter
Written by: Sabrina Carpenter, Amy Allen, Steph Jones, Julian Bunetta
Produced by: Julian Bunetta. Mixed by: Julian Bunetta, Jeff Gunnell

Now let's talk about a song that I feel encompasses most of these 'rules' of hitmaking and at the same time breaks them. Keeping in mind that the songwriters weren't thinking about the 'rules'; I think they are just naturally embedded into their songwriter DNA after many years of writing, honing their craft and experience. I know these songwriters personally and they are really some of the best in the biz.

This perfect pop song reached a billion streams in record time, the third fastest song to ever do that. It won a Grammy for Best Pop Solo Performance in 2025, was the No. 1 global song of 2024 on Spotify and topped the charts all over the world, a multi-platinum global smash that even had Adele's blessing.

I interviewed my dear friend who I've written many songs over the years with: Grammy-winning, multi-platinum songwriter/producer Julian Bunetta, who co-wrote, produced and mixed 'Espresso'.

> *With 'Espresso' it goes back to what I was saying about chemistry – just the four of us in the room, it went beyond math and it went beyond structure and it just was straight instinct. All of us in there have put in so many hours and have studied and are trying and striving to perfect our craft and we all have a lot of love and trust with one another and a lot of fun with one another. So we had come full circle and found ourselves for an hour or two or three in the studio, not even remembering that we're out here trying to write a hit. We're just kids and friends having fun, playing around in the studio, having the time of our lives, and the song 'Espresso' is what came out of that.*
>
> *The foundation of it is that we know when a part is really good or not or makes us feel good or not and we're being honest and truthful with each other, there was no ego, there was no pride. We were just four people that are at the top of their game coming together and making something with pure joy and fun in mind and 'Espresso' was the result of that, it was the love child of all of those components coming together. That's what you work so hard for – it goes beyond 'correct', beyond right or wrong, and it was just pure instinct and love and art and magic. It was just magic.* **Julian Bunetta**
>
> *'Espresso' has definitely opened doors that maybe would have taken a little longer or might never have opened at all. I've been writing professionally for about thirteen years, so I've been at it for a while, and to have a song like this connect the way it has is just surreal. It's been amazing to see how much people love it, and it's definitely reinforced that trusting your instincts and having fun with the process is always the right move.* **Steph Jones**

This song has everything!! I want to break down the tips I've given you and show you how this song incorporates them so effortlessly without it ever feeling too written or songwriter-y or forced.

Great title and concept ★ I mean, can you get a more unique yet simple title than 'Espresso'. Type it into Google and I promise you it will be the only song called that or the only song you've ever heard of called that, and immediately the song stands out, immediately I wanna hear it cos the title has grabbed my attention. An espresso is obviously a little shot of caffeine that we drink, but concept-wise they took an everyday average universal experience and cleverly twisted it to 'That's that me espresso', creating a new phrase, a slogan, using the espresso as a metaphor. It's confident, it's fun, it's cheeky and flirty and it catches you right away. A truly winning title and concept.

Hooks, hooks and more hooks ★ There's no 'don't bore us, get to the chorus' here... The song starts with a catchy musical hook that repeats throughout the song and by eight seconds goes straight into the chorus, the main hook. And this is a hook that will stay all day in your head rent free. It is catchy, instant, universal and ear-grabbing. From the pick-up of 'Now he's' perfectly setting up this masterful pop hook, to the way she holds and slides on the notes 'meeee' and 'oh' in the first two lines with such character, to the shorter more rhythmical 'I guess so' 'that's that me espresso' on lines three and four demonstrating how the rhythm, phrasing and the way it's sung also hooks us in. It's just jam-packed full of character, irresistible charm and hooks galore.

Sing-along-ability ★ Most great pop songs like this one are universal, where anyone can sing them. This song has that in bucket loads. And I don't mean everyone will sound like Mariah Carey singing it, but that's not the point. It's the perfect sing-along song that is melodically simple enough for all to sing but interesting enough that you don't feel bored. Just look at all the viral videos of the standout line in the song, 'I'm working late cos I'm a sin-Ger' – the way she gives it the hard 'G' makes it stand out with character and creates the perfect moment for all to scream the line at the top of your lungs.

Unique simplicity ★ Lyrically the song is full of clever witty lines and humour and lots of innuendos. It has the perfect balance of conversational lines like 'Too bad your ex don't do it for ya' to more visually quirky lines like 'My honey bee come get this pollen'. It goes perfectly between the two so it feels simple yet interesting and not generic in the slightest. The play on words is so well done. 'I know I mountain dew it for ya, that morning coffee brewed it for ya' and even the slightly incorrect grammar ('dream came trued it for ya') makes it all the more unique, cool and modern.

Rhyming and phonetics are eh-vuh-ree-thing ★ This song is a rhyming and phonetic masterclass. And it's not only the phonetics but how they are sung, the character in her voice and how she pronounces the sounds that are really ear-grabbing and easy to sing along with too.

Just look at the rhyming scheme and phonetics of the chorus:

Now **he's** *thinking* **'bout** **me**
Every **night** **oh**
Is it that **sweet** *I guess* **so**
Say you can't **sleep**
Baby I **know**
That's that **me es-pres-so**
Move it up down left right **oh**
Switch it up like **Nin-ten-do**
Say you can't **sleep**
Baby I **know**
That's that me **es-pres-so**

See how the chorus goes back and forth phonetically between '**eee**' and '**oh**' and the inner rhyming of the '**eeeee**' on the first few lines, and then they move away from '**eee**' sounds at the perfect moment. They switch it up (pun intended) to an '**uh**' (up) and '**ow**' (down) but continue to reinforce the '**oh**' sound. Finding another three-syllable word to match with 'es-press-so' ('Nin-ten-do'), the words all rhyming throughout the song — from the first listen it is so satisfying to the ear. Then in the first verse it stays completely away from '**ee**' and '**oh**' and instead uses '**ay**' '**aw**', and in the pre-chorus it's '**ooh**'.

Remember, switching up phonetics throughout a song really works well.

Start each section differently ★ Each section of 'Espresso' starts on a different beat. And rhythmically the verse is nicely spaced out in comparison to the pre-chorus, which moves into a more fast-paced rhythmical modern pop pre-, which builds so nicely into a pick-up into the chorus — 'now he's'. All these different sections starting on different beats with different rhythms and phrasing keeps the listener engaged and it never feels boring.

Trim the fat ★ There is not one ounce of fat on this song. It has been crafted so well, there's no section that feels too long or too over-written. Everything flows really nicely, leaving you wanting to listen to it again and again.

Make me feel something ★ Hearing Julian speak about the vibe that was in the room that day, the magic that happened, makes complete sense. Listening to 'Espresso' gives you the exact feeling of what they felt when creating it. Fun, joy, having the time of their lives. It's authentic. It immediately makes you wanna dance and have a good time and feels uplifting and fun and it makes you feel confident and empowered.

Repetition, repetition, repetition ★ The fact the song starts with the chorus already makes it a winner in the repetition race. There's a musical hook that repeats throughout the song. And without being told the title of the song you would instantly know it's called 'Espresso' due to it being repeated twice in the chorus and it being the bottom line and a great pay-off: 'that's that me espresso'. It never feels over repetitive either.

So there you go, it ticks all the boxes. I know it doesn't use the Four Chords of Pop from my list of tips but not every single hit does or has to. 'Espresso' uses a simple two-chord progression that's not over complicated and perfectly complements the melody.

I asked Julian if he knew from the day they wrote 'Espresso' that it was a hit and he said,

> I definitely knew it was a good one because I played it every day by myself from the time we wrote it for the seven months I had it before it came out. I felt it had a shot, it had a chance. You can only dream that a song will take over the world the way this song has, and I've thought that at times before about other songs I've written and been wrong but I just knew I loved this song and I was just proud to play it for people.

As well as 'Espresso' the entire *Short n' Sweet* album is really a perfect pop album. I went on to ask him why he thinks it's been such a huge success and he said,

> Sabrina is one of those artists that can write, can sing and can dance. There are so many factors of why I think it's become so big, I think part of it is that she crafted her own unique identity and voice that I think people can relate to. She's talking about things in a way that other people aren't. She's saying things that other people don't say. She had this momentum of 'Nonsense', The 'Nonsense outros' and that going viral, getting the Taylor Swift tour, 'Feather' going No. 1 at radio. So you could feel this momentum that culminated with the release of the first single off the *Short n' Sweet* album, which was 'Espresso'. Everything just aligned. It's like a slot machine, where all the sevens lined up, and it's all the little things she does behind the scenes to make that work. **Julian Bunetta**

Julian Bunetta, Amy Allen, Sabrina Carpenter & John Ryan

CHAPTER 4

BREAKING THE RULES: 'THE EXCEPTIONS'

"Songwriting is too mysterious and uncontrolled a process for me to direct it towards any one thing."

JAMES TAYLOR

"The best songs are arrivals: the 'Yellows' and 'Viva La Vidas'. You can craft them, that's true, but there's definitely an element that you can't control."

CHRIS MARTIN (COLDPLAY)

You probably read a lot of the last chapter and definitely thought of a song or two that didn't follow those rules and are just dying to tell me: 'Wait, but "Bohemian Rhapsody".' Trust me, I know! In this chapter we will talk about these songs that I call 'The Exceptions'.

These are the songs that broke the rules in the best way to still be a hit, or maybe followed some rules but did just one thing that defied the conventional commercial way. They did something really different AND achieved global hit song status and/or had a massive impact. To be honest I'm a bit of a rule-breaker myself; I love songs that defy the odds, that do something interesting and unique.

Sometimes as a songwriter we need to approach writing songs less like what a 'songwriter' would do and more what any normal person who knew absolutely nothing about songwriting would do. My biggest pet peeve is listening to something that sounds too crafted or too 'written', because writing a hit song is also about creating a feeling that millions of people want to feel.

It's refreshing to break the rules sometimes and it's a creative necessity to be free and not to box yourself in. When you're free you can really tap into magic that might not make sense at first but then actually makes all the sense. I call these 'creative accidents'. Sometimes the word that doesn't make as much sense but sounds good and feels good is the word to go with.

Don't be afraid to take a risk. Sometimes the word that stands out is the word that gets everybody talking about the song, whether they love it or hate it. This is better than having something 'meh' that strikes no thought or conversation, right? I'm sure a part of Taylor Swift wishes she did in fact write the lyric 'Starbucks lovers' in 'Blank Space'... that took on a whole world of its own as a misheard lyric for: 'Got a long list of ex lovers', but hey, it got everybody talking and listening to the song. I had my own inner debate about the 'it's my right to be hellish, I still get jealous' in the Nick Jonas song, 'Jealous'. The word 'hellish' bothered me at first but it was also the word that made me remember the song and stood out to me, and now I love that they used it as it was different and a clever near rhyme. Also, we can never forget the use of improper grammar in 'Are we human or are we dancer?' from The Killers.

> *I think with songwriters sometimes they worry 'Oh, I don't know if we should say this or that word, it sounds weird, or what will people think if we say this.' But you're then taking out what someone might love or you're taking out what someone might hate, then you end up with a song that people just like, and that gets you nowhere. If you're gonna have a song that people love, then that same song will also be hated by people, and that usually means the song is a huge hit.* **Julian Bunetta**

The great thing about songwriting is a thing called 'poetic license', which gives us the freedom to write whatever we want. We can even make up our own language like Destiny's Child '*Bootylicious*' or The Beatles '*Ob-la-di-ob-la-da*' or The Spice Girls

'I want *Zig-a-zig-aaaahhhhh*', 'De Do Do Do, De Da Da Da' by The Police or the classic 'Supercalifragilisticexpialidocious' from *Mary Poppins*.

You may even come up with a brand-new phrase like 'cake by the ocean', the smash hit by the band DNCE which frontman Joe Jonas said came about when the producers of the song, Mattman & Robin, kept confusing the phrase 'sex on the beach' with 'cake by the ocean'.

They got a hit title which turned into a massive song all by accident. I'm sure they were tempted to call the song by the proper phrase, 'sex on the beach', maybe they even tried it, but I bet it didn't have quite the same ring to it, the same punch. 'Cake by the Ocean' was a rule break and they had the guts and the smarts to roll with it unapologetically, and it became an instant pop classic. Most people might not even know what they meant by that phrase, but, guess what, no one cares… Sounded good, felt good and was unique.

And how about the change of key in the second verse of 'Please Please Please' by Sabrina Carpenter, produced by Jack Antonoff, who said, 'That key change was really a happy accident' but it worked and what's even more interesting is that it goes back to the original key for the chorus which feels fresh and unique.

Everybody breaks the rules sometimes and to step out of them can feel so good, freeing and inspiring, and who knows what song you could write if you are creatively completely free.

I have plenty more where that came from.

'I WANT IT THAT WAY' – BACKSTREET BOYS
Written by: Max Martin, Andreas Carlsson

Famously, this song is as abstract as they come, and it really makes zero sense, yet the melody gives you a feeling that it makes all the sense in the world. The truth is Swedish hitmaker Max Martin wrote these lyrics as more of a placeholder (and admits his English wasn't the best at the time).

The label wanted to try a more 'correct, makes sense' lyric version, which was written and recorded as 'No Goodbyes' but it just didn't have the magic of the original 'incorrect' lyric. They went with the original version, took the risk and released it and it became one of the biggest hit songs of the 90s – a pop classic to this day.

> You are my fire, the one desire
> Believe when I say
> I want it that way

Ahem, I'm sorry, what do you want what way? Confused? Same!

> That we are two worlds apart
> I can't reach to your heart
> When you say
> That I want it that way

HUH?

> Tell me why ain't nothing but a heartache
> Tell me why ain't nothing but a mistake
> Tell me why
> I never wanna hear you say
> I want it that way

Looking at the words, I get even more confused BUT I'm still so emotionally invested and feel something but I'm just not sure what!? Then another part of me does not care at all in the slightest what the song is about and I still find myself singing this at the top of my lungs any chance I get at a karaoke night.

Max is the king of melodies and lyrically he broke all the rules and just sang what felt right with the melody, and it worked.

> *Melody is the universal language.* **Max Martin**

NOTE TO SELF

The masters of the exceptions are the songwriters who know the rules, know when to apply them and know when to break them. I implore you to become so skilled at the craft that you can really do both. Strike the perfect balance and see what happens.

Now I'd like to talk about one of the most modern exceptions of recent times:

CASE STUDY

'drivers license' — Olivia Rodrigo
Written by: Olivia Rodrigo, Dan Nigro

I'm such a fan of Olivia and Dan's writing/production partnership because I feel they just get it. They've tapped into something together that is so strong and they bring out the best of each other creatively.

In a world where we are constantly told to keep our song lengths to 3 minutes 30 seconds absolute max, 'drivers license' already breaks that 'rule' coming in at 4 minutes 02 seconds, which for a radio single is pretty rare, especially these days. Songs are getting shorter and shorter, but I love how Olivia kept the integrity of this track, and, as I always say, we must always serve the song.

Let's take note of the key. Sad songs are usually written in minor keys, but 'drivers license' is written in the key of B flat major and yet the melodies, the vocal performance, the production is what makes us feel the emotion of heartbreak. The chord-to-melody tension is more intricate here than in most straightforward sad pop songs and I love that.

The first major rule break of this smash hit is in the title. As I said in the last chapter, everyone should know what the song is called without needing you to tell them, right? Hence why the title usually repeats several times throughout the song and/or is part of the hook so that it's very, very obvious. However, in 'drivers license', the title is only said once in the song in the very first line and then never repeats. Rule break, but I mean, who cares? It's still a great stand-out title, and how many other songs out there are called that? They made the title stand out even more by the artwork being a picture of her actual driver's license and how they cleverly start the song.

Intro:
What I love about the intro of this song is it starts with the sound of a car engine, a door opening and the chime of the open car door, and it's in the exact key as the song. That chime turns into a pulsing piano (technically known as an 'ostinato' — a repeated musical rhythm or phrase). This is such a different and uniquely clever way to start a song, by giving you a visual to lock into and further highlight the title.

Verse:
The verse sits over the pulsing piano and it's like a stream of consciousness. It feels natural and unplanned, like she just sat and sang what came into her head. I love it when a song doesn't feel 'written' because it taps into that heartbreak feeling that the listener knows well and those conversational thoughts we've all had.

The way the vocals are produced here also breaks traditional pop rules. Usually in pop songs, there are no breaths, no lip smacks, no voice cracks; all of that is normally pulled back or down to create a perfected pop vocal that is clear and pristine, but in 'drivers license', Dan (who produced the song) invites those real and raw vocal moments especially in the verses. It feels like Olivia is singing directly to you, her lips right to your ear and you can hear every breath, every vocal emotional fry, every lip smack — she sounds so present and raw. This gives the song the emotional character that is needed to make you feel the song and truly believe the narrative.

> I got my driver's license last week just like we always talked about
> Cos you were so excited for me to finally drive up to your house
> But today I drove through the suburbs
> Crying cos you weren't around
> And you're probably with that blonde girl
> Who always made me doubt
> She's so much older than me
> She's everything I'm insecure about
> Yeah, today I drove through the suburbs
> Cos how could I ever love someone **else?**

On that last line she lets go of the perfect rhyming scheme throughout the verse. Usually songwriters would rhyme the last word of the verse with the 'doubt' 'about' (ow) phonetic theme throughout here, but she ends it with 'else', which rhymes with nothing, doesn't follow the pattern, and... no one even notices because you're so hooked into the story at that point, so who cares!

Sometimes you listen to songs and get the sense that the lyrics were really thought out and hashed over and over to pop perfection, but in this song, it feels like they flew out of her from some divinely inspired place of pure emotion, and I believe that's the magic of this song and why it stood out.

Chorus:
The most interesting 'rule break' of all comes within the structure. On first listen, the next part after the verses appears to be a classic pre-chorus because in a lot of ways it does what a pre-chorus usually does: builds the tension for what usually leads to the big pop chorus. But in *this* case, this rising melody section is the actual chorus. The melody climbs up note by note against the backdrop of the fourth chord which creates a really interesting rub of tension, and this melody repeats twice. (See sheet music example on facing page.)

> And I know we weren't perfect but I've never felt this way for no one
> And I just can't imagine how you could be so okay now that I'm gone

Then out of nowhere it goes into new faster-changing chords which give urgency to the narrative as she then latches on to the highest note and stays on it, exclaiming in a big, belted emotive vocal:

Guess you didn't mean what you wrote in that song about me

Then all that build up completely quietens back down to the last line of the chorus:

Cos you said forever now I drive alone past your street

That is a very, very unique chorus that breaks all traditional structural rules in the best way.

Another 'rule break' is how the song has an up-tempo ballad feel. This is so hard to do well. Pace and urgency but with elongated chords that make you want to cry, and then from after the first chorus we're on to the third verse which introduces a big rhythmic drive and it feels like you could dance/jump/bop your head to it. Cry dance? My favourite kinda song.

As we make our way to the bridge, we get another unexpected twist:

Bridge:
In this section Olivia and Dan switch it up by going half time into an epic yet longer than usual bridge which feels more like a new hook part. It feels like maybe this was where it was leading to all along and in some ways feels like another chorus. She's taking us on an unexpected journey with twists and turns, and by the end you feel like every part of your heartbreak has been given words and melody. It's a very well-crafted song without it ever feeling like it was intended that way.

When this song was released, it had such a huge and instant impact globally. I believe this was because it was so unique and refreshing, and different from anything else out at the time. This song will go down in pop history, breaking rules and breaking records worldwide.

It's fun to break the rules, you should try it sometime.

SONGS THAT HAVE IMPACT AREN'T ALWAYS COMMERCIAL HITS

Another important piece of advice about being the exception is understanding that sometimes the exceptions were successful in different ways than what's deemed commercially successful, or some songs took years to finally get global recognition. Sometimes as songwriters/artists we want (or major labels want) instant gratification and get so bogged down in numbers and data we fail to see the impact our songs can have in the long term. The world is big, over 8 billion people big, so some songs will take a minute to find their audience. Sometimes it can take a sync in a scene of a movie or TV show with the right visual that matches the emotions of a song and then, boom, the song reacts. Sometimes songs become the soundtrack to special moments without ever having the awards or No. 1 accolades.

People are often shocked when I tell them that the song 'God Only Knows' (in fact, the whole Beach Boys album *Pet Sounds*) was a commercial failure upon release. It's rumoured that Brian Wilson was devastated by it and never got over it. This record was massively ahead of its time in so many ways. Wilson's genius wasn't appreciated until years later and now you'll see it on every list of the best albums of all time. The impact it went on to have is endless. Sometimes great songs take time, and that's worth remembering.

CASE STUDY

'The Vow' – RuthAnne
Written by: RuthAnne, Future Cut

To give another example of exceptions, I wanted to talk about my own first single I released as an artist called 'The Vow'. If you know it, you definitely know it, but if you don't, you definitely don't!! This song has had quite an eight-year journey and it's still going, and sometimes it feels like it's only the beginning.

I wrote the song at the end of 2017. I woke up from a dream, which I can't quite remember, at five in the morning and all the words just came to me like the song idea was floating in the air and I grabbed it. This was definitely a big magic moment. I wrote down these lyrics in a haze and when I woke up and read them I thought, 'Hmm is that cheesy or good?' I couldn't really tell...

> When time is up and the sun it dies
> Till the rivers flood and the ocean dries
> Hand in hand under the falling sky
> I will love you
> When I'm old so old that I lose my mind
> I'll still look at you like it's the first time
> So many say it and it's all a lie
> I will love you
> Cos you are the reason I make it through the day
> You give me the reason to better all my ways
> The beauty goes, the money spent
> When everything else fades away
> You are my constant

I knew it had something... So I brought it to my collaborators Future Cut, who I'd been working on my album with. I said the words to them and Darren said, 'Sounds like a vow you'd say to someone on a wedding day' and that's where we got the title 'The Vow'. Catch me breaking the rules, huh? It's said nowhere in the song at all... But that title in some ways manifested what it has become for people and the impact it has had around the world.

What I noticed very quickly was that everywhere I performed it, it would stop people in their tracks, you could hear a pin drop, and when you're a new artist going in front of crowds with a song no one knows it's very rare to fully grab the room and have them attentively listening. But it was this song... Something about it got people, it emotionally connected instantly. It was my first single released in 2018 through an indie record label, 'The Other Songs'. We had a small budget, so we did a £500 lyric video which has now had millions of views. This proves you don't always need the biggest budget to have an impact if the song can do it on its own, and it really became a song that was driven by discovery.

Music supervisors slowly picked it up and it started getting TV and film placements – *Greys Anatomy* (ABC), *Raising Dion* (Netflix) – bringing in good revenue for me. And the more it was synced the more people heard it. A ballad of this kind is a hard plug for daytime radio, so we were seeing nothing that side of things, BUT sync, streaming, downloading, people were slowly finding it. By the second year we got a big sync placement on the finale of *Love Island* UK Series 5, which was at the peak of its success and becoming a platform that was breaking songs and new artists. The song started charting in Ireland and the UK and more and more people fell in love with it. And in 2023, after singing it for a celebrity couple's engagement, it went viral and had its biggest chart moment, reaching No. 1 in Ireland, No. 2 in UK iTunes and breaking into the top 40 commercial main official chart in the UK at No. 31. Again, in 2025, it went viral on TikTok and Instagram with several wedding videos using it and again charting in UK, Ireland, New Zealand and Australia.

The biggest success for the song since its release is that it has become a massive wedding anthem. Every other day for the last five years I get videos and messages from couples all over the world walking down the aisle or dancing their first dances to it, being proposed to and revealing the gender of their babies, playing it at funerals of their loved ones who have passed, singing it as a lullaby to their babies. It has become the people's song in the most special way that no chart or no award could ever even come close to. And it has also brought so many amazing experiences and moments into my life.

When I get messages about the impact it has had on people and what it means to them, it reminds me that songs can play a huge part all our lives. Songs are the soundtrack to moments and moments become memories that live with us forever. As a songwriter, your goal should always be to create songs that can have an impact and 'The Vow' was the underdog and still is the underdog that continues to live on, a gift that keeps on giving and being discovered. Songs really can last forever.

NOTE TO SELF

There's no one path for a song, there's no one formula, one journey, one-size-fits-all and a song's biggest moment might still be yet to come...

EXCEPTIONS TO THE TITLE

There are a bunch of songs whose title never appears in the song, and guess what they all have in common? They were still all HITS, and let's be honest these titles are so unique they stand out in the best way.

'Iris' – Goo Goo Dolls
'Viva La Vida' – Coldplay
'Song 2' – Blur
'Smells like Teen Spirit' – Nirvana
'Blue Monday' – New Order
'Bohemian Rhapsody' – Queen (One of the biggest songs ever!!)

Speaking of which... We can't talk about exceptions to the rules of popular music without addressing possibly the biggest one ever written by the iconic one-of-a-kind genius that was Freddie Mercury. So, let's finish with a song that broke so many rules I lost count...

CASE STUDY

'Bohemian Rhapsody' – Queen
Written by: Freddie Mercury

There are so many ways in which this song broke the mould, it came completely out of left field. Queen's own label A&R said it would never be played on radio, being just under six minutes long, which was double the length of a usual radio record.

The acapella four-part chorale introduction is the first in a long list of 'rule' breaks that make this song a ballad-to-opera-to-hard-rock masterpiece. It has six distinct sections, all completely different from each other and the biggest rule break of all is that:

It has NO chorus
'Bohemian Rhapsody' broke every rule of the time but it was worth the risk. It's clear that Freddie was experimenting big time and, boy, did it pay off. It's the third biggest UK single of all time.

Originally titled 'The Cowboy Song', it's a song that lyrically is up for your own interpretation. We don't necessarily know what it's about, but it takes us on such a thrilling epic journey that we don't care!

The song took three weeks to record, which would be unheard of today. The year was 1975, so it was on analogue tape – no splice, no Logic shortcuts, no copy/paste. They recorded so many harmonies at one point they wore the tape out!

There were also some brand-new recording techniques used in this song that were ahead of the curve. A technique which has since become used in every recording known to man is 'panning' (distributing a stereo or mono track throughout the left and right channels of a stereo field). Throughout 'Bohemian Rhapsody' there are several moments of perfect panning of the vocals and guitar.

When listening to this song it's almost as if Freddie wanted to go completely against the grain of what was typical. It feels as if he was challenging and pushing himself as far out of the box as he could go, and I respect the courage and artistic bravery to do so. He put it all out there, and each section is so well done and fits together perfectly. He created something that has never been done again and probably won't be unless one of you reading this gets so inspired and are up for the challenge?

Now let's summarise:

HOW TO CHANNEL THE EXCEPTIONS

★ Find the perfect balance between implementing the rules and the right moments to break them.

★ Exceptions can happen by accident... Maybe there are no accidents, especially in creating music. The only way to know is to let the 'accidents' happen and explore them fully.

★ Let emotion override technicalities if it makes you feel something. If the listener feels something let it be because 'feel' wins.

★ Let go of perfection and channel the exception.

★ Be open, be free, be silly, let go and see what happens.

INTERLUDE 1

SONGWRITER STORIES

"Cher hated 'If I Could Turn Back Time'. I had to beg her literally on my knees just to try it, happens all the time."

DIANE WARREN

One of my favourite pastimes is hearing how songs are made. There are always such interesting and amazing stories behind the creation of a song, and so throughout this book I wanted to share some of them with you.

With song stories you often hear from the artists' perspective, but you rarely hear them from the songwriters' perspective. Some songs are written years before they are out in the world, and there's a journey the songs can go on in the background before they are even released. You'll notice a pattern of not only the writing of the song but everything needing to align for that song to have its moment.

I've interviewed a bunch of my favourite songwriters that I've been fortunate to have also written with – they are all at the top of their game and have been in the music industry for years. Let's get into their songwriter stories.

I'm starting with the amazing Emily Warren, who is one of the top female songwriters in the industry today. She told me the story behind co-writing Dua Lipa's breakthrough worldwide hit 'New Rules', which propelled Dua into a whole new stratosphere. The song went global, breaking records and is certified multi-platinum in 13 territories including five times platinum in the USA and UK.

'NEW RULES' – DUA LIPA
Written by: Emily Warren, Caroline Ailin, Ian Kirkpatrick
Produced by: Ian Kirkpatrick

So we actually wrote 'New Rules' at a writing camp for another artist... Me, Caroline and Ian. It was the first time I ever met Caroline, and we just were talking all day... so much talking. And she started telling a story about this guy that she was seeing who was not really good to her and she had tried to end it so many times. She was living in London at the time, and he had just told her he was gonna fly in from LA and she was like I really don't want him to come over. And then we were like, 'Why don't we write a song so that next time you're tempted to do anything with him you could play the song for yourself and you'll be like "no". So we'll write you out of this situation.'

When I first came out to LA, I was in sessions with only boys and older boys who would say to me 'Never make the lyric seem like the guy isn't gonna get some.' That was an actual writing tip – 'Leave the door of possibility open just a little bit because that's not gonna work if you don't do that.' Which I always thought was wild that it's a 'rule'. And then came our song, 'New Rules', which is not like that at all. That was the first time I was really like 'F*ck that, f*ck the stupid rule, that isn't even real and is just a terrible message to put out into the world.' We wrote this song which was the opposite of that because it was what we needed to write for Caroline's situation. It's super-wordy – I'd also been told not to write songs super-wordy. So really all the 'rules' went out the window and it worked. So it's such a good song for me to have to validate all the things that are important to me and none of the things that aren't.

We wrote 'New Rules' exactly how it is now. The verse lyrics were a tiny bit different, but the production was honestly pretty close to where it ended up, which is why Ian is a genius. We finished the song at the writing camp. The label A&Rs came in at the end of the day, they listened, and they were like, 'Um, this doesn't have a chorus, but if you guys want to work on it we'll come back again and listen in a little bit', so they totally bummed us out. It was 9.30 p.m. at this point and all of us were like 'Let's just call it a day. This is a great day but I'm good on re-working this.' When someone comes in and shits on your song right away, I'll never listen to that song again. It bummed me out to the point I didn't send it to anyone, I didn't listen to it again.

And I think it was almost three years later, and Caroline at this point had basically quit music. She had been working for eight years not making any money. She was like 'I gotta know when to call it, this isn't my thing' and she took a job waitressing in London. Right before she started this job she had one last session with TMS and had told them 'I'm basically quitting music, I'm calling it' and they were like 'You cannot quit, please don't quit.'

They ended up writing a song that day called 'In a Year From Now', and the whole point was in a year from now everything is gonna be different and better. So pause that for a second, cos in the meantime Ian's manager had sent 'New Rules' to Dua Lipa's team, who at the time loved it. They said 'We're gonna make it the single.' Originally, they were gonna add a rap feature on it and then they asked us to write a bridge. So this stuff was happening and I was thinking 'This is a weird choice, this is not a good song and you're gonna make it the single... Alright...'

It goes all the way down the road and it comes out as a single, and nothing was really happening, but then a few weeks later the music video comes out and suddenly, very, very slowly, the song started picking up steam and it was amazing. There were all these pieces about how it was like the 'Me Too' movement, and this song and what was happening, and it was sick to see so many impossible factors coming together to make this moment. I genuinely believe that song on another artist at a different time is like nothing, but everything that came together in this moment made it what it was.

I was with Caroline the night that 'New Rules' went No. 1 on radio, and we were celebrating and talking and up pops a lyric sheet on her phone – you know, when it shows this day a year ago on your phone – and it's the lyric sheet from 'In a Year From Now', the song that she had written with TMS, which was crazy.

I feel so grateful that 'New Rules' happened the way it did because it taught me that just because the song didn't get cut straight away it doesn't mean it's not a good song. Now I'm not worried about the song, the song's gonna be fine. There's no rush at all, it just needs to find the right home at the right time. It's better to wait and let it be right.

I'd also like to give a huge shout-out to everyone on Dua Lipa's team who saw the vision in

that song that I didn't. I was writing it because that's what Caroline needed with that guy in that moment, and that's validating to me just in terms of the intention behind the song and making sure that we love it, and we care about it and aren't just trying to write a hit.
Emily Warren

NOTE TO SELF
Break the rules, do what feels the best for the song.

Caroline Ailin has gone on to become one of the most successful female songwriters today – a Grammy, Oscar and Golden Globe Nominee for her song 'Dance the Night Away' with Dua Lipa from the *Barbie* movie. She's one of Dua Lipa's most frequent collaborators, writing 'New Rules', 'Don't Start Now' (with Emily), 'Dance the Night Away', 'Houdini' and many more with Dua and lots of other artists. Thank goodness we didn't lose such a prolific songwriter because think of the songs this world would not have heard.

Next up, one of the most sought-after songwriters today. This is Plested and his story about co-writing No. 1 global smash hit 'Before You Go'. This song is certified multi-platinum in 14 territories, including the USA, and four times platinum in the UK, going to No. 1 on American pop radio and becoming a Lewis Capaldi staple in his repertoire.

'BEFORE YOU GO' – LEWIS CAPALDI
Written by: Lewis Capaldi, Plested, Ben Kohn, Tom Barnes, Peter Kelleher
Produced by: TMS

Lewis was on tour, he had one day off and TMS messaged me: 'Lewis is coming to the studio if you wanna come and write.' I'd done one previous song with Lewis, so I said, 'Yeah, he's a great guy, I'm coming.' We wrote 'Before You Go'. When we wrote it, it was just a normal day and that's usually when the best songs come, when you least expect.

We wrote it about Lewis's auntie, who sadly committed suicide. He was like 'We should write a song about that.' I remember Lewis having the initial idea – the melodies mostly, verse, pre- and half a chorus melody – but I just remember it was very wordy. We were just going around and playing it on piano and then it was when someone just sang 'So before you go', which is so sing-along, we knew we had something then.

I think it was so important that day to go with what Lewis needed in that moment. A lot of writers in sessions would try pivot away from a heavy topic like that and go 'let's do something easier' or more a 'pop song for radio', but at that moment who am I to say I know better than this artist. Once we got the 'before you go' melody and lyric, then the song started to form and make sense as a song, and we all knew it was a good song but was it a hit song? I don't know.

Then it wasn't on the album, so I thought 'Yeah, this is gonna stay on a hard drive.' Then probably six months later, Lewis's manager was like 'we're re-packaging the album'. He'd gone through some emails and found the demo of 'Before You Go'. He said to Lewis 'Maybe finish this one'. They added a middle eight section on it and then they put it out as a single. And it just went wild.

And a song like that, a complicated song, there are a lot of words and it's a very deep, meaningful, heartfelt moment. For me, usually they are the last type of songs that I think are gonna go to American radio and then be at the top of American radio. I was like 'What is happening?' **Plested**

Everything aligned for that moment.

Now we move to the legendary songwriter/producer Lauren Christy who has been at the top of the game for decades. She told me the stories behind three of her biggest songs which were all hits in succession. We call that a run, and, boy, what a run this was. Lauren Christy met a young Avril Lavigne at the start of her career, Lauren noting, 'First of all, Avril's got one of the best voices I've ever heard' and it became a collaborative match made in heaven. Lauren was part of The Matrix, a writing/production trio at the time, and the rest is history.

Lauren Christy with Avril Lavigne

Let's start with Avril's debut single 'Complicated', which was a massive No. 1 global hit and launched her into pop stardom. Grammy-nominated, multi-platinum in 16 territories including four times platinum in the USA.

'COMPLICATED' – AVRIL LAVIGNE
Written by: Avril Lavigne, Lauren Christy, Graham Edwards, David Alspach
Produced by: The Matrix

Avril was 17 at the time, maybe even 16. She was very serious about writing songs and very serious about not wanting to be pushed too pop. So when she first came in to write with us we had prepared ideas, one being the verse for 'Complicated'. It ended up being the second song we wrote with her. I remember her showing up that day and we played her the verse idea which actually ended up getting replaced, we wrote a better verse. Avril had this word 'Complicated', and I was like 'frustrated'. We started to map it out and talk about how really everyone's pretty similar as humans, like 'Why do you have to make it so complicated?' Then the song just kinda of wrote itself and her voice on it was just so crazy good.

I'll never forget recording her vocal. It was just me and her and we had a vocal booth with no windows, so I couldn't see her. I said, 'Okay, let's just run it one time.' She'd been listening to me sing it because I always make a little recording at the end of the day with where I hear the phrasing and pushes. She sang a take down and I was so taken aback it was so good. It sounded so amazing the first time and I was like, 'Holy shit, can you do that again just like that?' And I think she maybe sang it three times in total, and I pulled a couple of lines from the second and third take into the first take, but she just nailed it. That was an amazing experience. **Lauren Christy**

It was one of those songs where everything went right. 'Complicated' was No. 1 for like six months.

Then Avril released 'Sk8ter Boi', another Grammy-nominated worldwide smash, reaching the Top 10 and certified multi-platinum in more than 10 countries, including three times platinum in the USA and No. 1 on American pop radio.

'SK8TER BOI' – AVRIL LAVIGNE
Written by: Avril Lavigne, Lauren Christy, Graham Edwards, Scott Spock
Produced by: The Matrix

'Sk8ter Boi' was really fun. After writing all day, we went back to my house to have dinner and Graham was just playing guitar. I said, 'Why don't we just do something super-punky and up-tempo' and Graham said, 'You mean like this – [plays what would become the 'Sk8ter Boi' guitar lick] da da da da da da'. I said 'Yes. Let's do something really obvious too, like "He was a boy, she was a girl, can I make it any more obvious".' Then Avril was like 'Let's make it about skaters', you know, because I think she had a crush on a skater boy.

So we were like 'He was a skater boy, she said, see ya later, boy.' And my story was that I was a ballet dancer, so we had 'He was a punk, she did ballet.' I was thinking back to my parents saying 'Please don't marry a musician', you know. And of course, I did marry a musician. So we just combined both of our lives in the lyric. And I remember sitting on the rooftop at the Le Parc Hotel that she was staying at and that's where we wrote the lyrics to 'Sk8ter Boi', on that rooftop. Graham's guitar lick which is the musical hook in the song is what kicked it off, completely genius, that was him. It was an amazing combination with Scott, Graham and I and Avril together, just so amazing.

Immediately after 'Complicated's success they put out 'Sk8ter Boi'. As a songwriter who right before this had thought about giving up, all of a sudden we were just continuously No. 1. And then they released 'I'm With You', so we were No. 1 for basically a year and a half with these three songs. It was totally life-changing for us. **Lauren Christy**

'I'm With You' ended up being Lauren's most special, best writing session she's ever had. It also went on to become Grammy-nominated for Song of the Year. Going multi-platinum all over the world and No. 1 on USA radio, it has become a classic Avril Lavigne staple song.

'I'M WITH YOU' – AVRIL LAVIGNE
Written by: Avril Lavigne, Lauren Christy, Graham Edwards, Scott Spock
Produced by: The Matrix

That day I was feeling a bit down. I think it was a rainy day, and in the summer, you know, which was strange. I remember Avril coming round and she was a bit down too, and she goes 'Just feeling a bit depressed.' I've been sitting at the piano noodling and I had this [sung] 'I'm standing on the bridge, I'm waiting in the dark, I thought that you'd be here by now' and she loved it. Then we started working on the next bit. And we're singing melodies, etc., and I said, 'What should we say now here?' And she's like 'Won't somebody come take me home' in this Canadian accent and the rest is history. We're just singing 'It's a damn cold night.' We had the whole thing after that, and it was just a really beautiful moment. I remember we got the first verse, pre- and chorus done and I ran to the studio. I honestly didn't know it was that good because it's a ballad. I played it to Graham and Scott and they both went 'That's it, that song is it! Let's do that one right now, let's cut it now.'

So we finished the rest of the song, and the rest is history. It started with two depressed women together in Sherman Oaks. I said, I'll keep that piano that we wrote it on forever because it's so special, and it's still my favourite song I've ever written.

Obviously when this song came out, and the other songs, I'm just so thankful to God for hearing my prayer that I wanted to be a songwriter and actually bringing it to fruition and having some evergreen hits like these. I'm just so proud of them. It was a collaborative effort, a great team effort, and it was very beautiful how it all came about. **Lauren Christy**

CHAPTER 5

THE PSYCHOLOGY OF A WRITING ROOM

"When I work with artists, I basically check my ego at the door and I become their bitch, and I'm completely comfortable in that role. Sometimes I'll steamroll them, and I'll realise I'm doing it. Because I'm so fast, for me, it's all channels. Words come out and it's just like 'bluh'. It comes out, and I'll just write the lyrics. I don't overthink it."

SIA

When I say the phrase, 'It's more than *just* the song' this chapter will help you understand just how important this phrase is. As well as the business side coming together in the music industry, it all goes hand in hand with what happens in the actual writing room. And there is so much more going on than *just* the writing of a song. This is what I call the psychology of a writing room and I truly believe that the dynamic in a writing room is EVERYTHING and it can make or break the song you write that day.

Songwriters must be extremely adaptable and patient. A huge part of our job is to know all the different creative types and processes, and then the key is being able to recognise and meet each creative where they are and be able to get the best out of everyone whilst getting the best out of yourself at the same time. If you can understand the psychology of a writing room, your song will be the better for it and you can up your odds of making something special.

I spent years as a songwriter not really knowing how important the chemistry behind it all was, and if I'd known this sooner, I think I could've been even more successful. And remember there is no right or wrong creative type or process. It's all about how you navigate it, how you work with people and find the rooms with dynamics that you can thrive in.

RuthAnne with Ed Drewett, Julian Bunetta, Damon Bunetta, Ian Franzino and John Ryan

People skills ★ When people say 'a session' or 'a write' in terms of music this is when writers/producers and/or artists go into a studio together to write a song. And like I've said before, there's so much more that goes into a song than just the act of writing it. There's a vibe, an energy, a dynamic, and striking that perfect dynamic leads to the great songs. It's not just your talent that's needed, it's also about having excellent people skills – that really is half the battle. Talent will definitely carry you far but having the people skills on top of talent will take you even further. I've seen people go a long way in music on their people skills alone. It honestly took me years to develop good people skills; it's something at 17 years old I was not at all ready for, being so young and having no experience whatsoever on how to 'work a room' or 'reading a room'. But I learned from being around other people, observing and taking it all in, so now I find it easier to navigate all the different creative personalities I come across in writing sessions.

> *I think being in bands most of my life, and also being one of three sisters has helped me really connect with artists, because I'm incredibly used to the balance of speaking my mind and listening. I also get what it feels like to know you're going to have to stand by each lyric, melody, and chord so whole-heartedly when you play it in front of an audience, which makes me want to help make the song as personal and authentic to the artist as possible.*
> **Amy Allen**

A lot of songwriters will say that most of us are chameleons — malleable, easily adaptable — for the simple fact that sometimes we only have a day with an artist, just a few hours to make a good impression, write a great song and form a trust and bond with creatives and most importantly create a reason for people to want to write with you again and have you in their rooms and vice versa.

> *The best writers can play different roles, we're chameleons. If someone's on a roll that day maybe it's their day, and it's knowing when to stay out of the way and when to jump in.*
> **John Ryan**

> *When I'm writing with the artist in the room, I usually like to spend the first hour or so just talking about anything except music because I feel like it kind of establishes a rhythm of bouncing off of each other and sharing things, and also I'd say 9 times out of 10, someone will say something that just organically turns into the song we end up writing.* **Amy Allen**

Being able to get the best out of yourself creatively and the best out of others is a skill, more of a people skill than a writing skill but a very important one in the music industry and a vital one as a songwriter/producer.

Stay in it to win it ★ Everything about the session beforehand is unknown. Some people prep before sessions — think of title ideas, start some tracks, chords, have some references to talk about to inspire everyone. I like to be a little bit prepped but not over-prepped. If you're over-prepped you can lose the ability to be open and free, you can be too set on your idea and miss the magic. Being a little bit prepared but staying open is key as it's the unknown and the unknown can be scary.

I've definitely battled with my own anxiety before sessions. The fear of not having any ideas that day, the fear of not delivering. A phrase comes to mind that I've told myself a lot of times to help me get out the door: 'You can't hit a home run every day.' And it's true, if you think you can write a hit song every day, a great song every day, you're already setting yourself up for failure. No one does that, not even Ed Sheeran… Though his bad songs are still better than most. The truth is, the bad songs will always lead you to the good songs because songwriting is like a muscle — the more you work it out the better it'll get, you just have to stay in it to win it. There are times where it may take countless songs to get the one that makes it.

Mindset is everything ★ Your mindset *is* everything. Being comfortable in the writing room to say every and any idea, being confident in your talent. You've got to protect your mindset and energy. You've got to be incredibly intuitive and know how to read the room and meet your collaborators where they are at in their heads. Artists can have a lot of pressures and stresses from other aspects of their job and life and the songwriter can have an important role with the artist. I call this 'the therapist'.

Imagine meeting someone at 1 p.m. on a Tuesday who you have never met before, and you have to get them to instantly like you and get them to feel comfortable enough to tell you their stories and secrets? Oh, and you also have to write a hit song that millions of people will sing that the artist also identifies with, feels attached to and loves all in the same day. The pressure can be immense for everyone. The best songwriters understand how important being a good listener is and being a good 'therapist' is and they know how to make an artist or fellow writer feel comfortable enough quite quickly to confide in them. This must be genuine and authentic where everyone you work with can feel disarmed, safe, comfortable and free to let their creativity take over and flow and feel seen, heard and respected.

Courage vs confidence ★ The truth is, more often than not songwriters aren't always confident. Like I've said, the writing room is the unknown and no one really knows what the outcome will be of each session. Some days I have so much anxiety about songwriting and sessions. What if I don't deliver that day? What if the other writers or artist thinks I suck and am the worst writer? What if they have this huge expectation of me that I won't live up to? What if I don't impress the artist enough for them to wanna work with me again? Trust me when I say most songwriters feel all these things at times.

> *Anytime I go into the room with a new collaborator I'm nervous. And when I'm super-nervous I'll usually bring my guitar and take it out right away because I'm like if all else fails I can just play guitar and hopefully they'll take me seriously as a musician.* **Ilsey Juber**

What I like to remind myself is that I don't have to be confident all the time, every day, at all times, but what I do try to be is courageous. Having the courage to step into the unknown every day creatively can be daunting. You just need to have the initial courage to do it, and once you have the courage to do that and you've stepped inside the room, remind yourself of how courageous that really is and the rest will fall into place.

Let courage lead you through the process and the confidence will come.

Dynamics ★ What I've learned over the thousands of writing sessions I've done is how important the dynamics of a writing room are. The dynamic between creatives can really make or break the song. If you get the dynamics right you are already setting your room up for success. And really it comes down to finding your role in the session that day and some days you may need to play multiple roles.

When I look at my diary now, it's all about looking at it in the sense of the dynamic, and if the dynamic makes sense, then it's all going to be great. **Jon Shave**

To be a great songwriter I believe being in tune and aware of what the room needs is vital. I've been offered sessions to join that I have turned down based on feeling it would throw the dynamics off or there would be too many people playing the same role, which can be counterproductive. I've also spent years really honing in on the people who I have great writing dynamics with and know my role and where I fit best. It's also very important for managers and publishers and A&Rs to understand dynamics in a room and to really be strategic about how many creatives are together in a room. Sometimes people throw seven strong writers in a room together, but that honestly can be too much. Just because everyone is strong at what they do doesn't mean it'll be the right dynamic because sometimes it can be overpowering and too many cooks in the kitchen. Always think ahead of the dynamics of a writing room because when you get the balance right it really can make the difference between a good song and a great song.

The psychology of a room is everything, the chemistry of a room is something that no one understands. It makes sense in hindsight, but chemistry is a mysterious force. Why these four people? If you took one person out and swapped them with another, you get a bad song, but if you swap with this person it's a great song. Why you consistently go back in with certain people. Maybe it's a combination of shared musical references, shared taste, shared communication styles. **Julian Bunetta**

Maintaining the flow of a room is very important as well. Really recognising where the shortage in the room is and trying to fill that gap as opposed to needing to be the one that has all of the ideas. **Ali Tamposi**

You have to be able to read the room. And some people have really big egos. I tend to disarm people pretty quickly. And the first thing I say is like, you know, especially with an artist who's written music before, is like, 'You don't need me to write a good song. Or you, you know, because you've already done it. You're here to write something different than the songs you write when you're alone, or when you're with some other co-writer, your job here is to write with me. And I think we should take a crack at doing something that sounds nothing like what you would normally do. Come back tomorrow and we'll try it again.' **Ross Golan**

THE CREATIVE TYPES

Over my twenty years of being in thousands of writing sessions I feel like I've truly been around every type of creative and writing dynamic you can be in. And there is a pattern of personality types in a writing room and what each type brings to the table. Knowing these kinds of creatives and knowing how to navigate them is a huge part of helping the dynamic of the room. Sometimes creatives can be a mixture of all these types and they see what role they need to play that day to get the best song and they go with it. Often, you arrive at a writing session with brand-new people you have never met before, and it's like speed dating. The sooner you work out the creative types in the room the sooner you can know how to get the best out of everyone without killing the vibe. Number-one rule in a writing session: 'Don't kill the vibe.'

> *My job may not be I'm going to do all the lyrics and melodies for right now. Sometimes my job fluctuates. I mean, I've produced records that have come out, my job is to be versatile. And if they need whatever in the room, I can do the part. You need a producer. I got it. You need the lyric guy. You need the melody guy. I got it. And if no one's around, I'll do all of them.*
> *Ross Golan*

Let's talk about all these different creative types. I've watched and learned from the best and seen first-hand how dynamics help make a decent song a great song, a hit song. And I've come up with my own little formula that I believe is vital in making a hit song.

I believe there are two vital roles in writing a song and if you have both roles covered in your writing room you are on to something good.

THE IDEA PERSON + THE SONG DOCTOR = THE HIT FORMULA

THE IDEA PERSON ★ This first vital role is the person I call 'The idea person', who has the spark, the inspiration and just starts blah blah blah-ing out amazing ideas, concepts, melodies like they've come from the sky. They have the access in that moment and they just get into their zone, they flow and they just go. This idea person doesn't overthink, they simply be, they let the music or the conversation, the chords, the vibe in the room lead them to the ideas. This role is so vital because it's often the magic part of the song. Often you need to record this person the whole time they're in a flow as they may not always remember what they've sung or said because that's how pure it is. You have to capture it before it's gone. And if you're the idea person that day you've got to be willing to let it flow, close your eyes and just feel and let everything out that you're thinking and feeling.

You must be confident as the idea person. A confidence to say something silly that doesn't make sense, because even something that doesn't make sense can still be a hit. There are no stupid ideas, so never be afraid to say them out loud, as you never know what could lead you to the hit song. The idea person feels first and thinks second. The inspiration and the emotions take over and they just flow.

I love being the idea person, especially if I'm full of good ideas that day. Some people bring out the ideas in me just from the energy they bring to the room, and when that happens it's exciting. It's creativity in its purest form, and the best thing anyone can do for an idea person is let them flow, help them flow.

How to be the idea person ★ Have you ever read the book *Big Magic* by Elizabeth Gilbert? If you haven't, you should. Every creative person should read it. She talks about how ideas float in the universe looking for hosts. They are all up for the taking. Ideas can pick a host and if that host doesn't feel inspired to run with it, the idea moves on and finds another host and keeps going until it's been used to its full potential.

To me, ideas are the closest thing to real magic in the world. Think about when Paul McCartney woke up from a dream singing 'scrambled eggs' to a melody which later became called 'Yesterday', a hit song that came to him in his dream. That's happened to me multiple times. Sometimes I wake up and immediately write down the idea or sing it down and sometimes I wake up and the idea is gone, lost forever... or is it? I believe to be a host for these great ideas you need to be open to them. You need to be able to access them, which means being present, being aware, tapping in and allowing the space for them to enter your consciousness. Be ready to receive these great ideas.

I always, no matter what, stop whatever I'm doing to write down a good idea. I remember clear as day breaking up with someone, and in the middle of the conversation a great song title came to me about this break-up. I politely excused myself, went to the bathroom, wrote it down, sang it on voice note and came back out to continue the break-up *and* I got a great song out of a very heartbreaking time.

Ideas have no time frame; they can come anywhere at any time. It's exciting as a creative to know that these ideas could pick you out of all the billions of hosts and they choose you.

NOTE TO SELF

Stay open, stay mindful and let the ideas flow in – one of them could truly change your life.

There can be more than one idea person. These ideas people can bounce off each other and that can be amazing to watch and be a part of, but it's what is done with those ideas that really makes the difference. Which leads me on to the next vital role in a writing session...

THE SONG DOCTOR ★ The song doctor plays such an important role in a song because they know which parts of all these ideas are the best and the strongest as sometimes the idea person doesn't actually know which parts are best for the song. The song doctor can seem to not be doing much but is also doing everything at the same time just by saying things like 'That part right there, that's the hook, sing that again' or 'That melody is so interesting, sing what you just did', 'Ooh, that's the title what you just said.'

It is the song doctor who has the perspective and can sift through the ideas and craft together the song with the idea person. Sometimes the song doctor can come into the session on a different day or later on the same day and listen to the ideas and have a fresh ear to know what's strong, what's weak, what needs tweaking, etc.

The song doctor is all about the craft – they craft the idea. The initial idea may be strong, but it needs everything to support it. The song doctor likes to craft it. Crafting a song is about figuring out a puzzle, cracking the code. Song doctors are incredible at crafting, they know when it's right and they'll keep at it until it's right, even if that means there are several versions of the song. They may eventually go back to the original first draft or by version five find that perfect verse lyric or chorus twist.

The best song doctors I've ever known are the most experienced. They've been around, they're wise, they think more; it truly is a gift and a massive skill. A lot of music producers make great song doctors because often they're not as strong at writing lyrics and melody but have a vision for the song, they know what feels right for the song.

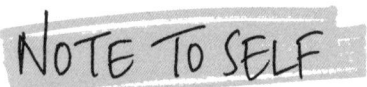

Reminder: The idea person + the song doctor = the hit formula

I'm pretty spur of the moment. When I look at the biggest songs I've had they are usually written fast – like 30 minutes or like two hours. That's just the way I work, and that's why I work well with someone like Julian because he's a little more methodical, he's a crafter and sees the bigger picture, and I just don't think about it. Then after I've got the spark of the idea, then I can sit back and listen and craft. **John Ryan**

You can play both roles at the same time when writing alone, or after taking an ear break from your magic moment you can listen back and be the song doctor yourself. In my experience, the best dynamics in a writing room work when you have people playing these roles as needed. Some sessions, especially with artists, you are needed to simply pull together their thoughts and ideas, help them craft what they want to say in the song, guide them, play the song doctor. Other days, you'll need to bring all the ideas to the table and be the magical element.

I think the foundations of a good writing room have a couple of components: you have to have the pessimist and then the optimist, someone who gets excited and is throwing out ideas and the encourager, someone who is like 'Yes, love that idea', and then someone who is not swayed by the encourager or the excitement and is like 'Hmm. I dunno, maybe we could do this...' like a filter that can distil it. If there's a third person in there that person can be the middleman who can translate it all. Sometimes that's the producer, sometimes that's the artist, but you can't have too many psychologists in the room because then you just over-analyse things and grind the character out of it. **Julian Bunetta**

Sometimes you have to play 1 or 2 or 3 of the creative roles, bring the ideas, bring the vibe. **Jamie Hartman**

The main thing is to tap into both roles, see where you're strongest. You should read the room and know what role to play in that particular room on that particular day. Ask yourself 'what is needed from me today to best serve the song?' Answer that question and pick your role.

Now let's delve into more creative types that you may come across in writing sessions. Maybe you'll even recognise yourself somewhere. You can be multiple types mixed into one or you may take on some of these roles depending on the writing room.

To me it's like trying to catch lightning in a bottle, and sometimes you're in the room and you get the lightning in the bottle, and then you got it and everyone's like, got the stopper in, and then, somehow, something happens. Occasionally, when someone actually just let the lightning out of the bottle a little bit, it can be the track goes wrong, all that stuff. So, I'm always like, super watchful, guarding that bottle. Let's go back to that initial thing at the end of the day that we did that sounded like a smash. What happened? Well, how is it, those live drums that we put on, is it, you know, what is it that's ruining it? **Lauren Christy**

Lauren Christy with Diane Warren

THE SEARCHER ★ The searcher is, as you've probably guessed, the creative type who is 'searching' and always looking for the bigger and better idea. They like to dig and dig and dig some more to really make sure they have the strongest idea possible. Often it's their own process to dig deep in themselves and get the idea through to bring to the table. This can be very useful in a writing room, especially if everyone is happy to search to get the absolute best idea. But it can sometimes be a difficult and long process to navigate, so you need to be patient. Where it can be particularly useful is when everyone is on the same page, has the same vision and agree that the ideas could be stronger. So you all continue searching together, digging a little deeper to see what you can uncover.

Some people come up with ideas quickly, some take time for their ideas to come through. Sometimes the song can feel like a good vibe, you're all jamming and it's vibey, but you may not have quite cracked the code, got the hook, got that section that feels exciting, got the lyric that gives it a unique edge. The searcher will keep going until that's found, and if there's more than one searcher in the room the searchers will talk, bounce ideas off each other and it's like a tennis match, hitting the ball back and forth until they find that great idea.

Where this process can be tricky for some is that it can mentally lead to a brick wall. Hours and hours of searching can suck the energy out of a room and kill the vibe if not everyone wants to keep searching. Some people in the room might feel they have found a solid idea to run with, but if a searcher doesn't agree it can stall things and the searcher may shut down, or the other writers might shut down because no one can agree what it is the song needs at that time. That doesn't mean there's not something good there but it's important to know when to keep searching and when to stop searching and take an ear break.

In this scenario, if the searching is leading nowhere, what I always suggest is to put down the best idea you have so far as a quick voice note or scratch vocal. Then move on and start something new, even for an hour, and then go back and listen to the first idea. Often, switching it up allows everybody to breathe and open back up. Then when you go back to listen to the initial idea it can inspire a new idea, or the searcher may find what he/she was looking for just from stepping away from it and coming back later. Or the new idea you start ends up being the one you all get more excited about, so then it's a win win. Creativity is endless, but it's better to keep a good energy in the room than to drain yourselves on one idea that isn't delivering. It's not bad to be the searcher but always be mindful of how it's affecting the other creatives in a room. If it's bringing the vibe down, park it, move on and come back when everyone is in a good zone.

Read the room, if the energy is dipping or people are hitting a brick wall creatively, switch it up, take an ear break and come back refreshed.

Learning to read the room is one of the biggest skills of a songwriter – knowing when to come forward and lead, knowing when to sit back and let that artist, who's quite a strong personality, do their thing and just drop breadcrumbs along it, or involve someone who you can tell is having an off day or feels overwhelmed by the room. **Ed Drewett**

THE DIRECTOR ★ The director is similar to the searcher but doesn't really ever say the lyric or sing the melody he/she is looking for, instead they try to direct you to it. Sometimes this role can be the producer who doesn't really write lyrics or melody but has a certain vision in their head for what they want it to be, or it might be the artist who may or may not be a songwriter but has a clear vision for what they want it to sound like. This can be useful in a writing session so that the writers aren't just throwing stuff at a wall to see what sticks, but instead have good direction of what's needed in a song in order to connect with the artist who will be singing it.

Artists usually bring in sonic references for their album or songs they love that inspire them which can pull songwriters in the right direction. This can also keep everyone on track if we start doing something that wouldn't work for the style or sound that they're trying to achieve.

Where the director role can be tricky is when he/she is not the artist and they don't actually come up with any ideas themselves but just keep trying to direct you to what they want. And if you're not coming up with what they want, the vibe in the room can go downhill. It's very hard to get inside someone's head if you don't understand what they want. And sometimes these 'directors' don't actually *know* what they want, they'll only know what it is when they hear it. This can take everyone on a wild goose chase that can either churn up something masterful or create a mess. With directors, if I feel I'm not coming up with what they want me to do, I usually try to pivot the session somewhere else so that we don't lose steam or waste time. How I pivot is I try to strike up some random conversation about anything else just to take us all out of our heads and back into the room. And if that doesn't work, I would usually say, 'I'm not sure I'm really getting where you wanna go with this, so should we start something else? How about...' Then I suggest a new idea or a new reference to get us into a more open space for ideas to come find us.

My tip for the directors out there: starting the session with clear direction can be so useful and helpful, and keeping everyone on track is good too, but try and balance direction with creative freedom and don't overdo it. Know when to direct and when to step back and let the magic happen.

THE ENERGISER ★ The energiser is a very important role in a room. There's something about good energy that can really drive a writing room in the best way. Walking into a room with a smile on your face and great energy can really change the temperature in any room and help make everyone's experience that day enjoyable. There's power in the energy you bring. I always try to bring good energy to my writing sessions. This can be tricky on days where I'm not in a good place, but before I step in that room I breathe and let go of any negative energy and bring my best energy that day. Good energy is infectious, and it really has a calming, comforting effect on all the creatives in the room, especially the artists. It can be so daunting stepping into that writing room with new people, dynamics, the pressure to deliver a great song. Bringing a good vibe means that everyone will enjoy their day regardless, and who isn't gonna write a good song when they're having such a fun time. The songs will come from all the positive energy being passed around the room. Chatting, laughing, bantering, dancing, being open and just remembering that everyone is there to write the best song possible and have a good time. I've been in sessions where at first the energy might not get us the best song, BUT it creates the relationships and a dynamic that everyone wants back in the room, and the more you write together with that energy the more comfortable you all are with each other and then, boom, enter the hit songs!

I believe everyone feeds off energy and the worst thing that can happen in a session is creatives being brought down by bad vibes. That doesn't mean you can't be vulnerable, upset or vent about things you're going through in a session (we've all been there and we're human) but there is a way to talk it out and also be there for people going through things. Try to boost their energy, support them and not be put off by it. Writing songs about heartbreak and sadness can be healing and also brings its own restorative energy.

Bad energy is infectious and I've seen it ruin writing sessions, and the best way to handle bad energy in a room is to not let it affect your own energy. Lead with good energy at all times and I promise you it will push out the bad and bring the whole room back to a good place. If bad energy is something that doesn't work for you remember you don't have to work with that person/people again. Find the energisers that give you great energy and watch the good songs fall out of you in droves.

> *Good energy in this space allows me to be creative. I hate it when I'm in a room where people aren't allowing me to shine and I'm kind of being held back or it's a cold environment. I like when if I wanna go and play the keys or if I wanna produce or bring a beat I like when I'm being encouraged to do that. Creative freedom, just feeling free. I like feeling respected in sessions and know that the person respects me and hears me.* **Kamille**

> *I just really love music. I'm not in the room trying to sell you my idea so I can get a publishing split on it. No, I just love making music, listening to music, talking about music. It's my love and passion for music. I'm spark guy, I'm energy guy, and I think energy can become really infectious.* **John Ryan**

Good energy is infectious — have an attitude of gratitude and watch everyone in the room light up.

THE THERAPIST ★ Now let's deep dive into the role of the therapist, creatively speaking. Most songwriters I know, including myself, are really unqualified therapists. Songwriters need to be so in tune with their emotions, feelings, the human condition, heartbreak, sadness, love, loss and everything in between and be able to create a safe space for an artist to spill their heart out, to be vulnerable, honest and LISTENED TO.

Being a good listener is so important for a songwriter. If you don't listen you may miss the story and the punchline that could become your title, your concept, your song,

THE BIG song. It's also about making the relationship and being there for creatives through the writing process. It's worth remembering that even if you write a song that day that helps the artist through what they're feeling or wanting to talk about, that is incredibly important too because even if that song isn't *the* hit, you've still built a trust with your collaborator and/or artist and that trust turns into friendship which turns into more sessions and more songs, and the more you write the more likely you are to stumble upon at least one special song.

The therapist is a vital role in the room, especially when writing with an artist. Making an artist feel comfortable enough to open up, talk about everything and anything they're going through could lead you to the song that might just change their lives and/or be the song that means so much to them. It creates a relationship, friendship and dynamic that they will want in the room again. The amazing artist Fletcher recently described the therapist role in a writing session beautifully, 'Climbing into the innermost chambers of an artist's heart to pull out what's at its centre.'

> *It's a fine line between therapy and songwriting sessions because ultimately what you do in therapy is sit down with a therapist and try to find the emotional truth in it, and that's really what we do in songwriting. We're basically just telling stories but you're trying to boil it down to what the true meaning is.* **Ilsey Juber**

Ilsey Juber & JellyRoll

Most writers who are this creative type are authentically and naturally this way. Supportive, nurturing, friendly and empathic, it should never feel forced or unnatural or not genuine, because that will have the opposite effect. There are lots of songs written in writing rooms just to help the artist or fellow writer get through the day. These can be magical because they come from such a place, and some go on to be huge hits. Even if they're not the song that sticks, you truly form bonds and creative trust in those moments which leads you to work together again and again and then the hit songs follow. If you are the therapist type, lean in and listen, and if you're not that type having someone in your writing room who is will always be an incredible asset to your session and your song.

> *Whenever I get in the room with an artist, I feel like the therapist digging into the artist's life, trying to see what trauma they've gone through, or if they're happy or if they're in love, if there's something that matters. And I'm looking for this one thing, that takeaway. Let's say you listen to any song for the first time and then the next day you remember something. That's the bit that I want to have before I start writing a song. Looking for that in a conversation with the artists. And once we've identified that phrase or that lyric or that line, then I feel okay, it's easy to fill in the blanks and make a song out of that.* **Toby Gad**

THE OVERTHINKER ★ Most times the overthinkers tend to be the creatives who have already had success, and due to lots of factors — like pressure to beat their achievements or maintain them, outside influences, label influence, reading comments on social media — take on the overthinker role.

I've mainly experienced it with artists and it's a tough one in a writing room. As with everything, it's all about balance. Some overthinking is needed — it's good to play devil's advocate in a session to a point — but watching someone spiral into worry, fear, panic and standing in their own way over melodies and lyrics can be difficult to navigate. Artists carry an immense amount of pressure once they've had success: 'You're only as good as you're last hit' or 'Was it a lucky fluke?' or 'A one-hit wonder'… During their first albums artists are usually creatively free and pure, untainted by the industry, so there's none of that pressure and that's usually why they're successful in the first place. They wrote from a place of inspiration with nothing to lose.

When you feel like you're on top and not wanting to go down or make a wrong move, that's when the overthinking hat comes on. I understand where it comes from and over the years have learned how to navigate it. Firstly, you've got to be patient; this could take a few hours, you've got to allow the artist to work through this and help them come out the other side.

The main thing is to take all the pressure away, listen to songs you all love, bring it back to the joy of music, bring back inspiration, creative freedom. Try to bring everyone in the room back to the feeling music can give, getting out of our heads and into feeling excited about making music. That's usually a good starting point. I also try to distract, tell a random funny story that makes everyone laugh or talk about something completely off-topic and that can get everyone out of their heads as well.

The other tip is if you have found an idea that is very solid but someone is overthinking it, definitely say your thoughts about it, such as 'This feels really strong to me. Can we just put down a scratch of it so we have the idea.' In doing the scratch vocal the overthinker may hear the magic whilst recording it and if they don't you still have the idea down so that you can come back to finish it yourself or with others who see the strength in it. Sometimes it's about time, place and where everyone is at. If the idea doesn't come to fruition in one writing session, it doesn't mean it won't in another.

THE ALPHA ★ The alpha writer is usually dominant in the session. They are ambitious and confident in their ability to lead, which can be positive if they are emotionally intelligent, can read the room and have earned their stripes, but some alphas can struggle in collaborations and instead can appear to be overly dominant and arrogant, which can kill the vibe. Sometimes newer writers feel they need to prove themselves so they try to take over with the intention of showing they deserve to be in that room, but the alphas who are purely serving the song will usually have the better results and not compromise the energy in the writing room. An alpha who can be a combination of confident, open to challenges, respectful and sociable can be a great asset in a writing room, knowing when to lead and when to step back and let other writers shine and thrive too.

> *I've been in situations where someone thinks they are the alpha writer in the room. The way I see it is, we're making sandcastles, like in a sandpit, and play this amazing creative game, and if there's an asshole in the room it just makes the game more interesting. Like, okay, we've got a writer here who only wants their ideas used. It's like sword-fighting with one hand behind your back. It's a good exercise and I never get annoyed or wreck the vibe in the room because someone's not that good at collaborating. A lot of people shut down and I've seen sessions end early, but I call that 'wave the hit goodbye'.*
>
> *At the end of the day I want to feel good, so I always try to see where they're coming from. I'm always open to learning. I'm learning stuff all the time from younger writers and older writers. If I really think someone is ruining the song then I will stand up and say, 'Actually, I think this is what we should do.' And the trick is to not make someone hate you – do it in an elegant and charming way: 'Oh, I like your idea but how about we tweak it a little bit and make it more like this.'* **Lauren Christy**

THE LONE WOLF ★ The lone wolf really needs and likes their own space to write. Often in sessions they'll be listening, then all of a sudden maybe walk off into a corner with a pen/pad or just their thoughts. You can see them working things out in their head and then a few minutes later they'll come back and be like, 'What about this?' and sing you an entire chorus or verse with full lyrics and melody. Some will actually leave the room and come back with full ideas. In a writing room there can be a lot of noise, people singing melodies, throwing out lyric ideas, and for the lone wolf they just need a second to think on their own, be with their own thoughts, and it doesn't always need the back-and-forth collaboration or debate on writing. They need space and time and then it will come to them. It happens all in their mind and they don't sing it out until they have more of a fully formed thought.

> *Sometimes creatives have a certain process, and that process is their process so you have to let them be.* **Jamie Hartman**

The lone wolf can be magic to witness but sometimes you wonder 'How do I write with a lone wolf? Does the lone wolf even need a co-writer? What role can I play here?' I normally let the lone wolf do their thing, especially if the ideas are great and strong because getting the best song is the most important thing. I support the lone wolf and there's always tweaks to certain lyrics or melodies that as a co-writer you can make to make their idea even stronger, or as they're writing one section on their own you focus on another section or write a second verse or pre- or bridge, or you focus on the music and helping the producer with the track.

You could also be the song doctor that day, making sure every section is the strongest it can be and help them craft it. Some artists who are lone wolves with their art are incredible songwriters themselves, so they just need a little guidance or a little help to craft the song. They might need you to pull that last 5–10% of a story, lyric or melody out or inject that last magical sprinkle on top – which is still a very important role to play.

The main thing is to not feel deflated or not needed and don't take it personally. The lone wolf is just doing the process that gets the best out of them. The room still needs you. If the lone wolf comes back without great ideas or ideas you don't feel inspired by, try and take their thoughts and expand on them, flip them around, find one line you like and work with that. Or say something like 'You wanna record that idea down so we have it and we can also try something else?' Never deflate, always acknowledge.

NOTE TO SELF

There is always a role to be played in every writing room. Find your role, don't fight it, lean in and see what happens.

THE 'OUT OF THE BOX' ★ These are the writers coming in hot from left field. Out of the box, with a different perspective, always able to channel something fresh, new and different. They want and seek originality. This creative type can be such an asset in a room. They go against the convention so naturally and effortlessly give your song a unique twist. I love it when I work with a writer who comes from left field. It's always great to have differing perspectives that can come together.

Sometimes these creative types can be quieter or more in their own zone and can be hesitant to share their ideas for fear of being too 'out there', but you should welcome all and any ideas. It's that quirky line, lyric or melody that can be the extra special sprinkle in a future hit. It's also a fun exercise to challenge yourself, no matter what creative type you are, to think outside the box, so get out of your comfort zone and try something new or in a different way than you have before.

Sometimes we can stand in our own way and ourselves creatively because of what we think the listener or artist wants, but being daring and brave enough to throw out ideas that go against the grain can lead somewhere new. Have no fear to say every and any idea even if you think it's too whacky or silly.

I like being around people who aren't afraid to try the weird and wonderful, because sometimes we're comfortable in the kind of bread-and-butter part of creative, and not as many of us are aiming for that Marmite song that might be awful or it might be the next biggest song in the world. So say something stupid, cos you never know, that could be what makes the song huge. **Ed Drewett**

Dua Lipa with Ed Drewett

There are no stupid ideas, say it all!

THE PRODUCER/MUSICIAN ★ The producer really has a vital role to play in every writing room. Most of the time the studio and environment you'll be writing in is owned by the producers. So he/she can really set the tone for the session. The producer has the sonic vision for the song, the sounds and the overall tone, so this will inform the song you'll write that day and knowing and being on the same page with the direction sonically is incredibly useful.

I always think the best producers are the most adaptable. They understand going with the flow of the room and not being bound by the tracks they may have prepped for the session, being open for anything to happen and being able to make it all happen sonically. They know when it's best to keep the song stripped down and simple and then work on the production after the session. The producer also is the leader in getting the absolute best from everyone that day, including the artist: getting the best vocal performance from an artist, or leading the room in terms of energy, ear-breaks, switching up instruments to inspire something else or trying new chords.

As I've said earlier in this chapter, producers can also be the best song doctors because they don't always focus on coming up with the ideas lyrically and melodically as they're focused on producing the music, BUT they have a fresh ear on the ideas and can help craft the song to a better place.

RuthAnne in the studio in LA

Some producers can be the biggest character in the room or the most shy and reserved type who likes to stick to what they know, which is the world of sonics and sounds. They can happily spend hours and hours on a snare drum or a kick or getting the perfect synth sound. However, the best producers know when to park the snare sound and keep the room flowing, get the song written and work the production around the song. I've written a whole chapter on production so more on this later.

Producers are often the glue of the entire session and great producers know how to get the best out of everyone in the room.

BEING A TEAM

When I was a young songwriter, I was so used to writing songs by myself, just me and my thoughts. I didn't have to debate with anyone other than myself about lyrics, melodies and chords, and when I started co-writing, I always felt this pressure to contribute and deliver so much of the song. If I was in a session and felt like I didn't do that I felt like a bad writer or not good enough, not contributing enough. But the truth is as you read through all these different creative types you can see that every day when you walk into a writing room you are walking into the unknown; nobody knows what's gonna happen.

> *If you have an idea that you're excited about and you don't bring it to life it's not uncommon for the idea to find its voice through another maker, this isn't because the other artist stole your idea but the ideas time has come in this great unfolding of ideas and thoughts, themes and songs and other works of art exist in the ether and ripen on schedule ready to find expression in the physical world.* **Rick Rubin**

Every creative type in a writing session has a role to play and each role can be incredibly helpful to the process if navigated correctly and fitting with the dynamic that day. It's okay for some creative types to not work well together. My best advice is to find the creative types that you work well with and stick with them.

One day you might be the writer who has come in with a killer concept, an amazing melody and/or the best idea and other days you may be with an artist who only needs you to help craft their ideas. What I learned along the way was that actually the best songwriters find out very quickly what role they need to play in each writing session to get the best result, and that will always change depending on who you are in the room with. It's all about working out what is needed from you as a writer that day.

What I'm getting at is that collaborating/co-writing is a team effort. From the minute you step into that studio and start conversing you are already, without even knowing it, contributing to the song that will be written that day. The song that you end up with would never have been that song without you in the room no matter how little or how much you feel you contributed. (Unless you said absolutely zero and sat silent and literally didn't speak, then that's different — that doesn't help write the song at all!)

THE SOCCER ANALOGY

I like to think of co-writing like playing a football game. Sometimes you will be the striker that kicks the ball into the net and scores the goal (comes out with the best idea or cracks the code of the melody needed or lyric) and sometimes you will be the writer who assists the striker's kick. And without that assist that goal may not happen.

There are days where my job as a songwriter is to assist the artist or writer and lead them to the goal kick and vice versa and throughout the session this can keep going back and forth. Just like a football game anybody on the pitch can score a goal. Everybody can take a shot and even if you miss, that attempt could be so close and help someone else to tweak the position of the ball sightly (tweak the idea) and then score the goal (say the lyric needed, etc.).

> *It's a team sport so whatever role you are playing that day, defender, striker, it doesn't matter as long as you are in a position where if someone else is having a brilliant day let them play, just pass them the ball and let them score and if they're having a bad day, step up.*
> **Jamie Hartman**

Sometimes talking through an idea, or explaining what the next line needs to say, like 'We need to now have a line that sets the scene of where we are in the song,' or 'That last melody needs to change and go somewhere new', or saying the wrong word can lead to the right word. Anything you say can inspire, influence, guide or lead even yourself to the answer, you just have to be ready to be part of the team. Some days you may have to carry the team, some days you might be on fire with ideas and just nail it and everyone else will assist you and craft with you. Again, it's still a team no matter what position you play.

THE PING-PONG ANALOGY

Sometimes you assist the striker and sometimes you engage in what is known as 'ping-pong'. This is an amazing creative flow that happens when collaborators enter a rally. Someone serves the first line and then you bounce the ball right back with the next line and then they come right back with the next one, and so on and so forth. It doesn't always happen but when it does it's pretty special.

When you hear about songs that were written in 20 minutes or 45 minutes usually that was just a great rally of songwriting ping-pong that the writers found themselves in, and it's really magic. It's when everyone stops thinking and just runs with the idea and the feeling, and every line back and forth of lyric or/and melody fits and works, and before you know it the song is written.

NOTE TO SELF

When you get into a songwriting ping-pong mega rally, run with it. Don't think, just flow because it is truly one of the purest creative experiences you'll ever have.

CASE STUDY

'Pocketful Of Sunshine' – Natasha Bedingfield
Written by: Natasha Bedingfield, John Shanks

During my interview with John Shanks for this book he told me an amazing story and great example of ping-pong songwriting that I want to share with you.

> When I played Natasha that track it was the end of the day and she needed to leave in 20 minutes, but we had the title. We had been talking and I said, 'Ya know, wouldn't it be great if you had this pocketful of sunshine that you could cure kids of cancer or if someone was depressed you could give them this pocketful of love.' She loved it and said, 'That's such a good idea – if someone needed money or love here's a pocketful of sunshine.' It really was more about overcoming sickness and spreading love.
>
> So I played her the track, and she came up behind me and started singing the melody with the title 'I got a pocketful, got a pocketful of sunshine.' Then I sang 'I got a love, got a love and it's all mine, oh.' We started rallying back and forth. And she said, 'I literally have to go in 20 minutes.' So we wrote the chorus as fast as we could. And then she said, 'Okay, I'll come back another day.' I said, 'Quick, you gotta go and record this chorus before you go.' So she went into the booth and started recording the chorus and I was like 'Oh, there's something wrong with the mic. Can you sing that again?' But really I was doubling her and layering it up. Then I'd say, 'Hey, just quickly do a harmony.' We got the chorus down as fast as we could. She had her coat on, and she's like 'I gotta go' and then she's 'Actually, wait, we need another section.' And I sang 'take me away, a better place', and she went 'a secret space', and I went 'take me away'. We had that next section, and nobody was overthinking or searching, we just felt it and went for it.

Ping-pong songwriting at its finest. The song went on to be a hit all around the world.

THINGS TO AVOID IN WRITING SESSIONS

SAYING THE WORD 'NO'

When you're in a creative flow there's only a certain amount of times the word 'no' can be said without you completely shutting down. Creativity is free, there aren't any limitations and there shouldn't be, but when someone keeps saying 'no' you slowly but surely start feeling trapped and bound creatively and you'll almost certainly hit a wall.

If you have someone who is pushing back too much or stopping the momentum it can be frustrating, like when they're not reading the room and just kind of want to be an obstacle in the way, and that can be a bummer. **Ed Drewett**

If you have a group of people that are having fun and want to make something great together and the synergy is right, then it's the most helpful thing in the world, but if you have somebody in there that's just shooting down ideas or singing melodies over each other, then you just end up hitting a wall. **Ilsey Juber**

I've learned to be so careful with how many times I say 'no' in a session. There are other ways to pivot from an idea you don't like by suggesting something else. Try this… 'Let's try it, let's hear it'. This is by far the best phrase to settle any debates musically, lyrically and melodically that no one can argue with or feel shut down or not heard or seen by.

It's worth it to try anything and everything because very quickly when you try something you'll know hearing it back if it works or not. Sometimes, what you think wouldn't have worked does actually work and/or what you thought was a no-brainer doesn't work at all. It's easier to pivot away from an idea that's not working by hearing it and trying it. There is always time to try, and you can always go back and keep the original idea.

SAYING THE PHRASE, 'IT DOESN'T FEEL LIKE A HIT'

Another phrase that is absolutely not productive in a writing session. Whilst making a song, it's so important to stay present in the moment and let the writing take you into the zone. You can feel that a song is stronger than others, but the word 'hit' just comes loaded with pressure and expectation and can bring everyone into their heads too much. Everyone in the room is already feeling that pressure in varying degrees.

The truth is there are many hits that have been written in 45 minutes with no thought, no conversation, just pure creative freedom and feeling. In a session you've got to know when you need to craft the idea to greatness and when to leave it alone because it's strong as it is. Comments like 'it's not a hit' don't do anything but make everyone feel like they failed that day and it sucks the joy out of the room.

Let the room be a sacred place where opinions like that just don't enter. Those conversations can come days later when you submit the song or listen back, but during the actual process of writing the song there's no relevant place for that phrase.

HAVING ANYONE IN THE WRITING ROOM WHO IS MANAGEMENT OR FROM A RECORD LABEL

The writing room and writing process can be incredibly intimate and vulnerable. Anyone who is not a part of writing the song should not be in the room (other than the studio engineer, or a videographer who the artist may want there to film for some of the session).

Keeping the room for creatives only is important because anything that anyone says, even just a passing comment, can have a direct influence on how everyone feels about the song, and if a manager or A&R says something negative or something irrelevant it can really throw off the dynamic and completely kill the vibe.

> *One of my biggest pet peeves is when a manager or A&R comes in the room when we're not finished or we're in a really good vibe and one look from them can just ruin the whole vibe.*
> **Autumn Rowe**

It can be so distracting having people in the room who aren't there to write. And I've seen it happen. When we go in to write songs we are opening up ourselves and getting into a zone together. A manager sitting on a laptop or taking calls or reminding the artist about scheduling things, it just takes everyone out of the zone. To write a song we need to be present and stay in this creative moment.

I am also against an A&R coming in at the end of the day to hear the song and give thoughts. Usually, the song will be in a rough demo state, unfinished, rough vocals, etc., so it's not the time to present it to a label. It's best to stay in this beautiful creative place together and go home feeling good after a day's work that you're all happy with. Finish the song or get it to the best place for presenting it to the A&R.

It can be so deflating if an A&R comes in after you've spent the day working on something you're all excited about only for them to shoot it down or say it's not good enough or not a hit. I've been in situations where that has been said and then the song has gone on to be a hit. So the negative or average comments ruined our day and deflated everyone, but the A&R was WRONG... Moral of the story: keep the writing room to the creatives.

NOTE TO SELF

Never underestimate how important and vital the psychology of the writing room is. It can completely help or hinder the song you write that day.

CHAPTER 6

THE ART OF STAYING INSPIRED

"Sometimes you pick the guitar up and the songs come out of your mouth. I write when the writing is there and when I'm inspired. And I don't worry about not writing. It's simply not predictable and you've got to get used to withstanding that anxiety."

BRUCE SPRINGSTEEN

"With songwriting I spend a lot of time living life, accruing all these experiences, journaling, and then by the time I get to the studio I'm teeming with the drive to write."

ALANIS MORISSETTE

Something I get asked about often is 'writer's block' and the truth for me personally is it's not something I've ever really experienced. Sure, I've been in sessions where the creative juices run dry or I feel like I didn't really do a great job that day, brain fried lyrically, or melodically not at my freshest, but I can touch wood and say I've never not been able to come up with something, an idea, a start.

I've always made inspiration a priority. I do whatever I need to do to stay inspired. I stand by the motto, 'You have to live to write.' If you are experiencing writer's block or a phase where you feel your ideas have gone stale or need a little inspirational pick-me-up, then this chapter is full of my tips to stay inspired and avoid the dreaded block.

LIVE YOUR LIFE

The best songs come from life experiences, so without getting out there and living, where are the stories gonna come from? Without living and experiencing, succeeding and failing, trial and error-ing, great conversations, hard conversations, heartbreak, love, times of joy, times of pain, diving fully into the human condition, well, what would there be to write? Honestly not much. Get out there and live! Especially when you are struggling creatively, can't think of anything, feel uninspired – life is waiting for you, so put the pen down, close the laptop, get off your phone and get out in the world. The more you live the more you have to write about.

I promise you the more you experience what life has to offer, the less likely you are to ever experience a complete block to your ideas. The best storytellers have always experienced so much life, and when you look around you there are stories and inspiration everywhere. You just have to open yourself up to see it and run with it.

A certain T.I. and Rihanna song comes to mind here:

> 'So live your life ay ay ay ay, you steady chasin' that paper, just live your life, ain't got no time for no haters, just live your life.'

MUSIC DOCUMENTARIES/BOOKS/FILMS

One of my favourite ways to stay inspired is by watching music documentaries. I love watching how the greatest songs were made, the stories behind the songs, how artists got their big break, the journey they went on, the journey a song has taken. To me it is all so inspiring; it reminds me how big songs can happen anytime, anywhere and the magic of creativity.

Books and films also can bring on great concepts for songs. Movies have always inspired song — the great one-liners in a movie are all up for grabs in song lyrics, and books can be an amazing way to find other stories, other concepts that you may not have fully experienced per se but can still find inspiring.

LISTENING TO MUSIC

In songwriting we call it 'references'. Sometimes writers and artists make these reference playlists of their favourite songs or music they are inspired and influenced by, not to steal from but to be divinely inspired from. I grew up constantly listening to every type of music you can think of. So many different artists and genres and moods of songs. That's why it's impossible for me to ever pick just one favourite song, I have so many. And songs that I love can take me into a different universe and inspire me so deeply. They're like best friends, so if you're low on inspiration go back to the songs, listen, become a student of song. I promise you will be refreshed, revitalised and ready to go.

HOBBIES (NOT MUSIC-RELATED)

Sometimes you need to fully shut down the music side of your brain to really step away from it and get a fresh creative glow. Everything in life is about balance but sometimes, as creatives, the amount we write, the workload, the business side can take a toll on the juices to create uniqueness. I'm not saying to step away for too long, but just getting out of the zone when needed to jig things up is a good thing. Find something else — a hobby, a passion — that isn't music-related. For some, it could be table tennis, basketball, going the pub with friends, travelling, being out in nature, cinema, dancing, exercise, going to see live shows or musical theatre, watching reality TV, football… The list is endless. Don't underestimate the power of hobbies and activities outside of music to help ultimately inspire your music.

> *I go hiking, work out and I try to meditate and eat something healthy to put myself in a good space.* **Ilsey Juber**

> *I'll hear a song or I'll watch a film or read a poem and it gets my creative juices flowing again. If I'm ever feeling like 'I can't do this' I'll just stop and take a day off and go to a museum, go do something, and it gives me the top up that I need.* **Plested**

'You have to live to write.'

FIND LIKE-MINDED CREATIVES

You'll hear a lot of songwriters talking about writing with 'their people' — friends, writers, who they enjoy being around. Being among people who inspire you can really help when you're feeling empty creatively. There have been days I've woken up and thought 'I've got nothing to give today.' I look at my schedule, see who I'm in with, and when it's someone I have a really good rapport with creatively, I know it's gonna be a good day. Often their energy will get me out of any creative rut I'm in. They'll bring out the good in me just from talking and hanging with me like a friend.

Writing with friends takes away the pressure completely — it makes it feel more like a hang or a jam rather than a 'writing session', so another way to stay inspired is to stay around inspiring people who you like being with.

> *If I'm working with someone who's fearless, then I get less fearful myself and I become fearless. If I'm with someone who's really creatively free in their creativity, really unembarrassed and shameless about showing their ideas it frees me from any inhibitions that I might feel and I become much more creative.* **Dan Wilson**

TAKE EAR BREAKS

I've often been in sessions where we get stuck, we hit a wall, and we don't really know if anything sounds good anymore. We're not sure where to go next, needing inspiration, and the flow has dried up. One of the best pieces of advice I ever learned from top songwriters and producers in my earlier years was the magic of the 'ear break'.

Trust me, listening to the same beat over and over again, or the same hook blasting in your ears you can lose all sense of what is happening. The best thing to do in this case is to turn it off, step away from the process and do something completely different. Don't talk about it, don't think about it, just set it aside and do something else.

In a lot of studios in LA they have basketball nets outside or table tennis; or even stopping to go get lunch in a different environment, take some air, a walk in the park, a new place, can really make all the difference. Once during a session I was in we actually went to the cinema and watched a whole movie, came back and were all completely refreshed and felt like we had new ears to listen to the song with perspective and a new wind of inspiration. You can take an ear break or a writing break for as long as you need to get the creative juices flowing again. There are no rules in this music game so take ear breaks as and when you need them and step away from creating when you need to.

DON'T BURN YOURSELF OUT

One of the fastest ways to kill your inspiration flow is by burning yourself out. There's a lot of pressure put on writers sometimes to just be in a studio 24 hours a day, writing constantly, session after session, 'gotta stay in the game and keep your spot' mentality. Each to their own of course, but I've always found that it's quality over quantity and that comes with time and experience in the music biz.

Of course, at the beginning you will be doing your 10,000 hours like we've talked about, but it's very important at whatever stage of your career you're at not to go so hard that you hit a wall and crash and burn out. I definitely went through a phase of what I called 'paying my dues' where I was sometimes doing three writing sessions a day, or two a day all week long. I found it hard to say 'no' and felt like I would miss out on opportunities, but it quickly led to me being completely burnt out. I learned the hard way how much smarter and vital it is to replenish the tank, recharge the creative battery and not say 'yes' to everything. I always know I'm about to burn out when I'm in a room singing the same melodies that I just sang in the last session or I'm lyrically not at my freshest. Burnout can be so hard on you creatively and really deflate and un-motivate you. Songwriters have to give so much in the room and when you feel like you've nothing left to give it really is time to take a break.

The best way to avoid burnout is to look at your writing schedule and have days off to live and do other hobbies or interests that you enjoy. I personally love a day to catch up on my fave TV shows, hang out with friends, go for a walk in a beautiful scenic setting or a drive listening to my favourite music.

If you are close to a burnout, check in with yourself and your team and be honest with yourself about how you're feeling. It's all about knowing when to stop and take that break. Don't forget to listen to yourself and remember, what's meant to be won't pass you by. Avoiding the burnout will avoid writer's block.

MENTAL HEALTH IS YOUR WEALTH

We've talked about the psychology of the writing room but it's important to note how much of a key role psychology plays in your own self when it comes to creativity. A lot of songwriters, artists and musicians struggle with their mental health and a lot of the time it takes a huge amount of self-care, bravery and strength to overcome those struggles and walk into rooms where you may not know anyone and write a great song. The music industry comes with its own toxicity from the business side of things which can have a very negative impact on your mental health. I know a lot of creatives, including myself, who suffer with anxiety and it can often be incredibly challenging, especially when so much of songwriting relies on our emotions and our headspace that day. That's why it's so important to check in with yourself and your teams and your loved ones if you're struggling and do whatever it takes to look after yourself first and foremost. It's more important than any session to practise self-care and take as much time as you need to look after your mental health. Sometimes I also find writing can help my anxiety, it just needs to be with people I trust and feel comfortable with.

> *I'm always trying to reconnect to why I started doing this and why this is what I chose to do with my life. I feel like sometimes how the business is set up, endless sessions and the counter always being full, and all these things, are more like a capitalist approach to an art that should be left out of that. I have found a good rhythm of tapping in, doing it, meeting people and also pulling out and having people I love come to me in Wyoming.* **Emily Warren**

> *I went through a lot of trauma throughout this industry, the last fifteen years of my life with sobriety, with tremendous amounts of self-doubt, and I don't feel like you ever graduate from that. It doesn't matter how much success you have, like a bad session it doesn't stick with me as long, but it's still present. But when you're at the beginning it's this rush of just being in the room with someone you look up to, and that adrenaline keeps you going, and now I really think about, how do I want to go to a session today? What's the combination of things that I need to feel inspired?* **Ali Tamposi**

IMPOSTER SYNDROME

A lot of songwriters experience imposter syndrome (the persistent inability to believe that one's success is deserved or has been legitimately achieved as a result of one's own efforts or skills) especially after having a hit song. They often wonder, 'Was that a fluke? Can I do that again? Did I even do enough on that song? Am I a fraud? Am I even talented? I have no idea how I did that.' And there is a feeling of pressure to have another hit once you've had one because of the age-old saying in the music business: 'You're only as good as your last hit'. Like we've talked about already and as the title so aptly reminds us, 'It's not JUST a song', there is so much that needs to align for a song to be a hit.

Your focus should always be on writing the best song possible because great songs find a home when they're meant to and great songs always have their moment. The truth is, I won't ever be able to recreate the hits I've already had. Record label people ask me all the time 'We need a song like "Too Little Too Late". Can you write another "In the Name of Love"? 'My answer always is, 'I can't write those songs again.' Simply put, 'Those songs are written and anything I try to do to emulate them will never match the magic of those songs.' But that doesn't mean I can't write another great song... Chasing the hits you've already written is just going to lead to a lesser batch of songs. Instead, I put my head down, stay inspired and know that if I can write one great song, I can always write another.

There have been so many times I've felt imposter syndrome, feeling like a fraud or I wasn't good enough or that I was winging it, and in a lot of ways creatives *are* just winging it. The truth is, we never really know what we're doing because every time we step into a room we are stepping into the unknown. What will we create? Sure, we build up the tools in the tool kit but the outcome is not always guaranteed. This is where another golden piece of advice comes into play and it's one of my all-time faves…

'You can't hit a home run every day.'

One of the best nuggets of wisdom I've had was from Catherine, an amazing life coach in LA. I remember having a bad session followed by another bad session and I said to her, 'Maybe I've lost it, maybe I never had it, maybe I'm the worst songwriter in the world.' She looked at me and said, 'But honey, no one hits a home run every day,' and it really clicked with me. There are days where we all write bad songs or the session falls flat and you literally leave the studio feeling like you are the worst songwriter in the world.

When I interviewed Plested for this book, he told me his story about when his imposter syndrome 'was going mad' and his anxiety (which I think every single creative mind has dealt with). This story reminded me that everyone suffers from this at some point and we're all human at the end of the day and it hasn't stopped him from writing more amazing songs.

> One of my idols is Ryan Tedder – I love Ryan Tedder – and for years and years I'd been dying for a session with Tedder. I think it was my first or second trip to LA since 'Before You Go' – the song I'd written with Lewis Capaldi – had started opening doors. And it was like 'Ryan Tedder wants to work.' I was 'Yo, okay.' Basically, I suffer like most people do with mild anxiety – it's not severe but it's definitely there. I'd never experienced a panic attack before, but I could feel the session was coming up – it was with Tedder, Michael Pollack and Marshmello (a big writing room) – and I was nervous, had butterflies. My imposter syndrome was going mad, right.
>
> So I get to the session, everything is fine. I'm friends with Pollack, so that was the common ground. And I had done 'Leave Before You Love Me' already with Marshmello. I'd never met Tedder. And he, as everyone knows, is so lovely, he's so welcoming. His studio is incredible. He's got the biggest fridge of snacks you've ever seen and gets you any drink you want. The studio is like a museum, so it was this whole experience, but I can feel this anxiety building because I want to prove myself, I want to write something good. This is the biggest opportunity.
>
> Then basically I feel the anxiety just exploding. And I'm struggling to breathe a little bit. So I go to the toilet to take a break and just take myself out of the situation. I didn't realise at the time that Tedder has his Adele *21* Grammy for Album of the Year on the toilet. So I just see that, and all of a sudden I have a panic attack and I couldn't breathe. I was just trying to not pass out. I just kept saying to myself, 'Don't pass out. It's the last thing you want to happen.' So I went back into the room, sat in the chair and didn't say anything because I was just trying to keep my breathing going.

I said 'I'm sorry' to Pollack afterwards and he was like 'Yeah, I mean I could tell something was up, but it was fine, didn't ruin the session or anything like that.' You know, I've worked with Tedder since and that's been great and it's all fine and I got through it. And it's never gonna get worse than that. I just got too in my head. It's all about your creativity, so your mindset and where you're at mentally is such a big part of it. **Plested**

IF YOU CAN WRITE ONE YOU CAN WRITE ANOTHER

One of the best pieces of advice I ever got in my early 20s about songwriting was from hit writer Franne Golde. She'd been in the industry a long time and written so many songs. One day when we were writing I asked her, 'What if I never have another hit like "Too Little Too Late"? What if I've peaked and the only way from up this high is down?' And she said to me, 'Ruth, if you can write one great song you can always write another one.' It's a motto I have kept with me throughout the years, and it has really helped me get out of creative ruts.

> *You're just trying to do the best that you can every day. I've had terrible sessions with people that I love, that I've written hit songs with, and I've had amazing sessions with people when we've never gotten anything.* **Ilsey Juber**

Whether you're an upcoming writer and you've just had a session that produced the best song you've ever written or if you've just had a big song or a semi-big song or the biggest hit of the year, please remember you can do it again. You can write a great song again. What the universe will do with it can't ever be guaranteed and we should always approach songwriting through inspiration to write the best song possible, not in desperation to have a hit.

> *I learned a big lesson after I had my first global hit because of course you want more of it, it's a bit like a drug, you're kind of, well, this is amazing. I remember almost trying to make a record that was quite similar in terms of how it sounded and how it felt. This record was called 'Beg For It', which, you know, it did pretty well. I think it was top 10 in America, which in any other circumstances would be great. But the big lesson for me was, actually, you shouldn't ever really try and do the same thing twice. Once you've done it, it's time to do something completely different, and, you know, try and open a new door to something. I think the temptation is, oh, this is what people like, they must want more of it, and actually, and I think this is even more the case now, once something's been done, it's done, but you can write something new and something different that can be just as big.* **Jon Shave**

> *I've gone from wishing I was in the rooms, trying to get in the rooms, being able to get in the rooms, not being the guy, then being the guy and then not being then guy, and how do you deal with that? I had a lot of No. 1s in one year and won Grammy Producer of the Year, but I've had years with no No. 1s too and I'm still here doing it.* **John Shanks**

You won't write a great song every day as no one does, but if you've done it once you can do it again, I promise. Trust the process, do all the things that work for you to stay inspired, tap in, find the flow and the great songs will come, don't let your own self-doubt stop you from getting those songs.

I've never said I'm giving up but I've definitely wondered if I'd ever have success. I wonder if I'm not as good or if I'll never be as good as I once was. Maybe I suck, maybe I've lost it, maybe I don't have the thing anymore, all of that. I've found my own mechanisms for combating that and/or ignoring or blocking it out. It's a journey that everybody has to take to figure out their own way of navigating the inner voice and the doubts. You just have to figure out a way to talk to your own voice cos you're the only one that has to hear it in your head. That's the only way you're gonna ascend to the highest level of something or it will just hold you down. **Julian Bunetta**

Every songwriter has those moments where they wonder if it's worth it. What keeps me from quitting is the belief from the people closest to me and the fact that I genuinely love the people I get to work with. And without fail, every time I feel like I'm ready to quit, I'll have one of those magical days writing something I love with people I love. Those moments are unlike anything else and remind me why I do this. **Steph Jones**

I've always had the experience where something I do becomes astoundingly popular and then normal life resumes for like four or five years. So every time I've had a big success I always have this crash afterwards and then the self-doubt and 'why am I even doing this' and it all kind of rises up again almost every time. But this past year I won a Grammy for a song I did called 'White Horses' with Chris Stapleton for Best Country Song. And we've written a bunch of songs over ten years and this song had been sitting around for a long time. For some reason after that song became a big No. 1 on country radio and was awarded a Grammy, I didn't suffer the crash after that. For some reason maybe I'm at a point in my life where I'm just more even-keeled about things. **Dan Wilson**

CREATIVE EXERCISES TO STAY INSPIRED

1: A SONG A DAY

Give yourself 30 minutes to an hour to write a song. Write freely, write about anything, anyone, no rules, no boundaries, just set the timer and go for it. It doesn't need to be a full song, it can be a chorus, a verse, an instrumental hook, whatever comes out.

2: REFINE

Refining and refining until you know you have the best of each section of a song. Make it the best it can be. Sure, sometimes the first pass might be it but it's always good to write more than you need and then you really can see which lines fit the best.

Spend some time doing this with ideas and song starts and it might just help you get something over the line. Let yourself be open with lyrics and lines and go outside the box, or inside the box, wherever the inspiration takes you.

> *I find it much more inspiring and creative and exciting when it's like, 'What's everyone doing at the moment? Let's do the complete opposite and find a sound that no one's used.'* **Plested**

3: DEEP-DIVE YOUR FAVOURITE SONGS/ALBUM

This is one of my favourite ways to get inspired. Pick songs you love or an album and spend a few days dissecting it song by song, melody by melody, lyric by lyric. Why do you like it? How does it make you feel? What is it about that song that's special? Find out everything about the making of it, look up interviews, behind-the-scenes footage. I promise after doing this it will be incredibly inspiring and make you want to get writing your own masterpiece.

RuthAnne

4: WRITE SOMEWHERE NEW

Another go-to of mine for ultimate inspiration is to write somewhere new or change up your writing environment. Somewhere you can fully focus with no distractions, somewhere beautifully scenic or even in your back garden in the sun; somewhere that you feel relaxed, comfortable, happy and ultimately inspired. Switch it up and you'll surprise yourself with how inspiring a change of scene can be.

> The story behind 'History' [One Direction] was interesting. We were three days in and we had got nothing, so we went to the pub down the road from the studio and had a couple of pints and were consoling each other. Then a taxi pulled up outside and I was like, 'I've got an idea, just bear with me a sec.' I ran outside and asked the cabbie if he could wait and I said to the boys, 'Let's get in a taxi, give him [the cabbie] a couple hundred quid, get him to drive us around London all day. We'll take a guitar, a laptop and a bottle of Jameson's and some beers and we'll see if that will get the juices flowing. So the boys ran and got the guitar, got the laptop and in the cab we went. We wrote about five or six different ideas driving around Trafalgar Square and just all over the place. And out of those ideas we wrote 'Hey Angel' and 'Made in the AM'. And although we didn't start it in the cab, as soon as we got back that evening we wrote 'History', so it was kind of what got things moving. Sometimes just changing up your visual peripheral and having different things flow is good to do because it's not always easy when you're in a studio room and you've got very little visual stimulation, but moving and seeing stuff and changing up your environment is important.
>
> And the concept of 'History' came from Julian just going, 'We've written the "best song ever" (which ended up being the first single and we knew it was strong for the boys to release) so like what else can you write?' and I was like, 'Well you can write history' and that's how we got the title, and that's how we started it. It immediately started to feel like 'You've got a Friend in Me' stylistically and it just felt very stand-alone. It ended up being One Direction's last single. It wasn't actually meant to be – they were going to release a song called 'Infinity' and it was the night of their final performance and the decision was made to release 'History' instead. **Ed Drewett**

5: LISTEN

Spend some time away from writing and have conversations with friends, strangers, family, anyone… and in those conversations really, really listen, be present and out of those conversations a million ideas will flow. We're all writing from the human experience, so the more you listen to what we're all experiencing as well as listening to yourself the more you can talk about it. Most inspiration for lyrics comes from real, actual human conversations and connection.

6: JOURNAL

To inspire your lyrics I can't tell you how amazing journaling can be. You don't need to write essays and it shouldn't feel like another chore on top of your day, just little thoughts here and there. It can literally be a line a day, or something you see or hear that inspires or interests you or makes you feel something or sparks an idea. My notes app is full of lines, titles, phrases, things I've picked up in conversations, things that I realise I feel, and then whenever you're struggling for some inspiration you can open your journal or notes app or wherever you put your thoughts and pick one.

> My brother Matt once said to me, 'You can only enjoy the process of making something. If you write a song, and you have a great day writing a song, and then you have a great day recording that song, those are the rewards of what we're doing, because even if people love it in Miami or Vancouver, you're not there to enjoy that – you just hear about it or see it second-hand. So all the things that might happen, even other people's esteem or respect for you, you're never going to feel that as profoundly as you do the joy of doing the thing, finishing it and listening to it in your car a hundred times.' He was always very rigorous about only doing things where he could sense that he was going to really, really dig the process. He would never just grin and bear it and do something that he thought was gross or unpleasant just because a positive outcome could be predicted.
>
> I learned that principle from Matt pretty early on, and that's really, really helped me a lot. I feel like music for me is an experience that I get to have with people, and if I have success one of the greatest things that happens is that these other geniuses roll up and want to write a song with me. And so I get to deal with brilliant, interesting, funny people and that's the pay-off that I love; I love that I get to be with more creative, inspiring people. It's the experimental thing that is the absolute main thing. And I think that shows in the work in some weird way where you don't even know how but you write a song, and you have joy, and it's challenging, and maybe you argue, but maybe you just laugh the whole time. But in the end a huge amount of vibes and spirit and the feelings you had are sort of woven into the song for the listener. The listener is enjoying the heart of it, they're catching that wave that you were on that day that you did it. **Dan Wilson**

7: GO OUTSIDE THE BOX

When a song becomes a hit, all of a sudden everyone wants another song exactly like it and often a bunch of songs follow that hit sounding like it but rarely as good, and music trends form and run in cycles. Dance pop can be hot for while and then someone will go in a completely different direction and bring back 1950s rock and it'll be huge and then that trend starts and so on... Everyone jumps on trends and there's nothing wrong with that, but its worth remembering that hit songs can't be replicated exactly the same as each other. When you copy or try do something exactly like it often you end up with a song that's just not as good. There's a difference in being inspired by a song versus trying to exactly replicate it.

Often, the biggest hits are the songs that sound like nothing else at the time and that come out and set a new trend or bring back a trend that has been gone for a while. When 'All About That Bass' by Meghan Trainor was released there was no song on the radio like it, it felt completely fresh. Same with 'Greedy' by Tate McCrae. I always think, when a music trend has everyone releasing similar sounding songs that's when it's good to try to do something completely different. So I encourage you to try and predict the next trend and create a song that sounds nothing like what's in the charts and you may just write and create the fresh unique song/sound that will set the trend for the future. Jon Bellion said it best:

> *Sometimes I'll fish creatively 3 years in advance like, 'what would this sound like in 3 years or 5 years' and usually that will catch a fish (get a song cut) if I'm fishing forward. I never catch a fish on a pitch song if I'm doing what's already happening now. You need to be about a year and half a ahead and fish out and make a guess on what that artist would sound like, so in 6 months I could try this and it will still sound new.* **Jon Bellion**

INTERLUDE 2

SONGWRITER STORIES

"Songwriting is like trying to catch lightning in a bottle. Some days it comes easy. Some days you chase it all day."

CHRIS STAPLETON

Now this is one of my favourite stories behind the songs from legendary songwriter Dan Wilson. Dan is not only a Grammy-winning hit songwriter but also lead singer and songwriter of his band Semisonic whose hit 'Closing Time' was famously written in 20 minutes, was a massive worldwide hit and has become a classic in its own right. During my interview with Dan, he told me the story behind a songwriting session that would change his life: the story of him co-writing and producing 'Someone Like You' with Adele.

Dan Wilson

This song is a songwriter's dream come true. It's the song we all strive to write in our careers. An 'evergreen', as I call songs that become instant classics – songs that will live forever and truly stand the test of time. I think we can all say we've cried to this song, we've smiled to this song. We've all experienced the story of this song. It took the world by storm. The song broke records for Adele: her first No. 1 single in the UK and second No. 1 single in the USA, making her the first British solo artist in history to have two *Billboard* Hot 100 singles from the same album. It went on to be the first single of the decade certified six times platinum in the USA and UK as well as certified multi-platinum in 16 countries and winning a Grammy award for Best Pop Solo performance.

'SOMEONE LIKE YOU' – ADELE
Written by: Adele Adkins, Dan Wilson
Produced by: Dan Wilson

The first day we wrote, we did two days. The first day we met at this very, very small studio in Hollywood called Harmony, which had a really nice piano and really good light, very small room, good vibes and a little porch so that she could have smoke breaks. We spent the first hour talking and she played me clips of songs she loved, including Wanda Jackson, rockabilly songs and Chris Stapleton singing 'If It Hadn't Been For Love'. And this was before people had heard of him outside Nashville and his band The Steeldrivers. She played me a couple of songs she was working on. 'Rolling in the Deep' and another one and they both sounded amazing to me and then she showed me two ideas. One was the song that would eventually become 'Rumour Has It'. She already had it kind of worked out, the drama of that song, it's gonna be a 'rumour has it you're the one he's leaving me for', all that clever wordplay stuff. She knew the groove she wanted.

It was really cool and then she sang me the first three or four lines of what would become 'Someone Like You' and she said, 'Which one do you wanna work on?' and I said, 'I love "Rumour Has It" but I'm not funny in my songwriting. It never comes out right if I try to be funny in a song and that's a funny song so I can't do it, let's do the ballad instead.' So we started working on 'Someone Like You' and about halfway through the day we got to the chorus. She wrote that line 'Never mind I'll find someone like you' and it really all started to come together. End of the day we had a verse, a chorus and a bad second verse, a good second chorus and it ended abruptly and we recorded it. I played the piano part into ProTools and slowed it down and sped it up in different sections a little bit. Then she sang in those sections, good verse, good chorus, bad second verse, good second chorus.

Then I realised overnight that the bad second verse was more like a bridge/middle eight part, and I thought to myself, 'If we work on that song again that's what I'll propose.' So the second day we got together the first thing I said was, 'So what do you wanna work on today? Do you wanna finish the one we started yesterday or do you wanna start something new?' And she said, 'Oh, we have to finish the song from yesterday' and I said, 'Oh really' and she said, 'Yeah, cos I played it to my manager and my mum.' (And all I could think about was the bad second verse cos the song wasn't finished so I was a little bit dismayed that she had already played it for people but it was the right thing to do.) She said, 'My manager loves it and my mum cried.' A couple of years later I was talking to her about that moment and she said, 'I knew at the end of that first day that "Someone Like You" was gonna change my life,' so she knew that and all I was thinking was about fixing that second verse but even maybe instead of finishing that song we could start a new one.

By the time we started working on this second day, her voice was rougher. She'd been having some struggles with her vocal cords at that time so that day her voice was rougher and more kind of emotional sounding. So I asked her to re-sing the choruses because I said it's just going to sound more emotional. So she recut the choruses and they sounded incredible. She kept saying 'Can we not have those high notes?' I said 'No, it's just a demo and it sounds so desperate and powerful. We've got to leave it in for the demo and you can change it later.' Then we wrote a proper second verse and used the parts of the old second verse for a bridge in the 'Nothing compares no worries or cares' part. I wrote new chords under that part, and we did that section.

And then I had her sing the outro choruses. And by the end of recording her voice was going, it was tired and raw but so passionate sounding. When it was done, she had to leave at six o'clock sharp because she had to drive out to Malibu and see the people from Sony and Rick Rubin and play this for them. And someone from that meeting, not Adele, not Rick, one of the guys from Sony told my publisher, 'I think Dan has written a copyright*.' Then that's the last I heard of it for about six months. Except that I heard a version of it that they were working on which was kind of a slow R&B smooth jazz version which I was not super into. Then suddenly her management contacted my manager Jim and said, 'We need the parts for "Someone Like You" right away.' They said, 'We're gonna mix the demo version and put the song out like that.' So she kept the magic of that in it.

She sang it at the Brit Awards, and she did such a great performance, which I think anyone who watched that performance will remember. And that live version went to all the radio stations like BBC Radio 1, etc., and it became a hit the week it was released. Then they released the album version and then the two versions of the song were charting together, and the rest is history.

Everything about it, the history of the song, the song was so contingent. It was shaky. I chose that song because I didn't think I could do a good job of 'Rumour Has It' and we finished it because even though I knew it had flaws, she knew it was gonna change her life. And when the song entered the charts, I have to confess I spent some time exalting and feeling excited. But I also spent way more time than I wish feeling nervous that it had peaked and it was going to start going down, to somehow worried it wasn't going to connect with people or wondering what it meant for me to have this thing happening. I just spent too much time worrying about it. And it was all completely out of my hands. There was nothing I could do so there was no reason to worry, but I did. **Dan Wilson**

Dan has continually written hit songs throughout his career, and he was kind enough to share the story behind another huge co-write of his...

The Chicks had just experienced an intense amount of backlash about comments they had made in 2003 criticising President George W. Bush which led to the banning of their songs from country music radio stations.

This saying is part of songwriter lingo: a 'copyright' in this context means a big song, a hit song, an evergreen, a song that will last the test of time and be covered and sang all around the world forever.

'NOT READY TO MAKE NICE' – THE CHICKS
Written by: Dan Wilson, Natalie Maines, Emily Robison, Martie Maguire
Produced by: Rick Rubin

I had pitched them this idea that I had called 'Undivided' which was about how they stuck together throughout this crisis that they went through. And with the president and the country music business all turning against them and blacklisting them. So I had this idea of writing a song that would be about how they stuck together. I said, 'Maybe it's true about everybody, maybe people in general are less divided than the media wants to tell us and maybe we're more alike than the stories we hear. And maybe politics is not the most important thing in the world.' And Natalie, who's very, very insightful, cuts-to-the-heart-of-the-matter-type of person, she said, 'Well, okay, but if we wrote this song "Undivided", would we have to say somehow that we have to forgive the people that screwed us and blacklisted us?' And I said, 'Maybe' and she said, 'Nope'. So the next morning, I woke up and I was thinking about that conversation we had about that 'Undivided' idea and how striking it was to me. I had a bunch of espresso and I thought of those lines, 'Forgive sounds good, forget I'm not sure I could, and they say time heals everything, etc.' and I brought that to them on the second day. And I said, 'Okay, since we had that conversation and Natalie said "about unifying" and I said "yeah, yeah", well, here's another idea. And I sang them 'forgive, sounds good, forget, I'm not sure I could' and they were like 'woooooo, yessss'. They had played me songs that very obliquely and subtly mention or allude to the incident but nothing that really addressed it directly, so that's when I proposed this and said, 'We have to do something that's really taking the bull by the horns. There's got to be a song that answers all this bullshit and all this hate in a strong way that's really passionate and confronts head on all the issues they were going through because otherwise it would just be this weird kind of elephant in the room that nobody was talking about, and they didn't want that, they're not that kind of person.' So we wrote it and we made a demo with vocal, piano and acoustic guitar in LA and I thought it was great. I edited it and added piano back home in Minneapolis, and when it was done I was like 'Oh, I love this, this is so great, also they're gonna know exactly what to do with this.'

So, many months later, after I'd done three or four more sessions with them and written a whole bunch of songs, I finally called up Rick Rubin and said, 'Hey, any word or thoughts about those songs I did with the Chicks?' And Rick says, 'Oh, they're all great, we're gonna use almost all of them' and I was 'Oh, good.' I'm not great at following up, I'm shy and I'm like if they're gonna use the song they'll tell me. I like that because you're kind of letting the process happen and the stars align when they're meant to align. Because sometimes songs can be sitting, can be around for a long time before the artists uses it. It's about timing, and if you're holding on to it you just end up being disappointed. **Dan Wilson**

The song eventually did come out and was a huge smash, went multi-platinum and won three Grammy awards that year (Record of the Year, Song of the Year and Best Country Performance by Duo or Group).

I told Dan that what I loved about that story was how he presented an initial idea, 'Undivided', that they had a conversation about and was turned down, but instead of taking that personally or arguing back or pushing it, he went away, thought about the conversation they had and was ultimately inspired by that and came up with a brand-new idea to present. That idea was the hit idea that led to the song, proving why Dan Wilson really is one of the best songwriters and I learned a lot from my conversation with him.

Ilsey Juber is one of the best songwriters in the game and hugely sought after to this day. Let's start with Ilsey's memories of a song that I'm pretty sure everyone wishes they wrote. The multi-platinum global smash with over a billion streams...

Mark Ronson & Ilsey Juber

'NOTHING BREAKS LIKE A HEART'
MARK RONSON FEAT. MILEY CYRUS

Written by: Mark Ronson, Ilsey Juber, Miley Cyrus, Thomas Brenneck, Clément Picard, Maxime Picard, Conor Szymanski
Produced by: Mark Ronson, Picard Brothers

This song is one of my favourite songs I've ever been a part of. We were knee deep in working on this Mark Ronson album and he had rented out Shangri-la for a couple of weeks. He had figured out the direction of the album at that point, and he was like 'I want to do a kind of country disco-y feeling thing' and Tom Brenneck started playing this guitar riff that was super-cool. So we had the idea for 'Nothing Breaks Like a Heart', and listening back to it we were like 'Who could sound great on this song?' It was very obvious that Miley would be the perfect person to sing it. So I think Mark texted her and sent her the little idea and she was like 'I can be there tomorrow' and so she came in. She and I had never really met properly before, but I had worked with her sister Noah quite a bit. We started writing and it was the easiest song ever. It came out so quickly. We got the verse in like twenty minutes and then she started recording and that was the origin of our creative relationship.

It was so special to me to have it be in that environment and a really magical song. It kind of felt like it came out of thin air. I think we could all relate to the concept at the time because we were all dealing with our own things, and she had this angle on it. Her music video that she made speaks to it where it was like the heartbreak of the world. The pain that we all feel, not just from love, which I thought was a really cool angle. I was in heartbreak city at the time, so that's what it meant for me, but I think the cool thing about that song is it means different things to me and different things to other people with how we painted those pictures in the chorus and the metaphors. It feels deeply personal but also universal and connected. And production-wise it very easily could have just been like a stripped-down country song and I think Mark did a really good job making it fit his world that he was making. And it's danceable, which was important. A heartbreak song that you can dance to. Once I heard Miley's voice on it, I knew it felt really special and really big. I think that sometimes it's the artist on the song that can make the difference. **Ilsey Juber**

Now I'd like to tell you the story behind the hit song I co-wrote with Ilsey and why it's such a special song to me and one of my faves I've ever written.

'IN THE NAME OF LOVE' – MARTIN GARRIX FEAT. BEBE REXHA
Written By: Ilsey Juber, RuthAnne Cunningham, Matthew Radosevich, Steve Philibin, Martin Garrix
Produced by: Matt Rad, Steve James, Martin Garrix, Yael Nahar

This was my first session writing with Ilsey, and it was incredibly special because it was the day we wrote 'In the Name of Love' and that session wasn't even meant to happen that day. Matt Rad and I had a session booked with an artist and the artist cancelled that morning, and at the same time a different session Ilsey was meant to have was also cancelled. I got a text from my publisher at the time, Hannah Babbit, and she said, 'I think you, Ilsey and Matt should write today, all your sessions have cancelled.' So we got in together. I always think about how this song wouldn't exist if the day had gone differently. At the time I was really in a hard place with the music industry. I was broke, singing in wedding bands to make money so that I could pay my rent in LA and I was having a lot of almosts with songs almost going to artists or songs almost being big but then flopping. And I actually was really considering quitting the music industry. Of course I didn't tell anyone, I would go to sessions and write and just try my best, but inside I was struggling. I felt let down by the music industry. I was giving my all and felt like I was getting nothing in return. The day before this session I had written down the title 'In the Name of Love', which of course had been a hit title by U2 years ago, but the great thing about titles is you can use them again and again and again as they can't be copyrighted. I thought that's a great title and it hasn't be done in a while.

So I headed into the session and immediately loved Ilsey. I remember us all just chatting and she was talking about a love interest that she was going through some stuff with, and everything she was saying about this person I was feeling the exact same but not about love, about the music industry. I didn't say anything, I was really more listening to her. Matt was on the keys and Ilsey had the guitar and I just said, 'I think the title "In the Name of Love" could be something.' They both loved it, and then based off of what we had been talking about and how I was feeling I just started singing 'If I told you this was only gonna hurt' – the melody and lyric at the same time – and Ilsey said, 'Wait, what's that?' I said, 'I dunno, just came up with it.' And she sang 'If I warned you that the fire's gonna burn' and Matt started playing the chords and we just bounced back and forth melodically and lyrically. Ilsey is such a special lyricist so it was just amazing.

When it came to the chorus Ilsey said, 'It should just be something big and that everyone can sing and just repeat it over and over.' Of course there was a thought of should we change up the third line, etc., but it just felt so good to repeat it over and over so that became our chorus. And 45 minutes later we had the whole song. And we never changed a thing. We kept it stripped back piano and vocal, we sang all the harmony parts. Ilsey sang the demo and she sounded amazing.

I feel like both of us really needed that song that day. We were both needing answers and this was the song that came from that. So regardless of it becoming a hit it was such a great day, a process that was so organic and natural and it really just fell into place. Essentially it was a ballad but we knew it had the potential to be a dance song, and when Steve James added that amazing future bass drop and Martin and Bebe did their thing on it, well, it became something we all felt so proud and excited about. It took two years to be released, and that was a tough wait but it was worth it. It went multi-platinum all around the world and is currently on over a billion streams. It's a song I've got to witness people screaming at the top of their lungs at places like Coachella and it brought so much to my life, it's truly one of my proudest songs as a songwriter.

RuthAnne with Spotify Billions Plaques

CHAPTER 7

PRODUCTION

"Being a great record producer is being put into any situation and understanding what the best decision musically is for that. Making the best track, recording the best vocal, all the things. If you learn all of these tasks to the best of your ability, and you'll never be done learning, there will be no situation where you won't be able to do something to make that record better, that music better."

MARK RONSON

RuthAnne at Abbey Road

I always say:

★ **Songwriters are the foundation of the music industry.**

★ **Producers are the backbone.**

★ **Artists are the messengers.**

★ **Record labels are the vehicle.**

We've talked about the tools to help write a great song, a hit song, the 'rules', the 'exceptions' to the song, which is our foundation, and now I'd like to get into how we can bring that song to life, the backbone of the song, the production of a song. The music, the sonic journey that we take the listener on. The finished recording where your song goes from being sung in a room on piano or guitar to a fully realised sonic vision.

Production is really how to take a song and bring it to life and it's a skill and art in itself.
Julian Bunetta

Most songwriters are also producers, most producers are also songwriters. The two things intertwine in the creative collaborative process. And just like the songwriting process, having endless melody options and endless lyrical options, in production there is an endless choice of sounds, so many options of sonic palettes. A song can be produced in so many different ways, but a great producer finds the best way for the song and serves the song always. A great producer knows how to complement a song, bringing the lyrics and melodies to life, musically and sonically.

> As a producer I wanna always get that feeling that makes me wanna put it on again and again and again. What's the thing that makes me wanna put it on again, what's the moment that I look forward to in the song that makes me wanna play it again, to get that feeling again? That has a lot to do with production and of course, obviously, the song has to be there as well. **Julian Bunetta**

WHAT IS A MUSIC PRODUCER?

In short, a music producer is responsible for delivering a completed recording to the artist/label who hires them. Being a music producer involves a range of creative and technical roles, the main one being bringing a song to life, overseeing all aspects of the creation of a song or album. Think of a music producer like the director of a film, or a movie producer; they have a vision for the song and they make a lot of the decisions to execute that vision or work with an artist/label to bring their vision to life. Gathering ideas, sonic references, composing music, making the beats, choosing the musicians, arranging the song, coaching/directing the performers to get the best performance on the song, recording all the parts, engineering the sessions, overseeing the mixing/mastering process and really everything and anything to do with the making the finished product as good as it can be.

A SHORT HISTORY OF MUSIC PRODUCTION

The music producer's role has evolved over the years along with advances in technology. In the late 19th century, the **phonograph** was invented by Thomas Edison, and it was really the first thing to capture and reproduce sound. Then came **gramophones**. Then we get to the mid-20th century where it was **magnetic tape** and the introduction of **multi-track recording**. Then came the birth of electronic music and use of **synthesizers** in the latter half of the 20th century, which brought new effects and sounds along with new genres and styles. The 1980s saw the most significant advance in music production, the digital revolution in the development of the **DAW (Digital Audio Workstation)**. This meant that anyone with a computer could and can create a full production of high-quality music. This leads us to where we are today, where music production and mixing can all be done on a laptop.

Recording music used to require a studio, often with a big elaborate mixing desk like the ones you see in movies about the Motown or Rock 'n' Roll era. Music was often recorded as a live performance with musicians and vocalists all recording at the same time and the recording being mixed live. These days, there is no longer a need for a big expensive studio as most producers can create it all on a laptop. Every piece of music can be created and recorded separately at different times and it can also be mixed on a laptop. DAWs really are the most used and essential tool for music production now, which is why you'll hear the phrase 'making beats in my bedroom' a lot more. Of course, there are still times where you'll see big artists hiring out Studio 1 at Abbey Road for an amazing expensive live string section, but the days of budgets being that big for artists are mostly gone and you really can do it all with the bare minimum. Again, it all depends on your budget, your vision and a producer's skills and experience.

THE TWO TYPES OF PRODUCERS

It's very important to understand what producing music is and how you could be contributing to the production of a song because there can be some confusion around it. I think there are two types of music producer and you can certainly be one, or both, of these and bring equally the same amount of greatness to the song.

THE VISIONARY ★ Some of the earliest most notable producers were a lot more like directors. They didn't play any instruments and they didn't engineer the session, rather they hired studio engineers to handle all the technical aspects, musicians to play and singers to sing. It was really their direction, their taste and their ear, knowing when they had all the magic, knowing what to add or take away to make the song come together. They had a vision or knew how to bring the artist's vision to life.

Sometimes this type of producer would simply sing what they were hearing in their head to the musician or the beat they wanted from the drummer, and very often back in the day the producer was not a part of the composition of the song. The lyrics, chords and melodies would be already written, and then the producer would come in and the job of production started then, taking the song and working on the arrangement of it, the sound, recording the instruments and putting the music with the song to serve the song.

Even though music is made differently these days, the visionary producer is often still around. A lot of writers and artists are this type of producer, contributing massively to the vision and overall finished arrangement and production. Some would call it more of an 'executive producer' role, the sourcer who brings all the right people together to make the music, or the finisher who knows what to add or takeaway to make the sonic palette just right. This producer can add a huge amount to songs and albums just by being the ear, having great sonic taste, being the visionary and making all the right decisions musically to complement the song. This type of producer is incredibly skilled in making hit records and is often a crucial part of the process.

Autumn Rowe won a Grammy for Album of the Year in 2022 for her work not only as a songwriter but also a producer on Jon Batiste's album *We Are*. (It's not every day a female producer wins Album of the Year, which is huge for any aspiring female producers reading this book.) She had this to say about having the vision in production:

Autumn Rowe with Jon Batiste & Kizzo

Everything I do is based on emotion, like how do you want to feel? I think one of my strengths as a producer is the vision and knowing what the song needs and capturing an emotion. How do I feel when I'm creating this? And how do I want the listener to feel? So whether it's me starting with drums or some loops or whether that's me with someone who is a better producer than me on the technical side and using my vision to guide them. It's such a great asset to have a vision and getting to complete that vision. **Autumn Rowe**

Which leads us to the second type of producer…

THE ONE-MAN/WOMAN-BAND ★ Ever since the advances in technology meant that a lot of music production could be done on a laptop, we saw the rise of the other type of producer. A producer who really can do it all themselves using technology mainly instead of live musicians, or being the musician himself/herself. A producer is often now a part of the writing process, with most being songwriter/producers because they come to the sessions with music/a track already made to write to, or they play the chords to write to. Or, as you're writing the song they are making the music and track simultaneously whilst also bouncing back and forth with you on melody and lyric. They can engineer their own sessions, add instruments and effects digitally, record vocals, mix their own records, and usually they can play at least one instrument, so when they want a blend of real instruments and digital instrumentation they can do that all themselves or add instruments in after the fact. They are arrangers, conductors, you name what needs to be done, this producer does it all. This is why I call this producer 'the one-man/woman-band' and in a lot of ways this person is saving record labels a lot of money in the process. To become this kind of producer definitely takes the 10,000 hours. Most producers these days have spent years honing their technical skills.

PRODUCTION DUOS AND TRIOS ★ You'll often see production duos or trios where one is the musician, one is the engineer making the beats and digital instrumentation, one is the ears, one is great at vocal production, etc. There're a lot of producers who work together using each of their strengths to make the finished record and all are equally as important as each other. These production teams can be so effective because they fuse all the aspects of producing together.

I got introduced to these two other guys that I ended up forming a team with called 'Invisible Men', and we did that for fifteen years. When we started there was me and George and Jason. I'd come from production-led computer keyboards programming, that kind of thing, and they'd been in a sort of pop rock band called Orson. George was an amazing guitarist and Jason a brilliant singer-songwriter. It was a very complimentary trio, there was a good sort of chemistry there. I personally really loved being in a team. It meant that there were always people to bounce ideas off, so it kind of eradicated anything like writer's block because you always have another set of ears. In a really creative way it kind of took a lot of pressure off. Also sometimes in the music business you can just have the worst day ever, and if you're going through that on your own that's a very different thing to if you've got people who are there to go through that with you. **Jon Shave**

I've worked with every type of producer you can think of and over the years have become a producer myself. I wouldn't be the one-man-band type at all, mine is the visionary mixed with some technical ability to be able to record, edit, comp and process. It has taken me a while as a female producer to have the confidence to really step up and produce but it's now one of my favourite creative zones to be in. To write the song and then be able to produce that song to life is truly fulfilling. I've been in scenarios where a producer does very little but does exactly what the song needed, and I've been around producers who have taken the song somewhere I never would have envisioned, in the best way, with sounds that are out of this world. Being a producer is such a creative role, and seeing the magic production can bring to a song and how many different ways you can produce a song to make it the best it can be is mind blowing.

5 STEPS TO A FULLY PRODUCED SONG

1. The music for the song
Choosing the instruments, making the beats, choosing/creating the sounds, arranging the music, etc.

2. Recording the song
Recording the vocals, live instruments, the performances that make up the sound recording which are recorded to hardware and software as audio or MIDI data.

3. Editing the song
Then the audio and/or MIDI sequencing can be edited in a variety of ways to change and enhance the performances or entire arrangement.

4. Mixing the song
The individual tracks that make up the multi-track recording are processed using effects to create a final mixed stereo recording of the song.

5. Mastering the song
The song is then mastered, which is making all the final adjustments to the overall sound of the recording and getting a finished stereo mix for distribution as an audio file.

> *The producer is sort of the captain of the ship essentially. The artist is the yacht, the captain has to bring it to the right destination, and you hire your crew to get there safely and enjoyably.* **Julian Bunetta**

WHAT MAKES A GREAT PRODUCER?

The best producers really bring these main things to the table:

★ **Great taste and a great ear**

★ **A vision for the song**

★ **A vision for the artist**

★ **Creates a 'sound'**

★ **Evolves your sound**

★ **Connects with the artist**

★ **Gets the best out of the artist**

★ **Technical ability and sound design**

★ **Attention to detail**

★ **Knows less is more**

George Martin, the legendary producer and one of the most famous of all time for his work producing The Beatles was often referred to as 'The Fifth Beatle' because of his massive contribution and involvement in all their records. He wrote most of their string arrangements and he played piano and/or keyboards on lots of their songs. He once said, 'The producer is the person who actually puts the frame around everything and presents it to the public and **it's the producer's taste that makes it what it is.**'

Great taste and a great ear ★ Having great taste and a great ear isn't really something you can force or teach. It also depends on the genre and style and there's no right or wrong when it comes to taste as it's subjective. What can help you is immersing yourself into as much music as possible. Listen closely to music you love because your production will be inspired by the sounds you've heard and absorbed. Become a student of music: study how things like arrangement, tone, tempo, instrumentation, building, layering and dynamics all create a feeling and have an emotional effect on the listener. Go to live music events, feel the feels of live music, listen to songs on the radio and pick up track ideas and musical ideas from all these things.

The more music you study, the more your ear will be well-trained and in tune with what's best for the song. The more amazing taste you'll have for what sounds great and how to make the music you're producing impact the most people universally.

A vision for the song ★ The vision for the song really is the foundation of the production. You must ask yourself, what do I want this song to achieve musically? What emotion do I want to evoke in the listener? How do I want it to sound? What instrument/sound will complement this chorus, this lyric? What is the tone of this song? How can I create dynamic range?

This vision for the song will help you make the right musical decisions and that's why it's crucial to the production. Each song can bring about a new vision as you grow as a producer. Also, you can try a vision that might not work, take an ear break and come back with a completely new vision for the song. Remember a song can be dressed up many different ways and you can re-approach it several times with a new vision if it comes to you.

> *I think the best producers are people who think of amazing ideas and put them together and just think of moments that are going to create an impact to someone's ear. I think this is what it means to be a producer and not necessarily how technical you are or how trained you are in production. I don't think that actually matters at all. I think it's about your creativity and your brain and just doing fun stuff.* **Kamille**

RuthAnne & Niall Horan on stage

A vision for the artist ★ When I interviewed Grammy-winning producer Julian Bunetta I talked to him about how I had observed his superpower whilst working with him over the years. I always noticed that Julian was amazing at just knowing what an artist needed — that song/the direction sonically that would take the artist to new heights. I've watched him do it many times. For example, when we were writing with Niall Horan for his first album *Flicker*, there were a lot of strong songs and beautiful ballads. Niall had an amazing vision and sonic palette for his album and it was exciting to be a part of because it was bringing me back to bands like Fleetwood Mac and The Eagles. Julian knew, especially production-wise, that he needed something a bit edgy, sexy, cool, a real standout moment, and that moment was 'Slow Hands'. It was written over two days with Niall, Julian, Tobias, Xplicit, and John and I came in on the second day to write on it. I knew instantly that it was special, though I could never have imagined how big it would be. It felt so fresh and unique yet nostalgic and showed a side of Niall as an artist that we'd not seen before. It's now part of the Billions Club on Spotify and it went to No. 1 on American Pop radio, Hot AC radio and Dance radio (the remix) all at the same time, and has gone multi-platinum all over the world.

One of the biggest things as a producer is having a vision for an artist that sometimes they might not even have for themselves yet. That's my superpower, or my competitive advantage, and I certainly trust that now and listen to it. It probably comes from my knowledge of musical history, knowing artists when they've pivoted, when they've reinvented, things that have worked historically for people, and running game scenarios in my head. But maybe part of it is just attempting to see the obvious. Sometimes I think we over-complicate things, sometimes the simplest, most obvious answer is what people don't look at because they think it's too obvious or that it's too simple, but sometimes it's just very clear. And I try to put myself in the shoes of the fan and consumer. I listen to my instinct, like if I'm hearing that this album feels a little slow I would love after song six for there to be a little pep in the step. **Julian Bunetta**

Julian worked with Teddy Swims when he was a new artist, before Teddy had big success, and produced his breakthrough song 'Lose Control', which again was exactly the song and sound Teddy needed. It paid off massively, not only breaking Teddy as an artist globally but also giving him an evergreen song that will truly last the test of time. A song that has broken records all over the world, climbing its way for 32 weeks to the No. 1 spot and has become the longest-running song on the Billboard Hot 100 chart, achieving a record-breaking 100 weeks. This makes it the longest-charting song in the chart's history.

It's my job as a producer and a writer to make the best song that the artist can possibly make, so that's my philosophy. The reason I wanted to work with Teddy was because he just had this magic voice. I could sing my whole life and never develop that tone that Teddy has. He has this absolutely magical tone, and he has incredible ability and just gives me goosebumps. And he had a cool look, I was compelled by how he looked and then I was compelled by his name, his stage name, and when we met, we had chemistry, it was fun, we laughed, we had a great time together, the hours flew by and I chose to keep doing it because it was always enjoyable and we always made something that I liked. **Julian Bunetta**

Teddy had been building a good following online singing covers and had been writing and releasing some original music, but it was 'Lose Control' that changed the game, leading him to his own Grammy nomination for Best New Artist. Once again Julian's strength as a producer came into play – he knew that Teddy was just one song away.

> *With Teddy I realised as a producer I wasn't finding songs for him that showed off his voice, his actual vocal ability, and then the songwriter in me was like wow, I haven't written melodies good enough to show off how exceptional his voice actually is. Taking it back to his voice was what worked, showcasing it, and it worked, it really worked.* **Julian Bunetta**

Julian Bunetta with Teddy Swims and Mikkey Ekko

Having a vision for the artist can make the difference between you producing one song or being brought on board to produce the album and becoming a key collaborator for an artist. When I interviewed John Ryan, who wrote and produced eight songs on Sabrina Carpenter's Grammy-winning pop solo album, *Short n' Sweet*, he said:

> *Sabrina likes to work fast. I do too! We did 'Taste' and 'Bed Chem' back-to-back on a Wednesday and Thursday. She's such an amazing songwriter and is always coming in with a lyric/title/melody ready to go. It just gets the ball going right away. Although the album does genre-hop a bit, her voice is the glue that ties it all together. Her lyrics are so personal to her and her perception too. It really makes her stand out. As producer, working with an artist that really knows what they want to say helps me do my job better. It's really about finding what's unique and original about that artist, then helping them bring it out as much as you can in the production and so on.* **John Ryan**

Creating a 'sound' ★ Mark Ronson once said, 'Aside from all the technical production tools that you learn as a producer, if there's one thing that I can convey that is the most important is to take all these tools and find your own voice, incorporate what you learn and make it into **your own sound, your own thing**.'

Beginning to create your own sound, your own style as a producer, will truly make your music stand out against the rest. Of course you'll be influenced and inspired by productions you love, the music you grew up listening to. It's about taking little pieces of all those influences and turning them into your own sound. The best producers have their own style, their own sound that can be recognised instantly.

John Ryan & Sabrina Carpenter

Some notable 'sounds' were created by legendary producer Phil Spector in the 1960s, with his '**Wall of Sound**' production technique. What is the Wall of Sound? Firstly, it was a room full of musicians. Phil Spector often overbooked musicians so the room would be overflowing. The next part was a hard-walled basement filled with speakers and microphones called the 'echo chamber'. The musicians would play in this cramped studio space and the overhead microphones would capture the sound in the room and that sound would be pumped into the echo chamber where it would bounce off every wall and get picked back up by the microphones and sent direct into the recording booth. This gave Spector a whole new sound to overlay onto the already full sound of over a dozen musicians playing at once. To hear this in real time go listen to 'Be My Baby' by The Ronettes, or 'You've Lost That Lovin' Feelin'' by The Righteous Brothers. Immerse yourself in Phil Spector's Wall of Sound and you'll see how important making your own sound can be.

Or have a listen to any of the Beach Boys songs to hear a their unique 'California Sound' created by the absolute genius, the late Brian Wilson. You'll instantly recognise a Beach Boys song, you turn it on and know who it is straight away because of the unique sound Brian Wilson produced.

Below are many other notable producers and some of their most notable songs, whose production sound and style is so recognisable every time. Go through these songs, listen and you will hear for each producer there is a sound, a style, that makes you instantly know who it was produced by.

Quincy Jones: 'Billie Jean', 'Man in the Mirror', 'The Way You Make Me Feel', 'Rock with You'

Nile Rogers: 'We Are Family', 'Good Times', 'Freak Out', 'I'm Comin' Out', 'Let's Dance'

David Foster: 'I Have Nothing', 'All By Myself', 'The Prayer', 'Feelin' Good', 'I Will Always Love You'

Linda Perry: 'Beautiful' (Christina Aguilera), 'Get the Party Started' (P!nk)

Missy Elliott: 'Work it', 'Get Ur Freak On', 'Lose Control', 'Lady Marmalade' (*Moulin Rouge* version)

Timbaland: 'Work It', 'Try Again', 'Sexyback', 'Cry Me a River', 'Promiscuous', 'Pony'

The Neptunes: 'Drop It Like It's Hot', 'Milkshake', 'Hollerback Girl', 'Hot in Here', 'Rock Your Body'

Mark Ronson: 'Back to Black', 'Rehab', 'Valerie', 'Uptown Funk', 'Nothing Breaks Like a Heart'

Daft Punk: 'One More Time', 'Harder, Better, Faster, Stronger', 'Get Lucky', 'Around the World'

John Shanks: 'The Climb', 'Pieces of Me', 'Rule the World', 'Everywhere', 'Come Clean', 'Breakaway', 'Pocketful of Sunshine'

Max Martin: 'Blinding Lights', 'Since U Been Gone', 'Blank Space', 'It's Gonna Be Me', 'Hit Me Baby One More Time', 'Can't Stop the Feeling', 'California Girls', 'Shake It Off'

Rodney Jerkins: 'Say My Name', 'The Boy Is Mine', 'You Rock My World', 'It's Not Right But It's Okay'

Finneas: 'What Was I Made For', 'Bad Guy', 'Happier Than Ever', 'Lovely', 'Ocean Eyes', 'Lonely'

HOW TO CREATE YOUR OWN SOUND

Experiment ★ Music production really has no limits. The sounds you can create and put together are limitless so don't be afraid to experiment. You never know what happy accidents can happen in a studio during the creative process. And there is no 'right' way to do it; go against the grain and see what you may uncover.

Create your own samples ★ I've seen everything from water bottles to feet stomps to traffic light noises be used to create sounds, sounds that can be effected to sound nothing like what they started as, that can add so much uniquely to a song. Go outside your environment and you'll hear ear-grabbing sounds everywhere and you can do much with those sounds. No one else will have these sounds, they will be yours and will help make your productions stand out and be unique.

Re-use your own signature chains ★ Once you've found your signature vocal chain, drum bus chain, etc, the best producers will often use these signatures on their projects so that their work is recognisable and in the same style. It'll be the foundation of your signature production sound. You might need to tweak things a little because every song is different, but it's a good place to start and it means the audience will recognise your production style easily.

Put your own spin on it ★ There will be producers and production styles that inspire you and that you will want to emulate. But make sure you put your own spin on it. Don't just copy, find a way to make it your own. Study genres, see what you can blend together. There are no rules, just make it sound good.

Create music that YOU love, that you are proud of, that makes YOU feel something. Always sonically serve the song and do what complements the song.

Evolving your sound ★ Whilst it can be hugely beneficial to have a sound that you are known for it's also important for producers to be able to evolve their sound and move with the times. You can still keep certain signature production techniques of your own whilst also making your sounds feel new and fresh. Music trends are always changing, genres are mixing and technology is always advancing. There're so many new and interesting ways to make sounds.

If you're building houses in 2024 the way they did back in 1980 you're probably gonna fall behind. You also have to use the newest tools that create the most current type of music.
Julian Bunetta

Connect with the artist ★ It's very important as a producer to remember that whilst you may be amazing at the music side of things it's equally important to have amazing people skills. A huge part of the job of a producer is to get the best out of an artist, a writer, a musician, and the best way to do that is to connect with them.

The producer to the artist is a very important and close creative relationship and there needs to be a lot of trust there. Often the producer and artist become great friends. A producer really must connect with the artist to be brought onto an album project or have a long-term creative relationship.

We've talked about George Martin being like the 'fifth' Beatle. A lot of producers are really a crucial part of the band – they may not be the face of the band or artist but behind the scenes they are integral, and this can play a huge part in the success of an artist.

Quincy Jones to Michael Jackson, Timbaland to Missy Elliott, Red One to Lady Gaga, Jack Antonoff to Taylor Swift, Dan Nigro to Olivia Rodrigo, Steve Mac to Ed Sheeran, Mark Ronson to Amy Winehouse. Once you find that connection with an artist they will always want and love to work with you. You become family in a way. Even a lot of your favourite DJs have producer teams around them who produce songs with them that you may never see or hear of and they are friends, a crew, a squad.

> *There are so many layers to what it means to be a producer. How deeply you have to listen to people and read the room.* **Julian Bunetta**

Whether you want to work one-on-one with an artist or be part of a production team, find the way to connect. Be personable, be warm, know how to make the artist feel comfortable and safe to go anywhere creatively with you. Allow them the space and energy to shine and always be ready to capture the magic and turn it into gold.

Grammy-winning songwriter/producer Jon Shave has worked with Charli xcx since 2013 and most recently wrote and produced on her Grammy-winning and cultural phenomenon album *Brat*. He said:

> The day we met was the day we made 'Fancy', which became a huge hit. And I feel like, sometimes you're lucky enough to find a collaborator where you just have this undeniable chemistry and spark where I know I can make some amazing stuff with this person, because there's that sense of you almost pushing each other. I felt that really strongly with Charli. Then every couple of years or so we've managed to somehow get back in the studio. I'm thankful to her that she keeps reaching out because she's always been one of those artists that inspires all the other artists. At the end of 2022 she reached out and said, 'I'm doing a new album in the new year do you want to do some stuff on it' and I was like 'Uh, YES.'
>
> It was amazing going back in this time because, working with her before she's always been so melodically driven because she's such an amazing freestyler, but this time she completely changed her whole process and she'd basically written pretty much every song she wanted

to write, at least conceptually, in longhand in a book, and she had concepts and titles and sort of moods in her mind. Then it was about trying to support that mood and enhance it because she really had a vision for the project.

She even had the *Brat* album title when she first texted me about working on it. And what made it so satisfying creatively was because she had the title and it was such a strong concept, then, because she's such a collaborative writer, we would be debating what is brat and is not brat and, you know, even down to the sort of nuance of certain lyrics, and it's debating and talking about how actually being a brat is more often than not a front for insecurities below the surface. It was just an amazingly well-thought-through thing that she absolutely just kind of walked through the door with so much of that just like fully formed, and to see her go on now to do what it's done, I don't think anyone was expecting that – least of all her. **Jon Shave**

GETTING THE BEST OUT OF AN ARTIST

Once you have that connection with an artist and they trust you, this is when you really can get the best out of them. You must invest the time it takes to get to know them inside out. How they like to work, what gets the best out of them creatively. How to get the greatest vocal performance. I've worked with and watched producers who are incredible at this, and it can be the golden asset as a producer – simply knowing how to get the best out of everyone in a room. Knowing how to keep the room inspired and in a great flow. Being honest with an artist but not deflating. Artists can be around a lot of 'yes' people, but producers know how to word the truth in a way that an artist understands, it doesn't bring them down, it will almost light a fire under them. There's a mutual respect there, the artist knows the producer is always trying to get the best and do the best for the project.

> *A good producer knows how to make creatives feel comfortable.* **John Ryan**

Some artists need a more sensitive approach. They thrive off being encouraged and nurtured, and they do their best when they feel good and comfortable and in a warm atmosphere. Some prefer a bit of tough love, they're perfectionists, they want you to be hard on them or to challenge them, they welcome constructive criticism, especially when they are self-aware enough to know when they could do better or aren't doing their best. Being a producer can require a lot of patience, a lot of trial and error working out how to get the best out of the artist but once you find that sweet spot and can unlock the highest potential of an artist you'll be up there with the best of them.

> *I love finding what makes an artist special and making sure that comes through in the music, really helping them create songs that feel authentic and unique to them.* **Steph Jones**

When producing a vocal it's really important to respect the artists, to give them a safe space where they feel comfortable opening up. I love vocal production and I love having an artist really live the lyric, and even if they cry on the microphone and have a hard time singing like Demi Lovato when she sang 'Skyscraper'. She was in tears and she was a mess after we recorded that vocal. She actually went to rehab after that recording and then came back three weeks later and said, 'Toby, I feel amazing now. I want to re-sing it.' We spent three days re-singing it and it was perfect but it had no emotion. So we used the original vocal she had sung through tears because it had that real emotion. **Toby Gad**

TECHNICAL ABILITY AND SOUND DESIGN

Now we have spoken about how back in the day a producer could come into a studio, have an engineer to run the session, musicians to play the parts and play more of a director role, and you can still stick to being that type of producer as it remains a vital role. But with budget constraints from labels, fewer studios with engineers being hired, fewer musicians being hired, it's always a good idea to have some technical ability and with the huge advances in technology it really is easier than ever to become a producer – one word… **splice**. If you know you know, and if you don't know get googling.

Splice has become one of the most used production tools. It still takes a lot of work and hours to become the best producer but it requires what any skill requires to be the best and the more you put in, the more you'll get out of it. At the very least, as a producer being versed in your selection of DAW – Logic X, Pro Tools, Ableton, Cubase, etc – is important because this is where the collection of sounds is pieced together. These DAWs are very user-friendly and the sooner you get started the sooner you'll be able to work on them and be comfortable using them. Having some type of home recording set up so you can practise recording live instruments, making beats, recording vocals, etc. is crucial. Understanding hardware and software and what you need equipment-wise to elevate your music, additional plugins or instruments you may need to create and be inspired, is also important.

Be around as many talented people as you can, seek good mentorship, ask questions, put your pride aside, be the fool in the room that doesn't know what they're talking about and listen. **Julian Bunetta**

Sound design

Sound design is when you create songs through **sampling** (using existing audio to create new sounds), **recording** (capturing acoustic sounds and processing them after recording), **synthesis** (waveforms and oscillators) and **manipulating** (taking any sound and processing it with FX and other devices to alter it). It's a technical and creative process. You can watch every tutorial about sound design and how to do it, but the best way to master it is just to dive in and play around. You can spend hours learning and practising sound design, deconstructing, observing and tweaking presets that come with your DAW. Find presets and sounds that grab your ear and start navigating your way around. Start tweaking the knobs and see what happens to the sound and save your own version and repeat this process as practice.

A.G. Cook, who sort of oversaw the whole 'Brat' project with Charlie XCX, he's a bit of a god to me in terms of production, he's got the most amazing brain. He's so talented. And every decision is like really thought through. He sort of designed the whole soundscape. And then in terms of the stuff I produced – so there were like two songs I produced on there. And it was, I guess, it's me trying to sort of get into that world a bit, you know. So luckily, he's even so cool, like spending time with him in LA was so useful, because he would literally tell me all the little rules he'd made for himself in terms of like 'These are the kind of sounds we're using, it's going to be from these kind of synths, we're not going to use any of these kind of drums, we're not using anything off splice on this record.' Because he's a sound designer, that's his whole thing. I think he really enjoys the 'what's the sound design for this record?' So, I felt very sort of privileged to spend a little bit of time in that sort of circle, because I learnt loads, but also it's really helpful in terms of me angling what I was bringing into the room and saying, well, how about something like this and making sure it's not way off base. And then there's a couple of other songs where like 'Sympathy as a Knife', he just brought in a sort of early prototype of the backing track. And we did a bit of work on it, but it was more like taking stuff away from it. And there was a moment with that one where that really sort of jarring melody going into the chorus could initially have been thought of as a mistake, but I kind of chopped out the backing track for those two notes really. And suddenly it's like everyone's eyes lit up. **Jon Shave**

Attention to detail ★ Being a great producer requires great attention to detail and being organised. It's really a collection of sounds put together, so being organised and attentive to the details only helps the overall finished product get to the highest level. Paying attention to your levels, adding effects, paying attention to anyone in the room doing something, singing something that could be added to the production. Save everything – the worst is when you're in a session and there's a technical glitch, which happens all the time, and the producer hasn't been saving… Magic can be lost! So press that save button often and have your session files organised where you can access the projects easily in order to make changes or add any extra sauce needed.

Say you're making a rap song or a pop song, take one of your favourite ones that's been big that's in the same universe as what you're making and listen to it, then listen to yours. You'll be able to go, 'Oh, theirs is much brighter sounding or the bass is louder or softer, their drums are more punchy or less punchy' and doing that will help you as a producer to get it to a place where it can sit up there with other big songs. **John Ryan**

LESS IS MORE

The best producers in the world understand that a lot of the time in music production less is more. You don't wanna ever pack too many musical elements into the one song. The song itself needs space and all you need to do as a producer is complement that space with elements that really support the song instead of making the song a chaotic, busy mess.

You also want to avoid frequency clashes and muddy-sounding mixes. I always think starting out with a smaller number of instruments/sounds is best and then add in extra elements where needed. Being able to know when to add or subtract is important. It's hard sometimes as a producer to know if the song is 'finished' and you may try lots of different versions to get to the finished one. Be open to trying it all but use your ear and your taste to know when less is more and when the production is in a sweet spot to send to mix.

> *You can get the essence of the song without over cluttering the production with unnecessary things. The best productions they're very clean. There's a lot of space for every instrument to breathe. And every note has its purpose.* **Toby Gad**

> *I always think every song is just a couple of clicks away from going from average, to good, to great, to exceptional. Sometimes it's the difference between a girl singing it to a guy singing it, sometimes it's making it fast instead of being a ballad. Something that makes the words have more meaning or more feeling.* **Julian Bunetta**

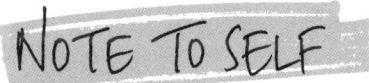

'Find good mentors, contribute to your community, have a circle of friends in the industry, cos no one knows what you're going through like other people that are doing it, so cultivate and nurture those friendships and be a good person.'
Julian Bunetta

PRODUCER – JOHN SHANKS

I also interviewed Grammy award-winning writer/producer John Shanks for this book. John has been consistently making hit records for decades. He's produced and/or written 43 No. 1 singles, 86 No. 1 albums and sold over 60 million records in the genres of rock, pop and country music. He won Grammy Producer of the Year in 2005 after a whirlwind year of non-stop No. 1s and created a production style that became such a sound many would try to emulate it.

PRODUCTION 157

'John's records have become the sound of top 40 radio,' legendary producer and music executive Clive Davis said. 'He's the father of that guitar-driven kind of pop sound.'

'First Cut Is The Deepest', Sheryl Crow; 'Everywhere', Michelle Branch; 'Breakaway', Kelly Clarkson; 'The Climb', Miley Cyrus; 'Pieces of Me', Ashley Simpson; 'Patience' and 'Rule the World' by Take That are just the tip of the iceberg. He has also been producing and writing Bon Jovi records for years and then joined the band as lead guitarist and toured all over the world with them. He had some amazing wisdom to share about production. So have a read, and take it all in.

Research:

Go listen to the artist and see what key he/she sings in. Go listen to their other songs, so when you're in the room with the artist and you're playing your ideas or beats they're in the right kinda key. Such a simple but effective way to start a session. You gotta research them and know their music. Because, basically, if you're gonna be presenting them a musical idea, you want it to be something they can melodically come up with something over, and if it's not in the right key or range it's not gonna work.

John shanks, Gary Barlow and Jon Bon Jovi

Making the best decisions for the song and artist:
You've got to keep your ears open and decide: Is this the best key for the artist? Is this the best tempo? Is this song really not a ballad, it's really a dance song? Being in a room with people you respect and collaborate with where someone goes 'Maybe we should put a four on the floor or make this a dance song, or make it a little bit folk.'

Teaching yourself the basics:
What was super-important for me as a writer and a producer was I got a drum machine and a 4-track recorder when I was probably 16 years old. I started learning how to record myself, put stuff down on tape, learned how to overdub, counterpoint, arrangements, background vocals all on my own, and one of the pieces of advice I always give to young creatives is don't think that the time you're putting in in your room alone is a waste of time. No idea is stupid because they will all lead to something.

Building trust:
There's a trust thing that needs to happen. Number one, I try to move somewhat quickly and trust my instincts, feed off the artist and tap into where they're at or what kind of sound. Even in a guitar or keyboard sound, I'm thinking 'Is this what it is? Are we going in the right direction?' And both of us talk about what we're listening to and what kind of record it wants to be. Then when you get a song and you record it and it goes well, eventually the artists say to managers or the record labels, 'I'm gonna stay with John because he doesn't just care about having a hit, it's the whole making of the album.'

Focusing on the body of work:
The thing I like about making albums with anyone is that it's not always about the single. I think part of the problem with the music business is when they feel the need to have fifteen different producers and songwriters work on a record because then what happens is that everybody's trying to write the single, which is a normal thing, but when everyone's trying to write the single, you don't get this beautiful mid-tempo or ballad, or the song about the artist's mother, or maybe there's something personal that's happened in the artist's life that they don't get to explore because we're all trying to come up with the single. And that doesn't make for an album that I wanna listen to very much in the long run. It becomes a collection of singles, but that doesn't lend itself well for something that will last the test of time.

Being open to producing songs you didn't write:
I've had situations where the artist is like 'Can I play you this song' and I'm gonna listen and support it and put on my producer hat. And you just become a fan of songs and production and I go into my studio-musician past and I just try to create the best version of that song and leave my songwriter hat out of it. You tweak it, you know, but that comes with the package. **John Shanks**

CASE STUDY

'Who Says You Can't Go Home' — Bon Jovi
Written by: Jon Bon Jovi, Richie Sambora
Producer: John Shanks

There was a Bon Jovi song that I produced that I didn't write. The story of this song was, we were at the end of making the album and I turned to Jon and said, 'Play me every song you haven't played me.' And he's like, 'No, no we're good, man.' I said, 'No, no. The band's still here, we're all set up, this is our last day, play me every song you haven't played me. Go to your house – I know you have a box filled with CDs, cassettes.' So he walks off and ten minutes later he comes back with the box with all these CDs and cassettes. I said, 'So, I'm gonna play smash or trash.' This is what I call it. I'm going to go through this dirty laundry, and I'm going to sit here and say, 'Nope, yes, nope, nope.'

On one CD, song 11 was him and Richie Sambora, playing an acoustic guitar, singing, 'Who says you can't go home.' I'm like, 'What is this?' Jon says, 'Oh, I don't know, it's an idea.' I say, 'That's a hit song, that's it.' And I always say this to artists, I say, 'Give me an hour, give me one hour and just humour me for an hour, and let me do my thing.' Richie grabbed an acoustic guitar. I grabbed my guitar. I say, 'Hugh, plug in the bass' and Tico and Jon say, 'We need a lick', so I picked up a guitar and played the lick, the opening lick. It's not my song, I'm the producer, but there it is, I wrote the opening lick. Great. Keep going. We cut the song. Now let's go over the drums and the bass, boom. Now go out there and sing the song. So, in a day we had basically done the song.

And there's a funny story to this as well. There's a part in the song where Jon wanted to do this call and answer – 'it's alright', 'it's alright' – and to me it felt cheesy, and I questioned it. He was like, 'Trust me.' The trust goes both ways, artist to producer, producer to artist, so I said okay. We ganged it up around a mic… Cut to three years later, they're playing Madison Square Garden and that song's the hit song and has won a Grammy. He's playing the song and the whole crowd is singing the very part, 'It's alright', lifting their hands in the air, singing 'It's alright', and he turns to me on the side of the stage and he goes, 'I told ya so, I told ya.' Jon is so focused and driven and awesome that he's in the middle of performing and he remembered that debate we'd had over that section. **John Shanks**

A hugely important part of this story is John listening through CDs and cassette tapes of old ideas and recognising this song being special, and then immediately having a vision for it and acting on his instincts and vision. Putting his producer hat on and producing what started as an acoustic idea on a CD that might never have been heard again to what would then become a hit song, a Grammy-winning song. So I asked him, 'What was it about that idea you heard on that CD that made you think it was a hit?'

I guess I was looking for a good chorus, looking for a good melody, looking for something I understood lyrically, a lyric that's universal, and this song had all that.

I hope just by this one case study alone you can see why John Shanks is a legendary writer/producer. I've worked with John many times and he's honestly one of the best.

Jon Bon Jovi with John Shanks

NOTE TO SELF

The best producers in the world always have their ears open, they have the vision and execute it to the highest levels, they build that trust with their artist and they have the skills to make a hit record that the whole world will connect with. This is the level to strive for as a producer.

INTERLUDE 3

PRODUCER / SONGWRITER STORIES

"I knew 'Lose Control' was going to change my life."

TEDDY SWIMS

To kick off this Interlude is the story behind one of the biggest songs of 2024. A song that has broken records all over the world.

You've just had some gems of wisdom from hitmaker Julian Bunetta, whose songs have amassed over 40 billion streams. From writing and producing over half of One Direction's catalogue including, 'The Story of My Life', 'Night Changes', 'Steal My Girl', 'Perfect' to writing 'Slow Hands', 'Nice to Meet Ya' and more on Niall Horan's solo albums to No. 1s galore with country superstar Thomas Rhett to writing and producing the Grammy-winning song 'Espresso' with Sabrina Carpenter and becoming one of her closest collaborators. Julian has solidified himself as one of the biggest and best in the world, and reading the story behind 'Lose Control' it's easy to see why.

'LOSE CONTROL' – TEDDY SWIMS

Written by: Jaten Dimsdale (Teddy Swims), Joshua Coleman (Ammo), Julian Bunetta, Marco Antonio Rodriguez-Diaz Jr. (Infamous), Mikky Ekko
Produced by: Julian Bunetta, Ammo

We were at a songwriting camp, me, Teddy, Mikky and Ammo. Ammo played some chords and I was like, 'Wait, stop stop stop' and I luckily put my recorder on my phone and the chorus, 'I, lose, controooooolllll', just came to me instantly. I said, 'Play that again', I sang the chorus down and I was like 'Yes' because I was looking for a real vocal moment for Teddy. We had been talking together about the kind of chords it should be and anyways we got the chorus. Teddy and Mikky came in and I said, 'Guys, I have an idea I think we should do.' I sang the idea to them – it really was based on a conversation that Teddy and I had the night before about what he was going through.

The guitar solo was really a jokey mouth solo that Ammo sang in and then we were gonna have a guitar player, a pretty famous guitar player, do the solo. They were lined up to play it but then that didn't work out at the last minute, so I just went back and re-played Ammo's mouth guitar solo on guitar.

I didn't send the demo to the label from the writing camp. I held that one back because it didn't have Teddy's voice on it yet cos his voice was gone from all the singing at the camp. I didn't wanna send it to the label without his voice on it and blow my shot so I didn't send it until I had Teddy come over and we spent an entire day on that vocal, getting the perfect vocal, and there were still things we changed from the demo because Mikky had done the demo his style and then Teddy sang it and changed things to his style, so the song was constantly evolving and changing. I knew that it was special, and I knew it was gonna do more than any of the songs that he'd released before, but I didn't know it was gonna be as big as it became. **Julian Bunetta**

Next up is Grammy-winning, multi-platinum-selling songwriter/producer John Ryan, who is also writer/producer royalty. His catalogue to date has amassed over 30 billion streams and he has collaborated with some of today's most iconic artists on their biggest songs. Songs like 'Don't Wanna Know' (Maroon 5) to 'Taste' (Sabrina Carpenter). With Julian Bunetta he also wrote and produced over half of One Direction's catalogue, including 'The Story of My Life', 'Night Changes' and 'Steal My Girl'.

Julia Michaels, Amy Allen and Sabrina Carpenter

'TASTE' – SABRINA CARPENTER

Written by: Sabrina Carpenter, Amy Allen, John Ryan, Julia Michaels, Ian Kirkpatrick
Produced by: John Ryan, Julian Bunetta, Ian Kirkpatrick

'Taste' was a 1-acoustic-guitar demo for a really long time. It's funny how some songs need to wait in the wings for a bit; need to stew before you go back to work on them. I think if we tried to produce the song the day we wrote it, it would've been completely different.

Again, writing the song came quick, maybe three hours. We always loved the lyrics and topline and how she blended poppy with sexy with funny all-in-one. But maybe three months later we finally added the live, almost country-leaning drums, plus the heavy electric guitars etc... and it really started to take shape. Then hearing the BVs and ad libs ... she just makes everything sound so expensive and classy, instantly. And deciding to start the album that way? EPIC!

I remember we did a lot of iterations of the intro... 1 acoustic, 4 acoustics, 12 string...1 electric, 4 electrics etc... I think she made the right choice!!!! **John Ryan**

'DRAG ME DOWN' – ONE DIRECTION
Written by: Julian Bunetta, John Ryan, Jamie Scott
Produced by: Julian Bunetta, John Ryan

Myself, John Ryan and Jamie Scott would get together every Jan/Feb for three weeks to write songs and ideas for One Direction. And the first day we had this melody which was the start of the chorus melody of 'Drag me Down' and we did like 18 ideas. John and I are sitting at midnight and we're recapping the day and I'm like, 'I think we got some good ideas.' One of us said, 'What was that very first idea we started, the one that's kinda like Mumford "Counting Stars"?' And we're like, 'Did we voice note it?' and we hadn't voice noted it but John remembered that one weird note in it. I was like 'Yes, that's a really cool melody', just that little bit, and we were like, 'We should write that tomorrow.' But that song was almost just lost to the ether – if John hadn't remembered those notes it would not have been written. And then we wrote it as a more up-tempo, four on the floor Mumford and Sons style. At one point it was called 'Bring Me Down', and we were fighting over the lyric 'Bring me down' or 'Pull me down' or 'Drag me down' and someone just said, 'We gotta go with drag me down – it just sounds phonetically better.'

Then when it came to the production Jamie had gone to bed and John and I stayed up and completely changed the whole production and did the half time The Police-style vibes. The reason we changed up the production was because I was like, 'I know the melody is catchy and I know the words sound cool, but why aren't I getting that feeling emotionally when I listen to this? Something isn't right.' So like in a seven-number jackpot on a slot machine I know we're not hitting the jackpot. I know four of these numbers are lined up but it's the last few numbers that aren't quite doing it. So we just changed acoustic guitar to electric guitar, and it had attitude, I liked that attitude, and maybe instead of being this softer song it needed that attitude, that more middle-finger-in-the-air, and so we played it in a way that made the song come alive. **Julian Bunetta**

John Ryan now tells us how they wrote 'Story Of My Life' for One Direction.

John Ryan, Jamie Scott, Louis Tomlinson, Julian Bunetta & Liam Payne

'STORY OF MY LIFE' – ONE DIRECTION

Myself, Jamie and Julian had done two weeks of writing for One Direction for their third album *Midnight Memories*, and they were just about to do a stadium tour, so every song was like 80s rock, made for stadiums. We wrote all these songs and most of them made the album, but by the end of the two weeks of writing we were tired of writing rock. So we were just like, let's do something different, let's pretend we're a band and do some Paul Simon fingerpicking, and we started noodling and Julian hit 'record' on the voice note. I was playing keys, Julian and Jamie were playing guitar. Jamie just starts doing the melody and went into the pre-, and then Julian sang a thing, and then I sang a thing. And Jamie sang 'the story of my life' and that was the title.

Then, instead of sitting and writing and thinking about what the song was about we just listened back to the voice note and wrote all lyrics that he kind of said, we just wrote the phonetics of it. That song isn't really about anything, it's just gibberish: 'I'll be gone, gone tonight, the ground beneath my feet is open wide, the way that I've been holding on too tight, with nothing in between.' It's the phonetics of it that sound so good.

So we had a meeting with their record label, and played all the stuff from the week, and right at the end of the meeting one of us said, 'What was that other one we did? The fingerpicking one?' We played 'Story of My Life' and Tyler, who was their A&R, was like, 'I think that's the one.' We said, 'What?' All this work into these other more rock-guitar riffs but this song was the standout one.

I just learned so much about giving the audience room to interpret a song in their own way and not being so on the nose or having to tell a story. The lyrics sound deep and everyone's relating to 'the story of my life'. Even if you don't know what it's about you still feel it, and the feeling is more important without having to explain it. It's as much about feeling it as it is about it meaning something. That song was my first real big song where I felt like I made something with artistic integrity and knew from the beginning that I loved it. It was a pivotal moment in my career. **John Ryan**

I spoke to Grammy and Brit award winning songwriter/producer Jon Shave – the songs he's written have amassed over 21 billion streams. He told me the story behind one of his biggest hits...

Charli xcx with Jon Shave

'FANCY' – IGGY AZALEA FEAT. CHARLI xcx

Written by: Charli xcx, Jon Shave, Iggy Azalea, Jason Pebworth, George Astasio, Kurtis McKenzie
Produced by: Jon Shave, George Astasio, Jason Pebworth

One of the biggest records I've been lucky enough to be involved with is 'Fancy' by Iggy Azalea and Charli. And that was the result of a whole load of work and process that had gone into the whole sort of Iggy world and that song came out of it. So basically, we were working with Iggy on her first major label album and she'd done a few mix tapes and was

PRODUCER/SONGWRITER STORIES 167

sort of a big figure in the blog kind of world, but we were helping support her development into a major label artist. So we'd done a lot of time with her. We started in London but it was too distracting, there were just too many other things going on, so we ended up going out to Wales to a studio in the middle of nowhere. And we made a record called 'Work' there, which was a really good insight into what the album could be. And everyone felt really excited by that. Then it was about building an album around that.

We were spending a lot of time in LA, and it was during that time, it would have been late 2012, early 2013. And I remember hearing in LA, vocals that just kind of really slap around the face, you know. And when we're getting towards the end of making the Iggy record, we had a lot of really cool rap records, but we needed a few more hooks to make it have a bit of a broader appeal. We had this really cool club track that had a rapped chorus on it. And I remember thinking, 'God, this would be really great if we could relook at the hook on this.' And it just so happened I had a session with Charli xcx the following week. And I remember thinking that sort of Gwen Stefani-ish punky vocal on a kind of electronic sort of hip-hop thing could be really interesting. I played it to her and she got it immediately, and probably within about an hour and a half, we'd sort of pieced the whole thing together. But then it kind of sat around for a while and no one was really jumping up and down about it. The label were aware of it but there weren't any plans being made. And in the end the early demo ended up leaking. And it started to get club play in America and get played on some of the hip-hop stations. And this was the version without Charli on it. But that was enough, suddenly the label paid attention. And it was like, actually, this is really reacting, we should push the button on 'Fancy'. And so that happened, obviously. Iggy made an amazing, stunning visual that really elevated it. It was just amazing then to watch week by week these two previously pretty much unknown artists just climbing the Hot 100. And then once we were at No. 1, it was there for seven weeks, and then the rest is history.

A big song like that changes everything really because it's such a powerful thing to have a No. 1 song in America. I remember a few weeks after it had come out and I was back in LA, I was actually doing some more writing with Charli, and we were in the studio. We were going home quite late, it must have been about 1 a.m., something like that, we were sharing an Uber and we were just going along Sunset and stopped at traffic lights and this car pulled up next to us – this car with the hood down with like about eight girls crammed into it all screaming along to 'Fancy' at the top of their lungs. We just thought this is amazing and I remember saying, 'Look, there we go, there's the target audience.' You know, those are the really special moments when you see it sort of takes on a life of its own and it's kind of not yours anymore, it belongs to the world. **Jon Shave**.

Autumn Rowe told me a fascinating story about how she came to meet Jon Batiste and went on to win Grammys for her work not only as a songwriter but as a producer on his five-time Grammy-winning album, including Album of the Year, *We Are*. This is a great reminder to trust your gut, and how vital a vision for the artist is from a producer.

WE ARE – JON BATISTE

I definitely felt it was a time of the 'boys' club' and I also felt I didn't fit into it. And I'm thinking, 'How do I navigate this world where I've already done some stuff but what do I do now?' So I had to ask myself, do I want to be someone who navigates in the space that's already there or someone who creates a space that doesn't exist? And how do I do that? So I basically started only working with pure intention. I made a conscious decision to only do things with intention. And with that mindset I cut 90% of writing sessions because I realised I was doing a lot of free artist development for record labels and not getting paid. Another mindset I adopted was deciding I was gonna work like I was a very rich woman because a rich woman is only gonna do what she wants to do. So I started saying no to things that I didn't wanna do or I didn't believe in.

I got a session one night with one of Ricky Reed's team. I got an Uber to the session and I was chatting to the driver and he said, 'You know, when I feel really down, sometimes I just sing.' It really touched my heart, so when I was in the session and they were playing me tracks and I just couldn't hear anything over the beats, I said to them, 'Can I just sing something into the room, something just on my soul and you guys can figure it out later?' I just started singing, on the verge of crying, and I wrote this whole song called 'Sing'. The Uber driver had totally inspired me, I just really felt it when he said it, and the song came out from that.

About six months later I got sent this full New Orleans-style production on it and this guy was singing it. And he sounded incredible, and I thought to myself, 'I don't know who this person is but, wow, I've never worked with an artist who has interpreted my lyrics and melody this way. Whoever it is I need to meet him, and I need to do more of this. It's not a hit song but it's special and I need to find this guy.'

I find it's a guy named Jon Batiste. And I'm like, I don't know who that is. Months and months of me trying to find him on socials, DM-ing him, tweeting him, never sees my message. I fly to New York on my mom's birthday to surprise her. As soon as I land in New York, Jon sees my DM. And he goes, 'I just saw your DM. I would love to meet, let's do it.' And I said, 'Wow, this is so crazy because I've just landed in New York and I'm here for 36 hours. Can you meet me tomorrow?' So I booked my mom brunch right next to the Colbert Show (where Jon was bandleader and musical director). So I ran to Colbert for an hour, we played a bunch of songs for each other and vibes started again. And I'm like, 'Well, I don't know what's going on, I don't know if you're working on music or whatever, but you sound really good on this song and I really wanna make more songs with you. So can we do that?' He's like, 'Okay.' He basically gives me all this control and says, 'Why don't you set up all of our sessions?' So I start making a wish list. I had Mark Ronson and Salaam Remi on this wishlist. Because what I did know, he was highly musical. He is definitely some kind of genius. And whoever we were going to work with needed to be able to match that genius and know how to hone it. I knew they needed to be on a certain level. I start making calls and texts, and I'm trying to figure out how to get to Mark Ronson and all these people. I don't know Mark Ronson. And I get up on a Sunday and get a call from Jon and he's like, 'Hey, I'm in town, let's get to work.' And I'm like, 'Oh, so it's Sunday and there's no way I can get any of these people by tomorrow. I'm not a big writer like that. I don't have that kind of, you know, I don't have that network.' I said, 'But I'm sitting next to my friend Kizzo.' So I play him the one song I had with Jon like, 'I did the song with this artist. It's very like artsy and, I don't know, I really like it. Would you do a session with us?' He goes, sure. So Jon comes in the next day. We do a song, and he comes in the day after. The second day that we three were together, we wrote a song called 'Freedom'. Then it came. It came so fast. It came so easy. It came because of Jon. Jon was dancing with a broom, and I was like, oh, this is how I could see the music video for this. When I wrote the chorus in like ten seconds, I was just, 'I don't know, I feel like freedom.' Jon starts going at the verses. I mean, we probably wrote the whole song in an hour.

But before we started writing, and when I met him, I think the important thing to know is that I already had a vision for what to do with him. When I met him, I was like, okay, he could be what you would do with Marvin Gaye and James Brown today. So, what would we do with that today? How do we break him from jazz to cross him over gradually? You don't just go into pop. How do we gradually move you over, with all his cultural background, the New Orleans and jazz and all this stuff. How do we do that? And basically, that was it, you know, we did those two songs.

And then we were like, there's no label involved. There's no management involved. There's no one involved. I believed in him a lot. I was like, you are who I've been waiting for. You're why I have been turning down sessions because I've been waiting for this. And I knew it. I just knew it. We flew to New York a few months later and we built the studio in his dressing room. And that's when we wrote 'We Are', 'Show Me The Way' and a bunch of other songs that haven't come out. We probably did the whole album in about ten days writing-wise. Production, of course, took way longer because we got choirs and marching bands and all kinds of stuff on it. But, um, yeah, that was it.

I remember the last day of our sessions in his dressing room. I will never forget I said it that day, I said it to my husband, I said it to everyone in the room, I said, 'Jon, you're gonna get a Grammy for this.' I knew it. After we made the *We Are* album, I wasn't able to write for about four months after that. I was drained, it was like, I gave so much. I can't even explain it because it's a completely different process than writing a pop song. It was so much more than technical rhyming and storytelling. There's a deeper aspect to it. And I know for a fact that making the album, I was 100% channelling because that night when we finished it, my husband saw me and I told him, 'You can't touch me. I need a minute to calm down because I feel like electricity is coming off of me.' I felt like I was so charged that I could explode. I felt like I'm out of this earth. And I don't even know what that is. And I can't understand it. But that is part of songwriting which I would love to learn more about. I think that's something that's very magical and doesn't happen all the time.

We finished it in 2019. Then the album came out – I think we started putting songs out during COVID in 2020. So the first we put out, it wasn't necessarily a commercial single, but it kind of coincided with the BLM movement. Jon had all his musician friends come by and it was a joyous, but you know, painful gathering with music and marching. And, you know, he started singing 'We Are' at these marches. BLM actually named some of the marches the 'We Are' March. And then then we started leaning towards the more fun side of the album with 'I Need You'. And then eventually 'Freedom'.

Jon Batiste & Autumn Rowe

So the Grammy – I won as a producer for Album of the Year, and as a songwriter for Album of the Year. That's why it's so huge because it's not often that females are winning, you know, as producers on Album of the Year. It was mind-blowing, by the way. I knew Jon would win a Grammy. I didn't know we would win Album of the Year. I didn't think he would get five. I didn't think it would get eight nominations. I didn't think any of that. I was just happy for one Grammy. But I didn't realise it would make him the first Black artist to win Album of the Year in fourteen years. This album, you know, that was created in a time when everyone's telling you to follow algorithms and follow trends and follow this. And this album was not that. This was not a pop album. This was not an album going for radio. This was an album made of creativity and pure love of music.

People ask what does a Grammy do for you, like does your whole life just change? Not necessarily, but what it does, especially this particular Grammy, when we created a project without a label, without people guiding you, and I'll be honest, I didn't have a lot of support, even from people I worked with. So I didn't have people saying this is gonna work. I had the opposite, which makes the story even better though because it proves you need to trust your gut. Well, what the Grammy does do is it opens doors. There are meetings I couldn't get that I can get now. It's a key to like, oh, I wanna go here. Oh, here's my key. Oh, it works. And then it's what you do with them. You still have to work like crazy and no one's knocking on my door, you know, to do things. I still have to go after them. And the biggest thing it did to me, though, was it validated to me that I'm not crazy. I'm not crazy. And if you believe in something, you believe in an artist, you believe in a movement, you believe in a sound, just do it. **Autumn Rowe**

CHAPTER 8

SAMPLING

"I wrote and produced millions and millions of selling records, so my publishing company alone was worth millions of dollars. I didn't have to work anymore in life because when the rappers started sampling... I'm the most sampled artist in history."

RICK JAMES

WHAT IS SAMPLING?

Sampling is when you reuse any part of an already existing song in a brand-new composition. It became the foundation of hip-hop music dating back to the early 70s at hip-hop parties in the Bronx where DJs would spin already released funk and soul records whilst MCs rapped over them live. It grew from there and has since become incredibly popular across all music genres.

One of the first *Billboard* Top 40 hits that used a sample was the 1980s Sugarhill Gang hip-hop song 'Rappers Delight'. Unless you've been living under a rock you definitely know it for more reasons than one.

> 'I said a hip, hop, the hippie to the hip hip hop a you don't stop the rock it to the band band boogie, say up jump the boogie to the rhythm of the boogie, the beat'

This song also sampled the very famous bassline from the 1970s Chic classic 'Good Times' and it is an excellent example of how amazing sampling can be done. They rapped over the bassline and guitar part of 'Good Times' with new lyrics, concept and title, essentially creating a brand-new song with the music of Chic as the backdrop, and it really was the foundation for a lot of hip-hop hits to come.

WHY USE A SAMPLE?

Sampling became a staple in hip-hop music because of a genre that was largely based on freestyling and rapping lyrics. It was the fastest way to get a great beat done quickly (and cheaply) to rap over and also a clever way of making something feel instantly familiar, and that's one of the biggest reasons people sample.

When you use parts of a song that's already been a hit, and you do it well, it means people will already recognise your new song because of the old song you've put in it. This increases the odds of people liking it, wanting to sing it instantly, and it takes them back to a time or a memory or something nostalgic about the original sample.

When sampling first started it was mainly the beats of the song that were two- to four-bar loops from funk and soul records, but now thanks to vast developments in technology, sampling possibilities are limitless and you can use any element of a previous song in your song. You can edit it, stretch it and/or manipulate it, or sing a pre-existing melody with a brand-new lyric. It can be a creative and fun process, and another great tool for songwriting and production.

SAMPLING vs INTERPOLATING

As I've explained, a sample is when you use a snippet of the actual master sound recording and copy/paste it into your new song. You may have changed the tempo of the sample or the key, but you still used the actual sound recording.

Whereas an **interpolation** is a re-played and/or re-recorded sample. So, when you use a melody or parts of a melody from a previously recorded song, but you re-record it (sometimes with newly written lyrics) instead of directly sampling it that's called interpolation. Say if you use the famous musical or melodic hook from an existing song but you re-play it with a different instrument or you re-lyric the melody and re-record it with a new vocal, that's interpolating. You've still used part of a previously copyrighted composition, so whether you directly sample or interpolate both need to be cleared for use from the original copyright owners.

Sampling/interpolating is reincarnating, reimagining parts of existing music in a brand-new way. It's a form of expression where you can use your imagination to create something fresh and new.

Now that we understand the difference between sampling and interpolating, let's delve into some examples of the most famous songs containing samples and interpolations.

EXAMPLES OF DIRECT SAMPLING

'Big Yellow Taxi' by Joni Mitchell. Directly sampled in 'Got 'til It's Gone' by Janet Jackson feat. Q-Tip

When you put Janet Jackson and Joni Mitchell in the same sentence it may feel genre-wise very far apart. But this really was a sample match made in heaven and such a clever use. 'Big Yellow Taxi' was released in 1970 and Janet Jackson has always been very vocal about how much she admired and loved Joni Mitchell as an artist. When it came to creating 'Got 'til It's Gone' Janet wanted to fuse the folk elements of Joni with Q-Tip's poetic rap and her own R&B/pop signature sound. The foundation of the song was built around the sample from 'Big Yellow Taxi' of Joni Mitchell singing repeatedly as the hook.

> 'Don't it always seem to go, that you don't know what you got 'til it's gone'

The song became a huge hit, and gave Joni Mitchell a boost in relevancy in terms of pop culture at the time. She's quoted as saying, 'My stock has risen lately with Janet Jackson sampling me in her hit "Got 'til It's Gone". More heads are turning at the airport these days.'

'Gimme, Gimme, Gimme' by ABBA.
Directly sampled in 'Hung Up' by Madonna

Another hit song with a huge sample as its foundation. Madonna and her producer Stuart Price made very good use of the famous instrumental introduction from ABBA's 'Gimme Gimme Gimme' released in 1973 which runs throughout Madonna's track, 'Hung Up', which was released in 2005. They only used the instrumental section and wrote an entirely new song over it. So, it felt familiar but fresh and new at the same time.

'Straight to Hell' by The Clash.
Directly sampled in 'Paper Planes' by M.I.A.

Another that uses an instrumental section with a newly written song on top is this captivating and wildly unique M.I.A. smash 'Paper Planes'. This was produced by Diplo who at the time in his earlier producing years loved to sample songs from vinyl and had the idea to sample 'Straight to Hell' by The Clash. Between the Clash sample and the gun shot sounds in the hook and M.I.A.'s opening lines...

> 'I fly like paper get high like planes if you catch me at the border I got Visas in my name'

... you have yourselves a monster smash!

Now let's talk about famous interpolations.

EXAMPLES OF INTERPOLATIONS

'My Favourite Things' by Rogers & Hammerstein.
Interpolated in '7 Rings' by Ariana Grande

One of the most interesting and successful interpolations of late was the use of the verse melody from 'My Favourite Things', known famously from the movie *The Sound of Music* released in 1965, sung by Julie Andrews. This was reimagined by Ariana and her co-writers in '7 Rings', released in 2019. They used the existing verse melody whose original lyrics were:

> Raindrops on roses and whiskers on kittens
> White copper kettles and warm woollen mittens
> Brown paper packages tied up with string
> These are a few of my favourite things

And they interpolated the existing melody by re-writing these brand-new lyrics:

> Breakfast at Tiffany's and bottle of bubbles
> Girls with tattoos who like getting in trouble
> Lashes and diamonds, ATM machines
> Buy myself all of my favourite things

The song became a massive worldwide hit and fans instantly recognised the clever use of 'My Favourite Things' and applauded Grande for her interpolation.

'Blue (Da Ba Dee)' by Eiffel 65. Interpolated in 'I'm Good (Blue)' by David Guetta feat. Bebe Rexha

Of course, we all remember the 1998 absolute dance tune 'Blue (Da Ba Dee)' whose hook consisted of an infectious melody with the following words repeated over and over again.

> I'm blue, da ba dee da be di, da ba dee da ba di da ba dee da ba di

Fast forward to 2017 when Bebe Rexha and her co-writers re-lyriced the existing chorus melody and decided to put new words to it. But they didn't actually release it until 2022 after a TikTok of David Guetta playing it out live from an older DJ set of his a few years prior went viral.

> I'm good yeah, I'm feeling alright,
> Baby, Imma have the best f**kin' night of my life
> And wherever it takes me, I'm down for the ride
> Baby, don't you know I'm good? Yeah, I'm feeling alright

The perfect interpolation, and upon its release it became a global smash.

I interviewed one of the song's writers, Grammy and Ivor Novello award-winning singer/songwriter/producer/artist Kamille about how that song came about, and she said:

> *I remember being in the room with David Guetta and Bebe Rexha at like 2 a.m. writing songs and not having any idea what I'm doing there or what these songs were gonna be. It was just a really, really fun night, but I remember thinking nothing's gonna happen with these songs. Then, three years later, the song goes viral on a TikTok video of David Guetta playing it live at a show and all of sudden the song goes to No. 1.*
>
> *David had a bunch of ideas and samples and he was like, 'Do we bring this back?' And I was thinking, oh my god, this is never gonna happen. Will they even clear the sample? And then I just thought, whatever, and typically as a lot of songs do, they just kind of fall into an abyss, a Dropbox folder on your laptop, and never see the light of day. But then it came out and was massive. I had just had a baby, so it was nice that it happened because it gave me a lot of confidence, because it's easy to feel like 'I've had a baby, my career is over' but that song just took over the world.* **Kamille**

WHAT IS THE MOST SAMPLED SONG OF ALL TIME?

A song called 'Amen, Brother' by The Winstons is the most sampled song of all time, having been sampled in over 6,000 different songs since its release in 1969. It is a drum break known as 'Amen Break' that was performed by Gregory Coleman and it has been sampled in such songs as 'Straight Outta Compton', NWA; 'D'You Know What I Mean', Oasis; 'I Desire', Salt-N-Pepa; 'You Know I'm No Good', Amy Winehouse, just to name a few. This four-bar drum break really became the foundations of a lot of early hip-hop records in the 80s and continues to be used in songs even now. This sample is so popular because it's versatile and easily manipulated but still sounds good when sped up, slowed down, chopped, distorted, and it's always recognisable.

The Winstons / Michael Ochs Archives © Getty Images

Now before you get all excited and run to your computer to rip every hit song's acapella or every guitar riff known to man, or re-lyric an old ABBA melody, we need to talk about the very important side of sampling and interpolating that can also be a reason that creatives avoid it or only do it once in a while. This is essential reading for all you budding samplers out there.

Let's say you have thought of a great old song to sample. You sample it in your track, and it sounds amazing and you want to release it. Well, hold your horses because you actually **can't** release any song that contains a sample without getting it cleared. You also can't release a new song with a re-played sample or re-recorded copyrighted melody with new lyrics without permission and the correct licensing. So, what's the next step? The next step involves two important things, copyright and clearance.

WHAT IS MUSIC COPYRIGHT?

Copyright is all about the ownership of a song. It essentially is a 'property' right. And the copyright owner authorises the use of the song in all the various ways and reserves the right to prevent its use. Usually, the first owners of the copyright of a song are the songwriters, and that's when the split conversation comes into play of how much of the new song you each own. If you write the song 100% yourself then you own the copyright 100%. If you write a song with another writer you may split the copyright 50/50 and so on and so forth – the more writers on a song, the more the pie gets split up. Where sampling is concerned, it's very important that you fully understand how copyright works and what you need to do to use a sample in a song so that you don't end up in a lawsuit.

HOW DO I COPYRIGHT A SONG?

It's worth noting that you don't need to be a signed, published writer to copyright your music. When I started writing songs I'd record an extra copy on a mic and a 2-track tape recorder (it was the 90s!) and my dad would take the tape with the title and marked date of writing on it to the post office and post it back to our address using special delivery, which also notes the date, and we would leave it unopened in a secure place. He did that with all my songs for years before I was signed. This meant that we had essentially copyrighted my songs with proof of date.

If you are a published writer, part of your publisher's job is to register your songs and make sure they are copyrighted.

WHAT IS CLEARANCE?

Clearing a sample/interpolation is an absolute non-negotiable aspect of sampling. You always always always need permission to use any part of someone else's work in your song. If you don't clear the sample/interpolation correctly it is an infringement of copyright which is plagiarism and will most likely lead you to a lot of angry emails, the song being pulled down and/or blocked and potentially a lawsuit.

Let's look at how you clear a sample correctly.

MASTER RECORDING vs PUBLISHING

In order to clear a sample, there are two types of sample clearances you will need.

The first type is clearing the **master recording of the sample**.

When I say the term 'master', which you will see several times in this book, this refers to the original sound recording of a song. Usually created in a recording studio or home studio or even sometimes from a live performance. It is the source from which all copies of the song are made: CDs, digital downloads, streaming or any other format. Think of it like an original painting. If you sample a piece of the original sound recording you have to get clearance for the usage of it from the master owner.

Who owns the master recording?

The master owner refers to whoever pays for the sound recording. Typically, in most instances this is the record label as they have the funds needed to invest in the artist's music by paying the upfront fees for the recording of the song. Those fees include hiring the recording studio, the sound engineer, the producer, any musicians needed and paying for the song to then be mixed/mastered. The label usually own the lion's share of the master if they paid for the recording of it. The artist also owns part of the master as the performer of it, as does the producer who produces it, but the label is typically who to go to in order to clear master recording samples first.

The second type is clearing the **publishing side of the sample**.

The publishing side of the sample refers to the composition of the song, which is also called the 'topline' — lyrics and melody. You need to clear the use of this which is covered by the publishing license.

Who owns the publishing?

Each songwriter/producer/artist involved in the original composition that you are sampling is a publishing owner, and they need to give permission for its use. If the songwriters are published it is the writer's individual publisher who you go to in order to clear the publishing side and they usually contact the writer directly and come back to you then. If the writer is unpublished then you need to track down the writer and ask them directly for permission.

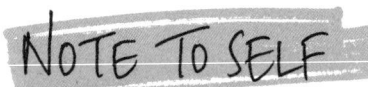

If you interpolate a copyrighted song into your new song, you only need to clear it with the publishing owners and not the master owners. BUT if you directly sample a song using the original master sound recording in your new song you must get clearance from both the master owners and the publishing owners.

SAMPLING A SONG vs COVERING A SONG

It is important to point out in case of any confusion, that performing a cover of an existing copyrighted song is always allowed because of something in place known as 'Compulsory Licensing', which basically means the owners of a song cannot deny anyone releasing a straight cover of their song if you don't add in any new parts of lyric or melody.

This has to be a straight cover of the song but can be your own interpretation. And the cover is credited to the original songwriters, so you won't receive any publishing royalties for your version. However, you will receive master royalties because it is a brand-new sound recording, which can be lucrative for artists and record labels who release covers. The only thing to do when releasing a cover is to get a compulsory mechanical license, which anyone and everyone can get, and credit the songwriters who wrote it so that all publishing royalties go to them. It's worth noting sometimes a good cover can become the biggest song an artist releases or can help launch careers of new artists.

Some examples of famous covers are:

'I Will Always Love You' – Whitney Houston
Originally written and sung by Dolly Parton, Whitney covered it as the title track of the blockbuster hit movie that she starred in alongside Kevin Costner, *The Bodyguard*. Her cover became a massive hit all over the world, holding the record at the time for most consecutive weeks at No. 1 (14 weeks). Winning Grammy awards and selling over 24 million copies, it became the best-selling single of all time by a female solo artist.

'Nothing Compares 2 U' – Sinead O'Connor
Originally written and sung by Prince, but it was Sinead's cover version that became a worldwide hit. Her emotive vocal performance paired with an iconic music video propelled her career into global rockstar status.

'Hallelujah' – Jeff Buckley
Originally written and sung by Leonard Cohen, Jeff Buckley truly made the song into his

own unique, stunning rendition. It was only after his tragic passing in 1997 that his cover became famous worldwide and is now considered a masterpiece.

'Valerie' — Mark Ronson feat. Amy Winehouse

Originally written and sung by The Zutons — a British indie rock band. But it was Ronson and Winehouse's cover version that made the song worldwide famous, so much so that often people don't even know it's a cover.

'Skinny Love' — Birdy

Originally written and sung by Bon Iver. Birdy's cover version was her breakthrough, launching her as an artist charting all over Europe and Australia.

HOW TO CLEAR A SAMPLE

A FOUR-STEP PROCESS

Step 1: Research

Find out who the copyright owners are. You can do this by searching the song credits, which will show all the songwriter's names and their publishing information. So basically, you need to know who exactly owns the rights to the sample/interpolation you are using.

Step 2: Contact

Once you know who owns the copyright it's time to make contact to start the clearance process. This can take a while and can be a longer process than meets the eye. Finding a licensing contact is a good place to start. Note that songwriters are often published by different companies and you need clearance from all the writers involved in the sample/interpolation.

Step 3: Negotiate

Now it's the fun part of negotiating the deal. You need to get each copyright owner to say in writing that they control the rights you need and that they agree to license those rights to you. It's important to note that it is never compulsory for a sample/interpolation to be cleared. The copyright owner can say 'no' if they want to. If they say 'no' you can't use the sample and that's that. If you use it without permission they can sue you for copyright infringement. This can be disheartening if you've spent a lot of time using a sample/interpolation that gets rejected.

Step 4: Agree the terms of the deal

More often than not, samples and interpolations are approved and once you get a 'yes', which is always great news, the copyright holders of the sample still hold the power because they can dictate how much of the publishing on the new song that they would like to have, no matter how much of their song is being used. There is no set percentage for samples and interpolations. It can get messy and there are instances where the original writers will want 100% of the new song that their sample is being used in. The deal must be agreed upon before the new song is released.

Let's use a case study from my own experience to see those four steps in action.

CASE STUDY

'Alibi' – Ella Henderson feat. Rudimental

Written by: Ella Henderson, RuthAnne, Maegan Cottone, Olivia Sebastianelli, John Morgan, Will Lansley, Stevie Wonder, Doug Rasheed, Artis Ivey Jr, Larry Sanders

This song was written in October 2023 and released under the record label Atlantic Records in January 2024. It became the biggest dance pop song of the year in the UK, going platinum, and was also nominated for Song of the Year at the Brit Awards 2025.

I had this idea to interpolate the chorus of the Coolio hit 'Gangsta's Paradise' and re-lyric the melody of that hit chorus, give it a new concept, and new title using the melody of the chorus. The writing session for this was so fun. We immediately came up with a fresh concept called 'Alibi' and we bounced around lots of ideas and the song was written quite quickly. Whilst we were writing the topline the producers in the session had also taken a direct sample from 'Gangsta's Paradise' of the famous choir section and this made the foundation of the music for our new track. Technically we used a direct sample AND an interpolation.

However, most people do not realise that 'Gangsta's Paradise' was also built upon an interpolation of the Stevie Wonder song 'Pastime Paradise', which was released in 1976 on his classic album *Songs in the Key of Life*, so they would've got clearance for the interpolation. They didn't use a direct sample from Stevie's version; instead they re-played the string hook so they didn't have to get master clearance from Stevie, just publishing clearance for the use of melodies.

In this case study you'll notice there are quite a few writers on our new song 'Alibi'. That is because we used not one but two interpolations in the song whilst also writing completely new verses and a new hook.

Interpolation 1:
Stevie Wonder – 'Pastime Paradise'
(Stevie Wonder)

Interpolation 2:
Coolio – 'Gangsta's Paradise'
(Artis Ivey Jr. (aka Coolio), Doug Rasheed, Larry Sanders)

'Alibi'
New writing:
(Ella Henderson, RuthAnne, Maegan Cottone, Olivia Sebastianelli, John Morgan, Will Lansley)

The original Stevie Wonder lyrics for the chorus and verse part are:

> They've been spending most their lives
> Living in a pastime paradise
> They've been spending most their lives
> Living in a pastime paradise
>
> Tell me who of them will come to be?
> How many of them are you and me?

Coolio and his writers then interpolated the melody of these parts, wrote new rap verse lyrics and tweaked/changed the Stevie chorus lyrics to be his chorus. Then they used what was a verse melody in Stevie's version as the bridge part of 'Gangsta's Paradise'.

> Been spending most their lives
> Living in a gangsta's paradise
> Been spending most their lives
> Living in a gangsta's paradise
>
> Tell me why are we so blind to see
> That the ones we hurt are you and me

And for 'Alibi' we came up with a concept about a woman who discovered her partner had been cheating on her and we decided to write 'Alibi' about getting revenge. We used the chorus melody from 'Pastime Paradise' and re-lyriced it as:

> You better run and hide
> Baby I know where you were last night
> So I'm lighting up the sky
> Setting fire to your paradise

SAMPLING

We then added a post hook with a brand-new melody:

> You ain't got no
> You ain't got no
> You ain't got no
> Alibi

Then we did a new verse with a new melody and lyrics, and then we used the melody from the verse of 'Pastime Paradise' as our bridge, changing it to:

> Tell me how you'd lie so easily
> You've been messing with her don't mess with me

We wrote the song and sent it to Ella's A&R at Atlantic, who loved it and wanted it to be her next single. Enter in the four-step process. This one was confusing because our topline did not actually contain any part of Coolio's 'Gangsta's Paradise' – we had interpolated only Stevie Wonder's original song – but as I mentioned earlier, we did directly sample the choir section from the 'Gangsta's Paradise' master recording. If you've been following, that means we needed to obtain publishing clearance from all writers credited on 'Pastime Paradise' *and* 'Gangsta's Paradise' plus master clearance from the master owners of 'Gangsta's Paradise'.

The first decision and change we made to make the clearance easier was we got the choir section sample remade/re-played. Once the choir section was re-played this then turned what was a direct sample into an interpolation which meant we only needed to clear it, publishing wise. It sounds like it's a direct sample BUT it is actually a brand-new master recording of the sample. Clearing direct samples from master owners can be incredibly expensive as they can charge any fee they want for the sample usage. There's more likelihood of the request for a direct sample being denied so most samples you hear nowadays have been re-played to cut the expense and headache of clearing an old master recording.

We'll go through some examples of both so you can fully grasp it. For this particular song it was best to re-play the sample, and when you listen to it you can barely tell the difference. It sounds exactly like the original choir section from 'Gangsta's Paradise' but it isn't, it's a brand new re-play of it.

Next was obtaining clearance on the publishing side. We'll use the four step process to walk through this.

Step 1: Research
We found out that Stevie Wonder's catalogue is now controlled by Sony. This means that Sony Publishing would have bought Stevie's catalogue or a portion of it. Therefore, we had to go to them for clearance first. And there are three writers on Coolio's 'Gangsta's Paradise' so they would all need to be contacted as well.

Step 2: Contact

Ella's team took on the task of contacting the parties involved and then came back to our own teams to relay the developments with the clearances. Everyone's teams did an amazing job at sorting all this out. There's always a lot of back and forth with clearing samples/interpolations.

Step 3: Negotiate

The good news was they cleared it!! As we discussed, they dictate how much they want to take. Of course they took a large portion of the publishing, but we knew straight away that we weren't gonna have much publishing on this song. The main thing for us was that we got some percentage of publishing, even if it was a small amount, and this is important to note. Because we've written a new title, new concept, new melodies and new lyrics we needed to protect that future copyright. In years to come if someone was to ever use our new writing we still have rights to it. So that was a deal-breaker for us on this song and something that took the most negotiating.

Step 4: Agree the deal

After much back and forth and negotiating everyone finally agreed and the deal was done. We were lucky to get publishing at all, as in some cases the sample owners have requested 100% publishing for any part of their song to be used. This can definitely be the drawback of interpolating or sampling songs and why some writers just don't do it ever.

Trust me, I get it, more often than not the writers of the new song will receive little to no publishing which means no revenue for their work. Which seems wildly unfair if you only use a small portion of an existing song and write a brand-new song and receive so little.

The examples I gave above of direct samples and interpolations were all cleared for use using some form of these four steps.

Janet Jackson contacted Joni Mitchell directly even though historically Joni has denied usage of her songs as samples/interpolations. The direct approach from Ms Jackson worked. Janet told Joni how much her music had inspired her in her career, sent her the song and within a few days Joni had given her permission for the sample to be used.

Madonna did the same with ABBA. She actually sent one of her assistants directly to Björn and Benny, the songwriters of 'Gimme Gimme Gimme', with a handwritten letter begging them to let her use the sample insisting it would pay homage to their amazing work. They also were not keen on samples of their music being used, but in this case they heard the song and really liked it and agreed for the sample to be used on a 50/50 publishing split basis. The cost for the use of the master recording instrumental section has never been disclosed but rumour has it, it cost a lot!! But the song's success I'm sure made it all worth it and everyone made a lot of revenue off the back of 'Hung Up'.

For Ariana Grande with '7 Rings', the catalogue of Rogers and Hammerstein, the original writers of 'My Favourite Things', is controlled by Concord Publishing, who asked for 90% of the publishing for the interpolation of the verses used in '7 Rings', which is a huge amount! This left the writers of '7 Rings' with a measly 1% each of the publishing... A phrase comes to mind in that instance which is important to live by if you're entering the sampling/interpolation world.

'1% of a hit global song is better than 100% of a song that does nothing.'

RuthAnne with Platinum Plaque for 'Alibi'

NOTE TO SELF

Clearing interpolations and samples can sometimes take months and months. It's not always straightforward as all writers must agree, so the more writers on a song the more tedious it can be to clear. I have a rule of thumb I stick to with sampling, and that is I always check how many writers in total there are and anything over four writers I don't sample. The fewer writers, the easier and quicker it will be to clear.

You never want to be in a situation where your sample is not cleared. A famous case of this was of course:

CASE STUDY

'Bittersweet Symphony' – The Verve

In 1997 'Bittersweet Symphony' by The Verve became one of the biggest songs of the 1990s. At the height of the Britpop era the song was everywhere, but it also became one of the biggest sample disputes of all time and a huge lesson in why it's so important to obtain the correct sample clearances.

What did it sample?

The very famous staccato strings riff sequence that is heard throughout the song was a sample taken from Andrew Long Oldham's orchestral recording of the Rolling Stones song 'The Last Time' released in 1965.

The Verve's manager at the time negotiated the right to use a five-note segment of that sample from the copyright holders, Decca Records.

But they didn't get permission or clearance from the Rolling Stones manager Allen Klein, who at the time owned the copyright to the Rolling Stones songs including 'The Last Time'.

The Verve were told that Decca had agreed to license a five-note segment of the sample for 50% of the publishing, making it a 50/50 split between The Verve and the Rolling Stones, but the royalty dispute arose when the song actually used a larger portion of the song.

By the time 'Bittersweet Symphony' had been released and was becoming a massive hit, Klein's company, ABKCO Records, sued and filed a plagiarism case against The Verve claiming that they voided any agreement by using a bigger portion of the sample.

The Verve's bassist Simon Jones commented, 'We were told it was a 50/50 split. Then they saw how well the song was doing and rung up and said, "We want 100% of the publishing or take it out of the shops, you don't have much choice."'

The case was settled out of court with Richard Ashcroft, the lead singer of The Verve and writer of the topline of 'Bittersweet Symphony', giving 100% of all the publishing and royalties to Allen Klein and the songwriting credits were changed to Mick Jagger and Keith Richards.

This meant that Richard Ashcroft and the band received no publishing royalties from the song, which must have been such a bitter pill to swallow (pardon the pun).

Let's just let that sink in. All of these lyrics and the melody that goes with them were written by Richard Ashcroft and he received zero publishing, zero royalty revenue.

> Cos it's a bittersweet symphony, that's life
> Tryna make ends meet you're a slave to the money then you die
> I'll take you down the only road I've ever been down
> You know the one that takes you to the places where all the veins meet yeah
>
> No change I can change, I can change, I can change
> But I'm here in my mould I am here in my mould
> And I'm a million different people from one day to the next
> I can't change my mould no, no, no, no
>
> Well I've never prayed but tonight I'm on my knees yeah
> I need to hear some sounds that recognise the pain in me yeah
> I let the melody shine, let it cleanse my mind I feel free now
> But the airwaves are clean and there's nobody singing to me now

What's so crazy to me and highly unfair is that as you can see Richard Ashcroft wrote an entirely new song, new melody and new lyric and received nothing for his work. It also meant that if anyone else interpolated his writing on this track, they would not need to obtain his permission or his clearance – it would always go back to Allen Klein, which is so massively unfair, right?

When you release a song without having obtained the correct clearance and licensing you are putting your song and your future revenue at stake. Once the song has been released the original sample owners will have all the power and it will leave you with very little choice.

An unlikely development

In 2019 Richard Ashcroft received an Ivor Novello award for Outstanding Contribution to British Music and at the ceremony he revealed that there were new developments around the publishing rights for 'Bittersweet Symphony' with Klein's son Jody and the Rolling Stones manager, Joyce Smith.

He said, 'As of last month, Mick Jagger and Keith Richards signed over all their publishing for "Bittersweet Symphony" which was a truly kind and magnanimous thing for them to do. It's been a fantastic development. It's life-affirming in a way.' What that means is they have given the copyright to Richard Ashcroft, so since 2019 he finally receives any revenue the song makes and his name is back on the writing credits. Anyone who ever wants to use the song again will have to get his permission, his clearance, and anytime it's streamed, downloaded, used in TV/film or sampled he will receive royalty revenue. But remember he missed out on 22 years of royalties at the height of its success, which I'm sure still stings a little, but at least the future of the song's copyright is in the right hands.

In 2022 UK artist Issey Cross sampled 'Bittersweet Symphony' in her song 'Bittersweet Goodbye', which did very well in the UK, so I'm sure Richard Ashcroft was relieved that it was him this time clearing the rights for this and receiving publishing on this new interpolation of his song.

As you can see by this glaring example of sampling and interpolating without getting proper clearances, it's messy, it's unfair and someone always ends up making a tonne of money and someone else loses a tonne of money and potentially all their rights.

Always have the business side of the sampling/interpolating done properly and correctly so that you aren't the one who gets sued and loses all your revenue and your rights.

How to avoid a court case
Please don't let that lawsuit put you off sampling/interpolating. If anything use them as cautionary tales. The truth is that more often than not, especially with the amount of interpolating these days, not every royalty dispute ends up in court. There's a very easy, less costly way to avoid the courtroom.

The first way is following the four-step process outlined earlier in this chapter and obtaining clearance/correct licenses to release your song with the interpolation/sample used. But what happens if you indirectly use an existing melody that you may have thought was similar to something, but not exactly it? Or you used it by accident or by complete coincidence and actually had never heard the existing song, and no one in your team spotted the likeness? This happens more than you think.

A great example of this is Sam Smith's 'Stay With Me'. The song was released and became a global hit in 2014. But some people immediately made comparisons of the chorus melody to Tom Petty's 1989 hit song 'I Won't Back Down' chorus melody. It took me a minute to see the likeness in the melodic structure but once I got it I couldn't unhear it. It was definitely exactly the same.

Was this done on purpose and they forgot to clear the interpolation? Or was it an accident? Or just a complete coincidence?

SAM SMITH SONG

TOM PETTY SONG

Tom Petty's publishers contacted Sam Smith's team after they noticed the similarities of the two choruses and this dispute was quickly and efficiently solved with no lawsuit action. Smith and his co-writers added the writers of 'I Won't Back Down', Tom Petty and Jeff Lynne, to his song's credits and they negotiated a publishing percentage of 12.5% each for Tom and Jeff, totalling 25% of the overall publishing of 'Stay With Me'. It was all very amicable and Petty since said, 'All my years of songwriting has shown me these things can happen. Most times you catch it before it gets out the studio door but in this case it got by. Sam's people were very understanding of our predicament and we easily came to an agreement.' Sam Smith said they had never heard 'I Won't Back Down' and that it was complete coincidence. And this, I completely believe.

I remember once being in a writing session years and years ago in LA and my American co-writers played me a song they had just written. After hearing the chorus I immediately started singing the song they had interpolated. It was a Westlife song, so I said 'Oh, that was clever using that Westlife song' and started singing it. They looked at me like I had ten heads and said 'Who is Westlife? And what song is that?' They did not know they had in fact used a melody of a pre-existing song. So, I played it to them and they could not believe their ears. They had never heard this song before and how could they? This was at a time before YouTube, Instagram and all the streaming platforms that made music so accessible worldwide. This was a time where certain music only made it in Europe and some songs only made it in the United States and didn't cross over. There are plenty of songs that if you'd never been to Europe you may never have heard. And this was one of them. Safe to say they were disappointed and had the task of having to re-write their chorus with a brand new melody... I don't think that song ever ended up being released, but it taught me a good lesson.

You may use an existing melody and not even know it. But the good news is, like in Sam Smith's example, you can agree a fair deal after the fact if this mishap ever happens. Lots of artists add songwriters to their songs in instances just like this and all ends well, everyone gets credited and everyone receives revenue for their work, and there's no court case.

Interpolating is a current trend that's not slowing down

I'm sure you have noticed just how many songs have interpolations and/or samples in them. It has become a massive trend in pop music and it's not going away anytime soon. I have a few theories as to why it's more popular now than ever.

You've probably heard of some of the big artists selling their catalogues to music companies, investors or publishers for millions and millions. Large sums of money are being given to artists/songwriters and producers to buy their song catalogues. These new owners now control the songs and can negotiate the deals for the samples/interpolations. Existing songs can go on to be hits over and over again when sampled or interpolated. So, it's become a business model and the new owners of these song catalogues want to make the money back from their investments. A lot of interpolations and samples are being used to make new songs and new revenue.

Another reason for this huge wave of interpolations and samples is how overly saturated music has become. With sometimes 100,000 songs being released daily, interpolations and samples are being used as a tool to stand out among the rest because of the instant familiarity the listener gets from hearing a song they may already know. And like I said before, using part of an existing hit song already ups the ratio of it being a hit again since it was before. I think people are being more inventive than ever with interpolations and it can really be a fantastic tool to take something from the past and reimagine it to make a new hit for the future. Definitely something to consider having in a songwriter's toolkit.

Some notable samples/interpolations of recent times

Central Cee – 'Doja'. Samples 'Blow your Mind' – Eve feat. Gwen Stefani

Beyoncé – 'Run the World (Girls)'. Samples 'Pon De Floor' – Major Lazer

Jack Harlow – 'Lovin' on Me'. Samples 'Whatever (Bass Solique)' – Cadillac Dale

Doja Cat – 'Paint the Town Red'. Samples 'Walk on By' – Dionne Warwick

Kygo feat. Ava Max – 'Whatever'. Interpolates 'Whenever, Wherever' – Shakira

Fred Again – 'Adore You'. Samples 'I Wish It Was Me' – Obongjayar

Mark Ronson feat. Bruno Mars – 'Uptown Funk'. Interpolates 'More Bounce to the Ounce' – Zapp, 'Funky Worm' – Ohio Players and 'Oops Upside Your Head' – The Gap Band

CHAPTER 9

THE BOYS' CLUB

"In my career I have never felt that my being a woman was an obstacle or an advantage. I guess I've been oblivious."

CAROLE KING

RuthAnne

This has definitely been the hardest chapter to write but when I started writing this book, I just couldn't ignore it. It's part of the industry, that is a fact, and every successful female in music has had to deal with it in their own way. It's getting better and it continues to improve but there is still a way to go. And, as a woman in music, in the interest of full transparency of how to handle it and navigate it, I simply had to cover this topic.

Every woman in music has experienced the 'boys' club' in varying degrees. In fact any woman in entertainment, in sports, in most to all working environments has experienced some form of the 'boys' club'. I want to make it very clear from the outset, I work and have worked with incredible men, men who I admire, respect, who have encouraged me, mentored me, helped me, believed in me, fought for me, respected me, and it's very important that I acknowledge the good ones because this is not a chapter to vilify or generalise all men or tarnish them with the same brush.

Unfortunately, however, there has been a misogynistic culture in the music industry paired with an abuse of power and gender imbalance, and I want the next wave of writers, male and female, to know how to handle those situations if and when they arise.

I think any man reading this book will gain a lot of insight from my experiences of this, things that as a man you just are a lot less likely to experience. That's why it's so important, more so now than ever to be aware of it. And if you're an up-and-coming writer or creative, it's important to know the good sides of the industry but also the ugly sides and how to protect yourself and stay around the good people, be on the right side of things and be an ally to your collaborators. Like I said, there are more good ones than bad ones out there, thankfully.

The truth of the matter is for as long as I can remember I have always been the only woman in a lot of writing sessions. For the most part of my career, especially in the beginning, it was me and two men, three men, four men, five men. And I noticed a lot of the other female writers would be in the same scenarios — them plus men. It was very rare to have more than one woman in a session unless the artist was female as well. I've been on albums where I am the only female songwriter on the entire album. Of course the songs aren't chosen based on gender — the best songs are chosen — but artists sometimes back then surrounded themselves with so few women that it made the odds of female songwriters getting those cuts harder.

At times I felt like I didn't get certain opportunities because of the boys' club culture in music and it was frustrating. It felt like I was losing out on opportunities because I didn't have a penis. Weird. Or my thinking was, 'Maybe I'm not talented enough and the boy thing is just an easier excuse for them to say.' It was hard to navigate but I did my best where I could to show up and make the most of every and any opportunity I got. I am so forever grateful for the writing rooms that welcomed me and gave me a shot.

Over time I learned what was expected of me as a woman in the writing session, and in some ways, some days I had to put on my big girl pants and put on a show and just act how I needed to act — to be fun, a good vibe, don't be over emotional, oversensitive, and most importantly know my place. The perception was, you can't go higher than the man, you need to stay where they wanted you to be and just play your role of an easy chill cool girl to be around and make everyone else feel comfortable, even if on the inside I was totally uncomfortable... What I felt, what I needed didn't matter. What I take away from all my years as a woman in music is how there really are different rules for men and women.

Taylor Swift said it perfectly when explaining how there's a different vocabulary for a man and a woman in the music industry.

> *When a man does something it's strategic, when a woman does the same it's calculated. A man reacts, a woman only ever over-reacts.*

I mean that could not ring more true in the music industry.

THE CULTURE

I was backstage at a very big TV talent music show in my early 20s and I was doing some work on it for extra money. A few of my fellow songwriting and producer friends were also working on the same show. At the time I was feeling a little deflated. I had just moved to LA the year before and I was still finding my feet. I hadn't had a hit in a while and I felt like I was on the outside of the industry looking in and trying to belong and be in the inner circle of it all, but I couldn't figure out how to do that.

A female who worked in the industry came up to me and said, 'You need to use your sexuality more, you need to flirt more with A&Rs and producers, artists and writers. You need to make them feel like you would sleep with them and sleep with them if you want to but definitely make them feel like they could have you if they wanted you, that's how you'll be more successful, talk about sex, flirt more, be more open and use your sexuality.'

I know what you're thinking right now: 'WOW', from a female... A female!! But, madly, she's not the only female who I'd heard talk that way. It's like it was embedded in the culture.

I'm sure you're wondering what effect that advice had on me. Call me old-fashioned, but I've never been the type to sleep with someone who I actually wasn't attracted to, or didn't connect with or like or fancy... so sleeping with A&Rs to get cuts or be 'closer' to projects was NEVER my thing personally. I'm all about a natural connection, I've never forced relationships or friendships in the music industry and sometimes I wonder if I'd be more successful if I did, but it's just not in my nature. My parents always raised me to believe that my gift and my talent would speak for itself and that was my power. My body, my sexuality, I just always kept it separate. I obviously did date in the industry, I was in a serious relationship for a few years with a songwriter and I also had my years of being single in LA and meeting other people in and out of my industry, but it was always a genuine romantic connection, never anything to do with work or trying to get ahead. I've also seen the other way it could go if you got involved with creatives. If it went sour they wouldn't always want to keep that writer around because it's 'too awkward now' or 'she's still in love with me' or 'I can't then talk about other girls I'm seeing or have them in the studio'...

I did, however, take on the 'be flirty, be sexy, be cool, be fun, bro down, keep everyone happy, be easy, don't be difficult' vibe, definitely. And I thought it was all harmless, but also I felt like if I was fully myself I wouldn't last a day in this business as most sessions I was actually very anxious, didn't feel good enough, didn't feel listened to or always respected, and I had to just smile and be the female that was cool and chill and fun in order to be the female chosen to be in the room.

Let me tell you the number of female writers who have come up with amazing ideas in a room only for them to be ignored, but then a male writer a few minutes later says or sings exactly the same thing and then all of sudden cos he said it it's a great idea... So frustrating.

I called it 'paying my dues' and it's the sad reality for a lot of female writers. And the truth is it was very competitive for women then – once you got that one slot in the room for the female you had to really fight to be heard in certain rooms and that can be incredibly exhausting, and you'd walk away wondering, 'Do they know how much I contributed there or will they just not even remember what I delivered today?'

Autumn Rowe recalls this same time in the music industry when:

> There was for a long time a crew of straight men who didn't wanna let other people in through that, they just didn't want to let other people in. And if you were a woman that was let in, it seems like there were consequences for you. You might be made to feel uncomfortable. I feel like a lot of female writers felt the pressure back in those days to be that cute, hot, fun girl that didn't cause any problems, that was malleable, that would almost be so down for everything, but at what cost? The cost of your mental health, there's always a cost that comes with that, and I'm not judging any of those writers because I get it, we need to eat and this industry can make you feel like they're dangling your dreams on a stick.

I'm glad to say that now that's changing. I've written songs with all women, and more times now than not I don't even notice the gender gap in the room. But back in my first ten years it was rough and I do think it had a lasting detrimental effect on me.

By the end of my time in LA the cracks were showing. I wasn't able to pretend anymore in rooms, my self-esteem was at an all-time low, my mental health wasn't coping and Hollywood had definitely got the best of me. And the crazy thing is, it was when I was getting the most successful as a writer – that's when I felt the most frustrated and let down by the industry.

THE DARK SIDE

Having been in the business now for 20-plus years professionally, I've been in a lot of writing rooms and I'd say I've probably seen and witnessed a lot of things. There is no union for writers, there is no boss who anyone reports to, there is no department who handles complaints. It's a free for all, it's the wild wild west and that's pretty scary when you think of how young a lot of writers/artists are who dream of making it. Look what happened to Aaliyah right under everybody's nose. It took 25 years to get R. Kelly silenced and in jail. Now the reckoning seems to be coming for P. Diddy, a certain saying comes to mind: 'what's in the darkness will always come to light', and I do believe that.

I was 17 years old when I first landed in Hollywood. My manager at the time had befriended my parents and he had a family of his own and promised my dad he would look after me, and to his credit he did. I was well-protected in those first years. It wasn't until I was old enough to be considered an adult that I had experiences of the dark side of this industry. Even though to me at 20 years old looking back I was still so young and naive.

I had a session with big UK producers who were a team of three men – amazing guys and I'm so proud of all their success. We had a session that day with a UK artist, let's call him 'C'. He was on the verge of a big break; he'd had a feature song do really well and it was time for his own project to fly. He was signed to a major label and I was excited to get the opportunity to work with him. So, it's twelve noon on an average day, one of the producers is making the track at his computer and myself and C are writing the topline, sober, no drink involved (not that I even need to say that but just so you have full context). This wasn't a party, or a club, this was a professional recording studio working environment. We're writing a song about stars in the sky, a dance anthem. And all of sudden he's talking about his manhood out of nowhere and how big it is. I laughed out of disbelief – I did the whole *woman laughs when uncomfortable thing* and he said, 'nah, I'm serious, look', and he pulled his trousers fully down, and flashed me, waving it around. I was in shock, I didn't really know what to do.

The producer who had his back to us facing his computer had heard everything and immediately turned around and said, 'Mate, did you just get your d*** out?!' C responded, 'Yeah, I did!' laughing. I still hadn't said anything at this point as I was still in shock. The producer immediately said, 'Mate, that's not okay. You can't do that. What is wrong with you, mate? Don't do that again.' He took me outside and he and the other producer who had heard what happened checked I was okay and asked if I wanted to continue. They handled it perfectly, I felt protected, safe, I mean, at the time I just thought, 'What a weirdo.' Safe to say he never made it. I don't know what happened to him but he's not a working artist or writer in the industry anymore. I'm sure he was the cause of his own demise in that department if that's how he behaved in the daily writing sessions!! To this day, when I see those producers, we still bring it up to each other, how odd it was and how messed up it was, but I always thank them for how well they handled it.

Another weird experience that comes to mind, around 2007 at 19 years old arriving in Miami on my own. First day writing with these producers who were really big at the time, the day was good, we got on well and wrote some good songs. Later that night the biggest producer, who is also now a big artist, arrived, proceeded to kick everyone out of the room except me and the engineer, completely ignoring me, turned off what we were working on and started taking pictures of his diamond chains and blasting his own music.

Next, a woman comes in yelling at him because he had forgotten to pick someone up, and he grabbed her by the neck, shoved her up against the wall, screaming at her, 'Bitch, don't you ever touch my m******** weed ever, you hear me?' She then left the room all shook up, he turned around like nothing happened and continued to blast his music. I was shaking with fear and finally the engineer came up to me saying, 'I think you should go now, this session is over, you can go now.' I ordered a taxi and got out of there as fast as I could. So grateful to that engineer as I was absolutely terrified in that room. To this day, that particular artist is successful, powerful and I can't ever listen to his music.

I know a lot of women who have experienced some kind of sexual harassment and/or sexual assault in the music industry and sadly I am one of them.

SOME MEN WON'T TAKE NO

The hardest, most heartbreaking moment in the music industry for me came when I was 31 years old. Imagine my surprise when I had protected myself from sexual assault this whole time in an industry that I knew it was rife in. I had escaped it thus far until this night in Nashville. It was an A-list artists' writing camp. This was a writer/producer that very clearly wanted to sleep with me, and usually when someone wants to do that and you say 'no', they take 'no', and it's all good and we move on... This was the first time I was ever meeting a guy who wouldn't take no.

It's hard for me to feel comfortable giving all the details of the sexual assault, given that my parents and family will be reading this book, and I know how much this has also affected them. Therefore, I won't go into any in-depth details, but I will share the feelings I had at the time.

It was honestly hard for me to even process what had happened. I didn't know who to call. I wasn't raped, so was what happened to me a criminal act? Did I do the wrong thing? Was it my fault? Did I lead him on? I was so confused. I blamed myself. I did tell my manager, my publisher and family and friends immediately. They got me to safety, and my manager at the time and publisher told the head of the record label who had hosted the camp. His response was, 'Thank you for letting me know' and that was it. This was at a time when women had no power and no one spoke up out of fear of losing their career. I was so scared of people not wanting to work with me or thinking I was being dramatic or overly sensitive, but I wasn't. I told the people I thought could make a difference. I assumed that I had done the right thing, told the right people and that he would never work again, but to my complete dismay he still is a working writer/producer to this day. I honestly don't even know if he remembers what he did, he was so intoxicated. I also don't think he would even think what he did was criminal... and that's the scary thing. How many other women has he done this to?

A few years after it happened I was in a session with a bunch of female writers and we got talking about these types of situations. I started to tell my story of what had happened to me but I didn't name him. Within the first few sentences one of the writers looked at me and said, 'I know who that is, he's done this to multiple writers, this is what he does, he's a scumbag.' She named who she thought it was and ding ding ding she was right. Hearing his name is still triggering for me — it really affected me to think how many other women he had done this to and how many possibly gave in or didn't fight back because he was so overpowering, manipulative and aggressive. I felt at that moment I had failed others because he is still out there. I go over and over in my head about how I could've handled it differently. Should I have gone to the police? However, there could be no rape kit as I wasn't raped... It would be my word against his and in those days before the 'Me Too' movement, who really believed women? Clearly the record label hadn't believed me as he still works with their artists.

THE AFTERMATH

I've chosen to heal through therapy. I've had incredible help and support dealing with this and an understanding that I did nothing wrong, but it's still a trauma that I'm working through. Part of me always wonders if I should name him publicly, but it's not something I'm ready to do yet and I don't know if I'll ever be able to. The sad truth is there are way too many stories from female creatives much worse than this. A lot of the men responsible are in high-powered positions being protected and so a lot of women are still scared to speak out against them, and I totally understand it. But a lot of the women have told people in the industry, people know about instances like this, people know the names of who has sexually harassed or assaulted or raped but still nothing is done.

This happens in all industries, not just the music industry. Where is the protection for our creatives? Where is the consequence for the bad guys? There is still so much to be done here. I want to believe it will change for the better. It has to. We owe it to our future creatives to protect them.

SESSION SAFETY CHECKLIST

★ Make sure someone always knows the address of where you are when in a writing session.

★ Keep your phone charged and with you at all times.

★ If someone is making you feel uncomfortable in a session, tell someone. This could be one of the other writers or producers there, or text your manager, publisher or a friend or family member and inform them so they can help you.

★ If something doesn't feel right, leave. You should never feel trapped in a session or forced to drink anything, take anything or do anything. Never be afraid to leave any situation that feels off.

My time as a writer in America taught me a lot. I have so many amazing memories there, I spent most of my 20s there, learned a lot, worked with the best in the business and some of the best songs I've ever been a part of were written there. I feel so blessed and grateful and lucky to have been a part of those amazing songs. I was young and naive and trying to navigate something, and I didn't always know how to navigate it and I own the part I played in it. I had so many amazing collaborators I worked with whom I still, to this day, dearly love and cherish but also some of the worst, darkest times of my life I experienced also happened there.

HOW I NAVIGATED THE 'BOYS' CLUB' TO SUCCESS

I will say that I had a lot of strength, courage and determination that I need to give myself credit for. I navigated the 'boys' club' the best that I could with the tools that I had at the time. That mainly was by finding the male creatives who never made me feel like the 'token woman in the room'. These were creatives who wanted me there because they loved working with me and respected me, listened to me and saw what I could bring to the table. Rooms where I didn't feel any different to anybody else. I worked with and still work with many creatives like that. Those are truly the best kind and I am so appreciative for them.

I also always let my talent lead first. I tried my best to drown out the noise and just show up with good energy, a good attitude and do my job. Find the role in the room that was needed and do my best. Put the music first and find the people who make great songs, as those songs will bypass anyone trying to gatekeep you. There are a lot of gatekeepers in this business and it can be frustrating, but make great music and no one can argue with that or hold you down – at the end of day everyone wants the best songs. Artists will find you through your work.

I kept it about the music, put my head down and did the work and that got me into so many amazing rooms where I was encouraged to thrive. I also had the courage to step away from anything that wasn't serving my creativity and my mental health. Sometimes leaving can be the hardest, but the best thing for you. The truth is, you can write music from anywhere. There are so many amazing music communities and hubs all over the world. No success is worth sacrificing your soul for. I'm here, still making music – nothing and no one will ever take that away from me.

THE TOOLS

Having healthy boundaries with collaborators
Just like with any profession, it's important to try and keep healthy boundaries with

your collaborators. This can be hard when it's not an office, nine-to-five, professional environment. A lot of the time your collaborators can feel more like best friends, family, your peers, your crew, which is amazing if you keep nice healthy boundaries. Writing songs is incredibly personal; your collaborators can end up knowing more about you and your deepest, darkest thoughts and secrets than your actual families! It's amazing to have close collaborators of course but as with everything, there's a line, and it's important for your own career to keep that line in place.

RuthAnne & Diane Warren

Show them how incredible women are

Grammy and Ivor Novello award-winning songwriter Kamille's advice about the boys' club are words to live by: 'I didn't give a shit about the boys' club. I do what I want. I'm here for a reason and that's anywhere I go into. I've got this "I don't give a f**k" attitude and I haven't got time for anyone's shit. So if I'm here, I'm here to be the best I can be. I actually love when it's just me in the room full of men because it just means I can show you even more how incredible I am. It's always a chance for me to show how incredible women are and remind a lot of men out there who still don't realise women are incredible, especially in the world of engineering, mixing and production.'

Stick with creatives where gender isn't even a thought

There are lots of writing scenarios where gender isn't even a thought and I mean that in a good way. There are lots of women in the session, there are men, it's not even a factor.

It's just creatives getting together to make music and everyone is respected and valued for their talent, and those are the creatives to stick with. I don't want to be in a scenario where I'm ticking a box or it's even about my gender. I wish things like the 'boys' club' didn't even exist and I do think it's a cultural change that is going in the right direction, especially since the 'me too' movement.

Hit songwriter Emily Warren says:

> *My mom who was a lawyer was the only female lawyer in her law firm so when I was growing up she was always 'I don't wanna think about how I feel as a woman in this context, I just wanna be considered in this context.' So my attitude was always trying to ignore that it's even a dynamic. Which is awesome in so many ways because I don't really walk into rooms being like 'Oh, am I the only girl in here?' I just was 'I'm here.' But things still obviously happen where you're like 'You didn't hear my idea when I said it but when HE repeated it right after me you loved it.' When that happens over and over again you're like, oh, there is a dynamic at play here. I remember really early on I was working with this producer on this vocal that an artist had just recorded. And at one stage I said, 'Can you turn this part up here.' And he like paused the music, turned around and looked at me and said, 'What did you say?' I was shocked that I was heard, so I said it again and he turned around and did it. 'Oh my god, he really heard me.' It was such a moment of, wow, I was heard. Which is so wild because it definitely shouldn't be like that. I realised in that moment how much conditioning I've had, we've all had as women. That you have to be so sure when you speak and you'd better be loud and aggressive about it so everyone hears you.*

Women supporting women

Women are working together now more than ever, supporting each other and lifting each other up and sticking together, and that's what will also make the change. There are so many female songwriters and producers smashing it right now and we all need to encourage this and support it.

> *As women writers people tend to think of us sometimes as like 'Oh, there's one girl in the room, one spot for the biggest female writer.' Whereas there's lots of spots for all these other guys. But there's something so powerful about two women, or more women, in a room. A lot of my successes come from writing with other women and I'm trying to make that a point. You just have to be intentional about it. If you have that choice, trying to go towards other women.* **Ilsey Juber**

> *The responsibility is on you to request female songwriters, as opposed to requesting more males.* **Ali Tamposi**

The female perspective

I've always said I feel there is such a power in having a female songwriter in the writing room for one very important thing... the female perspective. The female experience, the female emotions, we know more what a girl wants to hear from a male artist. We know what a girl definitely doesn't want to hear and that's why it's so important to have that female perspective in the writing room. It's a superpower we have that only we have, and embracing it and bringing it to a room can really make a song so much better. Male writers and producers who know this are the ones who love having us in their rooms because they know how vital the female perspective can be in a song.

'Work hard and you get respect' is hit Grammy-nominated songwriter/producer Lauren Christy's advice, 'Of course it's a male dominated business but what I've come to find out is that success has a way of minimising that problem.'

Amy Allen with the Grammy for Songwriter of the Year

Amy Allen won the Grammy award for Songwriter of the Year in 2025, making her the first female songwriter to have won this award. She is the most sought after songwriter in the industry at present and it is so amazing and well-deserved to see her journey and triumph to the top. To see a woman in music win this award and dominate the charts with songs she's written for the biggest artists in the world, from Sabrina Carpenter ('Please, Please, Please', 'Espresso', 'Taste', 'Manchild', 'Busy Woman', 'Bed Chem' and more) to Rosé feat. Bruno Mars ('APT') to Halsey ('Without Me'), makes it so inspiring for any female creative out there.

It meant a lot to me to win the Songwriter of the Year Grammy Award for so many reasons but mostly because I got to have my family from Maine there. They've supported me every day since I was just a little kid trying to write my first song in my bedroom, and tens of thousands of songs later it was great to share the moment of winning a Grammy with them. I felt like that whole weekend (hopefully, even just a little bit) made up for the thousands of bad songs I've played for them over the years!

It also felt really amazing to be representing women in music, and also getting to pay homage to all of the amazing songwriters that came before me who have paved the way for pop music, and really all genres, who didn't get to receive their flowers back then because Songwriter of the Year Non-Classical wasn't recognised as an award until three years ago. The moment was really overwhelming, but I really tried to take it in and pay respect and appreciate all the songwriters who have soundtracked my life, and the lives of generations through their songs. **Amy Allen**

A SEAT AT THE TABLE

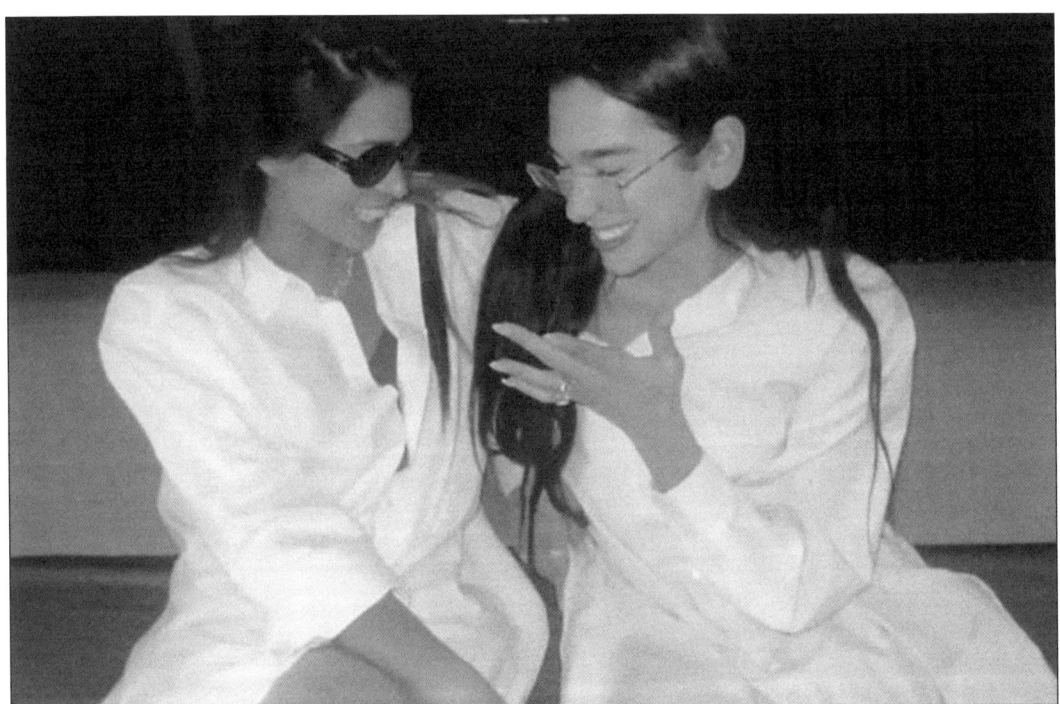

Ali Tamposi & Dua Lipa

I guess I'll end this chapter by reminding you that any and every successful woman in music has had to walk a lonely, long, screwed-up path to get there and I know what that takes. I achieved a lot of what I wanted to on my own terms without going to the dark side but not without experiencing dark twisted things. Man, it's not easy being a woman in music! So I salute every woman who works in the music industry – I know what you've been through to get where you are. The fight, the drive, the determination, the road blocks, the never-ending war just to be seen, heard and respected.

The tides are changing but we have to keep supporting and encouraging our female creatives and allowing them a seat at the table. If you're a woman in music who's in a work environment where they won't give you that seat then get up, leave that scenario and sit at a new table, create your own table and be the table that everybody else wishes they were sat at.

> *Now I feel very grateful to have the opportunity to be around so many incredibly talented women. And I see it not just in the songwriting. I mean, 90% of the biggest artists right now in 2025 are females. And it's so great to see.* **Ali Tamposi**

INTERLUDE 4

SONGWRITER STORIES

"I don't try to control the songs. I let them come through me. Sometimes I feel like I'm just the vehicle."

JONI MITCHELL

"I write 100 bad songs for every good one. You have to just keep going — the great ones sneak up on you."

BENNY BLANCO

Kicking off more amazing stories is one of the biggest female songwriters ever, the Grammy Award-winning iconic Ali Tamposi. Songs written by Ali have amassed over 50 billion global streams, including the diamond certified 'Havana'.

'HAVANA' – CAMILA CABELLO FEAT. YOUNG THUG

Written by: Ali Tamposi, Brian Lee, Andrew Wotman, Louis Bell, Brittany Hazzard, Adam Feeney, Pharrell Williams, Camila Cabello, Kaan Gunesberk
Produced by: Frank Dukes

The success of 'Havana' surprised me the most because when we wrote it, it just came out so quickly, the chorus. And we all left the studio like, 'That was cool.' But I remember listening back the next day and I was like, 'Oh, there's something here.' But the label put two songs out at the same time for Camila and nobody was that gassed up about it. I loved it always. I thought it was super-cool. And I remember seeing people with an A&R from her label and them being like 'but it's not as good as this other one.' I'm so glad that they actually put it out at the same time because they let the consumer decide. And it ended up being the song that really catapulted her career. **Ali Tamposi**

'IT AIN'T ME' – KYGO WITH SELENA GOMEZ

Written by: Ali Tamposi, Brian Lee, Andrew Wotman, Kygo, Selena Gomez
Produced by: Kygo, WATT

We were in a Kygo session writing camp for him. It was Brian Lee, Andrew Watt, Kygo and I, and we had started something and Kygo came in, and it was sort of this generic title type thing. It was just very generic. And I remember him coming in and being like, 'Um, this is um kinda cool.' And that to me, just like, this is cool. At that particular moment, I was like, no, this is not good. So Brian picked up the guitar, which was rare, you know, in a room with Andrew who usually plays the guitar. But Brian started playing the chords for the chorus of 'It Ain't Me.' And it came out so quickly, the topline of the song. I had been able to write about a breakup in that song that I needed to get out of me, and I remember him coming back into the room, I think he was on his way out of the camp. And we played him that hook of 'It Ain't Me'. His eyes just lit up and I could see him, his genius was working and it was like sort of coming out through his eyes. And I was like, 'I think we did it.' And he was like, 'I love this so much.' We finished writing the verses and – and it was just such an easy process through that point. But I remember just cause I love that song so much. I love the way that it all kind of just happened. So naturally, I love that place in my career during that time with, you know, we were all very much aligned, Andrew, Brian and I, and it was like all of our strengths in one song, we were going back and forth in lyrics in the room. And everyone was coming up with great ideas. And it just felt like that one is important to me because it was like the peak of our chemistry together in that room. And very vivid to me when I think back on that particular day and everyone was in a really good place and that one was really special. It just was so validating and also the song that we all love. **Ali Tamposi**

'TONIGHT (I'M LOVIN' YOU)' – ENRIQUE IGLESIAS FEAT. LUDACRIS

Written by: Lauren Christy, Jacob Luttrell, Justin Franks, Enrique Iglesias
Produced by: DJ Frank E, Carlos Paucar

Well, 'Tonight I'm f**king you' was the original lyric, and I was like 'ah, come on.' And that's the fastest song I've ever had a hit with – we wrote it, I got like an email the next day saying, 'Please do not play this to anyone. This is being released in two weeks.' And about three weeks later, it was No. 1. It's a crazy story how that song was written. Atlantic called me into work with DJ Frank E and Jacob Luttrell. And they said to write a song for Akon and they played some Akon stuff. I went outside, I said a little prayer like, 'God, I've got nothing, I prepared nothing, and I've never worked with a DJ before,' and so anyway, I had this little melody pop in my head and so I said, 'check this out.' I said, 'We just need to find a lyric that lines it up, so you say something like, "I never felt this way until I met you".' And I played it over his beat, and I was like, and, and everyone was like that's amazing. And Jacob said, 'Tonight, I'm f**king you!', like this! It is the boys' club – all the boys in the room were like, 'It's fantastic!' and I was like, 'No, we can't say that, that's awful.' They're like, 'Trust us, we'll cover it as "Loving you", too, but the one we're gonna send out is "F**king you".' So, by the next day David Guetta wanted to do it, Akon wanted to do it, and Lady Gaga was gonna do it with David Guetta. And then Enrique came in and he was like, 'I want this really badly' and I think he might have flown DJ Frank E to see the Dolphins game in Miami. And that was it, and he killed it. **Lauren Christy**

'EVERGREEN' – YEBBA

Written by: Janée 'Jin Jin' Bennett, Abbey Smith, George Moore
Produced by: George Moore, Abbey Smith

One of my favourite songs that I wrote was 'Evergreen' by Yebba. I had never heard about Yebba, and she hadn't done many co-writing sessions either. I think she had had a bit of time off from music, there was a tragedy in her family. Her mother had passed away. So she was trying to go through all of that. And she was in London for like a week or something over the Easter break. And I was due to go to Manchester with my family to spend it there. And my A&R at the time, Mark Gale, sent me a YouTube clip of Yebba singing her big viral song 'My Mind,' so I was like 'Wow, that's amazing. Who is that? Who is this artist?' And they were like, 'Oh, she's here in the UK. She's not really done any co-writes before. She's here for a few days. She's gonna do sessions with Jimmy Napes and Sam Smith and would love to work with you and George Moore. Would you be up for it?' And I was like, 'Oh my gosh, I've never heard of this artist, but she's absolutely incredible, love her voice.' So we got in the session, which was lovely. And, you know, 'Evergreen' was totally her story, what she wanted to write about, about her mom and the passing and stuff. And yeah, I was just so fortunate to be a part of that. And even though she was new to co-writing, I learned a lot from that session. She had this app on her phone called, I think it was called Looper Man. And she was singing the melodies down of different instruments. So say she wanted the bass line to do something, she would put it in the loop. It was a crazy process. And then she would send that reference to her friends in New York and say, 'Hey, can you put me down a bass line for this?' And she would have these amazing musicians who would send back the live bass or the other instruments. That's amazing, that's so cool. And she recorded the full song beginning to end just a few times. And that was it. So I was just like, wow. It's rare and it was amazing, and you know she doesn't really love the industry side. So I think that's why she shies away from all the business and the industry. She just wants to be in a room and jam with her friends. She's just a pure musician. **Jin Jin**

Drew from The Chainsmokers and Emily Warren

'DON'T LET ME DOWN' – THE CHAINSMOKERS FEAT. DAYA
Written by: Emily Warren, Scott Harris, Andrew Taggart
Produced by: The Chainsmokers, Gino Barletta

So I had just started writing for other people and I sent my publisher, Rhea, two songs, one of which The Chainsmokers ended up producing and releasing called 'Until You Were Gone'. I had met them once or twice when that was happening and it was all fresh off the heels of 'Selfie', so then they asked to do a session and I went with Scott Harris. Beforehand Scott and I had met up in New York to have a coffee and chat about our plan for this session with The Chainsmokers, and it was one or two weeks after Coachella. I had gotten super-lost at Coachella, with no phone service, and couldn't find anyone and ended up having to go back to the Airbnb by myself. I was fully scared being alone, and I was telling Scott about this

and we were like it would be so fun to write a song that if you were lost at Coachella and you heard the song it would make you feel less scared and less alone. So we went to the session and wrote 'Don't Let Me Down' and it just so validates for me how important it is to have the song rooted in a true story. That was the first song I wrote with them and then the next Coachella I got to watch them perform 'Don't Let Me Down', our song, from side stage, and I just loved that whole experience. Now they're two of my best friends, I love writing with them and hanging with them. And that song was obviously a huge life-changing moment.
Emily Warren

Simon Aldred is a global hit songwriter who has written with Sam Smith, Liam Gallagher, Mick Fleetwood, Birdy and more. Here he tells us the story behind one of his frequent collaborators and friends, the late great Avicii.

'WAITING FOR LOVE' – AVICII
Written by: Simon Aldred, Tim Bergling (Avicii), Salem Al Fakir, Vincent Pontare, Martin Garrix
Produced by: Avicii, Salem Al Fakir, Vincent Pontare, Martin Garrix

The most exciting and instantaneous story behind a song for me is 'Waiting for Love', and it was definitely a hit that came as a surprise to me because I really didn't know much about EDM or anything about the dance world at all, and I ended up writing and singing this song with Tim (Avicii). The way it happened was, he rang me up because he heard some of my own artist music in a tour bus and was really passionate about my music. So he called me and said that he had basically written a song inspired by something that I'd written in the past, and he was like 'I really would like it if you would write the lyrics to it and help us finish it.' But there was a catch – so this was a Tuesday and he said, 'This Saturday I'm playing at Ultra Festival and I need you to write it and send it to me so I can mix it before Saturday.' I was in London, so I had to go back to Manchester on the train. He sent me the track idea and I just obsessively paced up and down my house writing lyrics, changing lyrics, it was proper deadline stuff, and I had never written to track before, and it felt like a puzzle to crack.

I really got into the lyrics, and even though it's not naturally my preferred genre of music, Tim, Avicii, was very musical, he made real songs and this song had changing chords and took me on a journey even though it was a dance tune, so I was able to put quite a bit of depth in the lyrics and it didn't feel throwaway. It's the only time I've done that, and I really enjoyed it. Then I had to sing it, and I wasn't intending on singing it but, obviously, I had to demo the lyrics I'd written and I kinda assumed that he would get someone else to sing it. So I had written the lyrics, recorded it, and sent it to him. He had said to me, 'If you send it at such and such a time I'll have Wi-Fi, so I can download the files and mix it on the plane and play it on Saturday.' It was all so fast and exciting because the turnaround was so insane. And I did it, and I thought I had nailed it, and it's two in the morning and just as I was going to bed I got an email back with like 30 bullet points of suggestions and changes from him, and I was up until like 5 in the morning making all the changes. I got all the notes done

and I sent him the new vocal as he was en route to Ultra Festival in Miami. He debuted it there and sent me the YouTube video of him playing it. It came out three months later, and it was so quick in comparison to how it usually goes with songs and song releases. Its success was the biggest surprise to me because I had no idea the reach that dance music had at the time. I was on holiday in France – and I was here, there and everywhere – and the song was constantly being played everywhere I went, and I was like 'What the f**k' and it was so exciting. And because now he's sadly passed away I'm just so glad I got to spend a week with him in LA as a result of that song and we became friends and it was so lovely. He was such an absolute sweetheart, a lovely, lovely guy. And so many beautiful things came from that song and me meeting Tim, it was a really positive experience from start to finish.
Simon Aldred

Ed Drewett is one of the top songwriters and has been a part of several No.1, billion streaming songs. This one was a worldwide hit...

'GLAD YOU CAME' – THE WANTED
Written by: Ed Drewett, Wayne Hector, Steve Mac
Produced by: Steve Mac

We had the topline and we left the studio that day and were like 'Okay, cool, we've done something and it was all right.' The song 'I'm Coming Home' was out at the time and I was like 'I love that song' and if you listen to the start of 'Glad You Came', although it's completely different, the emphasis of where the chords sit is in the same place as that song. Then Steve sent it to us the next day and he'd put the accordion on it that follows the chorus melody, and we were like 'Oh, this is really good.' That's what Steve does incredibly well, he did that musical hook and transformed it. Then I remember it just blew up and it was a No. 1 airplay record in the USA. I heard it in the car driving down the PCH in LA, and as you can imagine I lost my mind and was so excited to hear it on the radio in America. But I didn't even really get the enormity of that at the time. I knew it was big, but in terms of how hard that actually is to achieve, I didn't get that at the time.
Ed Drewett

Ed Drewett with The Wanted (Siva, Jay, Max, Tom & Ed)

CHAPTER 10

BAD DEALS VS GOOD DEALS

"Music is spiritual, the music business is not."

VAN MORRISON

"As for the music business itself, the key things have not changed that much. It operates like any business and money still keeps things moving."

TOM JONES

This chapter may be all about the boring business details and pop our creative bubble momentarily, but I cannot stress the importance of understanding this area to ensure a long and successful career in the music industry. It is a massively important side that we as creatives tend to ignore or not fully understand or be educated on because we trust our teams around us to handle the business side.

What I've learned, and it took me years to learn this, regrettably, is just how important and critical it is for a creative to be as educated as possible on the business side of this crazy industry. I talk to so many incredible songwriters, producers and artists who are trapped in very bad deals or deals they didn't quite understand when signing, and it can be incredibly frustrating to be caught in a bad deal with no way out.

I want this chapter to not only educate creatives but empower us all to fully understand what we are entering into and be a part of the process to push for the best deal you can get for yourself and your future. These deals can make or break careers, so studying this chapter and taking away in the simplest of terms what to look for, what to negotiate, what to avoid and how to know if there's a good deal on the table that you can jump up and down with joyous glee about will help you so much in forging a long and successful career.

I have experienced many different types of deals; publishing deals with various publishers, record deals, song deals… and the main thing I started noticing in my earlier days as a songwriter was how little I actually understood about the deals I was signing, so I started asking questions, lots of questions, and learning more and more. I've had the same lawyer for twenty years and I have always trusted him to negotiate the best deal on my behalf. (I'm sure it irritates him when I ask a million questions about each deal, but I promise you it's better to ask and fully know what you're signing than blindly sign something and then be confused as to why you are broke, not making the money back and/or stuck in a deal for years on end.)

Contracts and deals are always long, full of legal jargon that it is so confusing, and it feels like you need a law degree to dissect and understand what's even being said. So, for each deal I always ask my lawyer, Jeremy, to send me the main deal points in very dumbed-down language so that I can know exactly what I'm signing before I sign on that dotted line.

Main advice before signing anything is to always have a music lawyer look at it and explain it to you in a way you fully understand.

Now, let's get into it. For this chapter, I picked Jeremy's brain to help break down in the simplest of terms a good publishing deal. So you'll see quotes from *him* throughout this chapter.

If there's any music language that you don't understand in this chapter head to the Glossary pages at the back of the book for all the definitions.

The job of a music lawyer

The main job of a music lawyer is to protect artists/songwriters/producers and to advocate for artists and to make sure that he/she is first and foremost protected from a legal standpoint and most importantly working with managers and other representatives of the artist/songwriter/producer to make sure they are making smart and strategic business deals.

When is the best time to hire a music lawyer?

From the beginning and certainly before you put ever put pen to paper on a contract. The sooner the better.

PUBLISHING DEALS

Music publishing in every song is generally viewed as divided into two halves, the publisher's share (50%) and the writer's share (50%). The writer's share is most often retained by the songwriter.

When you sign a publishing deal you are often assigning a share of the copyright and a share of the total revenue, and how much or what that looks like depends on the type of publishing agreement you choose to sign.

There are two main types of publishing deals:

A co-publishing deal (aka co-pub deal)

This is the main deal you'll hear about in the music industry today. 'A co-pub deal is one where the co-publisher actually acquires a piece of the copyright (the songs).'

The songwriter and the publisher co-own the copyrights of the songs and the music publisher administers 100% of the copyrights of the songs. A standard co-pub deal revenue split is usually 75%–25%, meaning you receive 75% of the revenue generated (the writer's share 50% and half of the publisher's share 25%) and the publisher retains the remaining 25%. So in simple maths terms, for each pound a song receives in royalties, 75p goes to you and 25p goes to your publisher. And in this type of deal the publisher might give the songwriter an advance payment (keep reading, we'll get into advances).

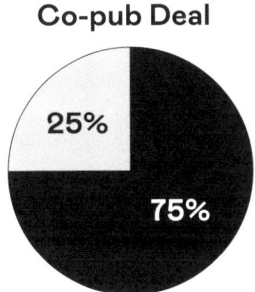

A publishing admin deal (aka admin deal)

The first difference between a co-pub deal and an admin deal is in an admin deal the administrator doesn't acquire any ownership of the copyrights in your songs, they just administer them for a fee. They are another resource/third party to help exploit your catalogue and find the songs a home whilst also making sure the correct amount of revenue from your songs is being paid and collected from all around the world. They help to make you more revenue by keeping on top of where your songs have been exploited. Usually the standard split is 90%–10% or 80%–20% depending on the deal. So that's 90% to the writer (50% of the writer's share and 40% of the publisher's share) and 10% to the admin company revenue. So again in simple maths, for each pound that comes in, 90p goes to you and 10p goes to the administrator. These deals can also come with an advance payment, although it's usually less than a co-pub deal advance due to the split being more favourable to the songwriter.

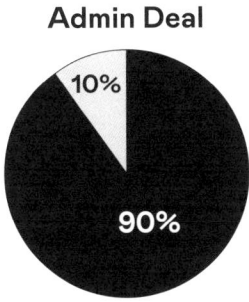

I have experienced both types of deals. In fact, my first very publishing deal was an admin deal and since then I've done co-publishing deals with varying advances and structures.

Why sign a publishing deal?

First of all it's important to note that what's most crucial in each publishing deal can be different depending on whether you are a new writer or an established writer.

So always ask yourself why are you doing the deal. Are you capitalising on a moment and you're doing it for money, or partnering with a publisher in the hopes of them advancing your career and getting your songs out there?

The **why** is very important in the type of deal you will end up signing.

The co-publishing deal: What to look for, what to negotiate, what to avoid, what is optimal

There are a few points that are crucial in every co-publishing deal, so let's break them down in digestible chunks.

The term ★ How long the deal lasts for, how long you are partnered for. *'It's important to think of it as partnering with a publisher rather than just giving them the rights to administer your songs.'* A favourable term would be around *three years* recoupment-based. (We'll get into what recoupment-based is further along this chapter.)

The retention period ★ Once the term expires how long does the publisher co-own and/or administer the songs that are covered in the deal. This is of critical importance.

Bad deal ★ You can be offered a deal which is life of copyright which basically means whatever rights the publisher is acquiring they'll have those rights forever... My advice is do not sign this.

Good deal ★ You could have a deal with no retention period which means once the deal is up all your works/rights come back to you fully. This is rare. *'In most modestly competitive deals the retention period is four to eight years, which is a good deal but always negotiate the retention period to the best you can get it.'*

Full reversion vs partial reversion ★ So what happens at the end of your retention period? *'With most major publishers if you have a good amount of leverage you can get what's called a full reversion, which means whatever rights you've given to the publisher, they will all come back to you at some period in time, meaning the rights revert back to you. Or you can get a partial reversion which is what rights you've given to them in part come back.'*

What is covered by the deal ★ *'You want the publisher to control the smallest batch of songs. Most first drafts of co-pub/admin deals say that they cover any songs written prior to the term, during the term and any songs acquired during the term. You can negotiate what's covered in a deal depending on your leverage. You may want to exclude acquired songs altogether. When it comes to songs written during the term, if you can limit the publisher's rights during the retention period to those songs which have a found a home or have been commercially exploited* *in some form or fashion while they're your publisher, that's optimal.'*

This is so that when the term of your deal with that publisher is up, the songs that haven't found a home and haven't been exploited come back to you fully and you can take those songs with you into a new publishing deal or retain all the rights for those songs.

ADVANCES AND RECOUPMENT

So for most writers when they talk about deals it's all about the advance. And sometimes the allure of the advance makes them blind to the other crucial points of the deal, hence why all of the above is really important to take into consideration too because the bigger the advance you get the more the deal will try lock you in for longer terms or retention periods. So let's talk about the most attractive part of a publishing deal… the show me the moneyyyyyy moment… the advance.

What is an advance?
An advance is an upfront payment that you get as a songwriter/artist. It is money given to you by a publisher/record label like a salary for a job and it's usually given in a lump sum. Sometimes you get 50% of an advance upfront and then another 50% when you pay back the first 50% and other times you get 100% of the advance upfront. It can be structured lots of different ways but ultimately it is an advance payment against the royalties the publisher/record label hope your songs will make in the future. It is not free money and the royalties you make from your music is how it is paid back.

Advances are like a bank loan
When I was younger, I saw big lump sums of money on a page and thought 'wow, a lump sum of money, where do I sign?' However, I didn't fully understand that publishing deals and record deals are basically a loan, like a bank loan, the money they give you has to be made back. You owe the record label or publisher. So you may get a deal for £50k and you think, 'I'm rich' but that money may have to last you for years and that's a huge important thing to note when entering into a deal with an advance.

Recoupment
Whilst an advance is like a bank loan, in some ways it's not the type of loan that you HAVE to pay back from any of your earnings, there's no monthly payments back. Publishing advances are only paid back (recouped) from the royalties generated from your released songs and your released songs only are what pays back the advance and it's the same with a record deal. This is called recoupment.

Recoupment-based deals

The most common structure in favourable co-pub deals right now are what we call recoupment-based deals. The term might be three years for recoupment, so if you get £100k advance at the start of your publishing deal and you get to the end of the three-year term and you have not recouped that 100k advance money back, this means you are unrecouped and so the deal continues until you recoup the full amount of the advance.

'In most UK co-pub deals there is usually something called a "hard stop" where the deal is over whether you've recouped or not, so in a three-year term deal if you are unrecouped the deal will only continue for one more year with the hard stop at the end of the fourth year. This is way more optimal to have a hard stop because it means you can get out of your publishing deal without the advance debt hanging over your head and you can move on and sign a brand-new deal.'

It is the publisher/label's own risk if they make the money back or lose the money. And if you decide to work in a restaurant on the side, or do some backing singer work on the side none of that money has to be given to pay back your publishing advance — it is only song royalties that pay it back.

If you've signed a USA publishing deal, the deal continues indefinitely until you have fully recouped. They haven't adopted the hard stop yet, which is one downside of signing out of the USA. Even though American publishers tend to give bigger advances, there's the downside that you could be stuck in the deal until you recoup the advance amount fully. *'It's important in deals like this to implement a right for you, the writer, to have the options to pay yourself out of the deal or another publisher can buy you out of that deal.'*

If you have huge hits and have recouped your deal during or by the end of the three-year term that's the best scenario because then you are a free agent again and can renegotiate a new deal with the same publisher or sign with a new publisher. The more money you take, the longer it can take to recoup. And that's always something to consider when taking advances. If you take a large sum, you must be prepared to live off that sum for a long time because it can take years to recoup the advance. The less money you take, the faster you'll move through your deal, but each person has their own set of circumstances and needs financially so it's all case-by-case. It is important to remember that your advance is recouped from YOUR share of the publishing — not from the publishers share.

WHAT TO DO WHEN OFFERED A PUBLISHING DEAL ADVANCE

Sit down and fully calculate what you will actually receive after:

* Tax
* Management commission (20% typically)
* Lawyer's fees

And then after that you will see the amount you will actually receive from the advance.

Next step:

Work out your cost-of-living expenses, rent, mortgage, bills, etc. per year and make sure the take-home advance amount you are receiving can cover this for at least three years.

This is the true reality of the industry. It may take three to five years or longer for you to have enough revenue from your songs to pay back your advance and move through your deal. If you write the biggest song of the year then you'll pay off your advance quickly, and that's the best-case scenario, BUT there are always delays in song releases that are out of your control, plus it can usually take six months to a year for the royalties from released songs to start flowing through to you, so just be aware the advance may have to last you for longer than you think.

 **from my lawyer**

'What I always want for my clients is the ability to move through a publishing deal as quickly as possible and preserving elements of flexibility throughout the deal.'

Getting stuck in an un-recouped deal

When you hear the words 'advance' and 'recoupment' these are two crucial parts to a co-pub deal. You hear of so many artists going bankrupt or not making money for years, and songwriters having to live off an advance for maybe five years before their songs have paid it back and not being able to pay their bills. If you're in a position where you get a very large advance, be smart with it, invest it and remember it may need to last a long time.

HOW TO GET A GOOD ADVANCE

For publishers it's mainly about pipeline and hype.

Pipeline

For example, you are an unpublished writer and you've just got word you have the next Dua Lipa single. A publisher will view that single as pipeline, meaning if they sign you there will be a song out already by a big artist, meaning more recoupment towards the advance they've paid you, so it's less of a risk. The more pipeline you have, the bigger the advance offered will be. If you have a good track record as a writer and have had hits before, your market value will be in a good position to get a big advance because you've proven you can deliver. If you're a brand-new writer, bringing lots of unpublished songs to the table that you've written is very appealing to a publisher because they already have lots of songs to work with and find homes for, and so bringing songs to the new deal as a new writer might help you get a bigger advance.

Hype

Hype is a BIG component in getting a bigger advance. If everyone is talking about you like you are the next big songwriter and you have great teams around you, getting you into great rooms with big opportunities, your market value for an advance will go right up even if you are yet to have a hit. The potential in you to have one if it's presented the right way with all the hype in the world can make a huge difference to the deal, and I've seen some ridiculous amounts of advances be given to new writers and new artists just based on hype. It's all at the risk of the publisher, so if they're offering you that big cheque, take the money and run because if the hype runs out the money offer will go down. BUT be smart with the advance money and don't spend it all on the same day, because, like I've said before, the bigger the advance, the longer it will take to recoup. It's not free money and it may need to last you a number of years.

RED FLAGS IN CO-PUB DEALS

Options

We've spoken about the term of the deal. Let's say you've got through the term of, for example, a two-year deal, there is an 'option' by the publisher to extend the term for another contract period. Sometimes it's one option, sometimes it's two options. For example, if you sign a co-pub deal and the term is two years, after the two years is up the publisher can then exercise the option for another two years and so on depending on how many options are in the contract. I know a lot of writers who sign deals with options not knowing or fully realising what it means, and the truth is 'options' are really only a one-way option completely for the publisher's benefit.

'So think of it as "a publisher's option" meaning that you, the writer, have now got no flexibility if you decide your publisher is not what you thought it was going to be, or your person has left the company, or you don't wanna be in a co-pub deal anymore or you want to do a new co-pub deal with a different publisher. Basically you are not the one with the option when there's "options" baked into your deal. It's optional on the publisher's part not yours. There is no scenario where an option is beneficial to a songwriter.'

Always look out for that in your deals and try take any 'options' off the table or at the very least keep the options to a minimum. The best deals are all about moving through the deal and maintaining options on your side, the writer's side, and not having to re-sign for another contract period is what you really want to have in your deal.

'Options' in publishing deals are not ideal, try to avoid or negotiate to a minimum option period.

In summary the main most crucial points in all co-pub deals are:

★ The term
★ The retention period
★ The advance
★ Recoupment-based
★ The splits

Always negotiate these terms to get yourself the best deal possible.

RECORD DEALS

A song is split into the publishing side and the master side, a publishing deal is for the publishing side (song composition), and now I want to talk about the record deal which is for the master side (the sound recording of the song).

Record deals come in all different shapes and sizes depending on the artist, the label, indie label or major label and you should always have a music lawyer hired to do the deal on your behalf. I'd like to arm you with the crucial terms here to know about and dumb down the complex legal jargon that can be really overwhelming and hard to decipher, so at least you can have the knowledge about what you are signing. In a record deal there are similar things to a publishing deal to look out for, although there is often more to negotiate in a record deal, so let's break down the most important parts.

What is a record deal?

The purpose of a record deal is a legal agreement between an artist and a record label to enable the label to legally sell and promote an artist's master recordings in return for royalty payments: physical sales (CD, vinyl), public performance and broadcasting of the music, digital sales (downloads, streams) and audio visual.

Let's talk about the main points to look for, what to avoid, what to negotiate and what is optimal.

The term ★ Just like with a publishing deal the term is an important point. Labels will want you to be tied in for as long as possible so that the investment is not as risky, but for an artist the shorter the record deal the better so that if it's not going well you can get out of the deal quicker and sign somewhere else or be independent. Again, flexibility is key. And again, watch out for those 'option' periods and try to minimise the amount of options.

Exclusivity ★ A record deal will typically want you to sign to the label exclusively meaning the artist can't record for another label without their permission and the artist can't just leave the contract if they're not happy. And if the artist wants to feature or guest on another artist's song, they would need a 'sideman' provision in the deal to cover this. A lot of DJs and producers sign several deals under different aliases so that they can have projects signed to multiple labels.

Territory ★ Most major labels will sign artists to a worldwide deal. But some record deals can just be for a single territory which means that an artist in theory could sign different deals in different territories.

Royalty split ★ This is a crucial one. Most indie labels will do a 50/50 deal with an artist, meaning the artist owns 50% of the masters and the indie label owns the other 50%. They'll invest the money into your project and once they've recouped back their expenses the profits are split 50/50. It's important to clearly define what expenses are allowed and include in your contract that larger expenses you must have approval on before they are spent.

Major label splits are a lot lower because major labels usually invest more money and have more of a budget to invest than an indie label. Typically an artist royalty on a major label is between 15–20% ownership of masters and the label owns 75–80% of the master. Again, the artist only makes that 15%–20% after the label has recouped what they spent on the project, which on a major label can take years… if ever. And the reason for this is:

Rights granted ★ In a record deal, the artist assigns copyright of the master recordings to the label. Usually for exclusive recording contracts this is for the full life of copyright, which is 50 years from release… A long time, right? Even unreleased songs remain the property of the label and even when the artist has repaid all the recording costs. Sometimes an artist can negotiate a reversion of the copyrights, allowing the return of their masters in the future, but it's rare.

You may have heard about labels selling the masters. I'm sure unless you've been living under a rock you've heard about Scooter Braun buying Taylor Swift's master catalogue, which caused a huge fall out as Taylor Swift wanted to get her own masters back. Taylor, being the bad ass boss that she is, came up with a plan. She re-recorded all of her albums as brand-new masters (incredibly smart move) and called them 'Taylor's version' so she now owns the new masters and her fandom, ever so supportive, have been streaming, downloading and loving these new masters, and Taylor took the power back.

Release commitment ★ The record label's job is to release your songs. So, it's very important that an artist has a good release commitment from the label, with a minimum marketing budget to support the release. If the label fails to release the record, an artist should be able to terminate the deal and/or get back the master recordings so that they can be licensed to another label or self-released. This is happening more and more these days.

In the case of Raye, she was signed to a major label for years and years and they refused to release her album. She famously went public with what was happening and they parted ways. A few years later she went on to release the album independently through a distributor, and is now more successful than ever, winning a record-breaking six Brit awards. Prince also famously had a big falling out with his label, Warner Records, in 1993. It got so bad he would appear in public with 'Slave' written on his face. He said at the time, 'I believe record contracts are just like slavery', which I think was code for 'Know what you're signing and negotiate the best deal possible in your best interest where you can or you're screwed…'

360 deals and non-record revenue ★ This is a crucial thing to look out for these days with record deals. Record labels are often now asking for a piece of every pie of revenue from an artist – touring, merchandise, publishing – and this is known as a '360 deal'.

Before you even consider doing a 360 deal you need to know what the label is prepared to do to earn their share of every pie. For example, if they want part of your touring revenue will they provide funding/tour support? Or with publishing, will they be providing publisher services, find your songs homes, securing syncs in film/TV? It's important to remember that if you're giving a share of the pie from all these extra revenue sources to your record label plus paying your management commissions, it may leave you with not much revenue after, so weigh up the pros and cons of this type of deal and always do what is in your best interest.

Key-man provision ★ Something to make sure an artist bakes into a record deal is a 'key-man' clause just in case the A&R (artist & repertoire) who signed you then suddenly leaves the label or is fired (which is happening more often than not these days). A key-man clause means you can leave the label as well and can sign a new record deal elsewhere instead of being what they call 'shelved', where an artist's music is prevented from release because they lost the one A&R who was fighting for them or was their only contact/supporter at the label.

Advances ★ Just like with a publishing deal a label will give an artist an advance payment against future royalties. This is usually paid when the artist signs the record agreement. And the same principle applies here as the publishing advance. It must be recouped before you receive another advance or profits. Always make sure your record deal advance is recoupable not repayable (that would be personal debt which we never want to see in deals).

Recording costs ★ When you hear of an artist getting a 'million-pound' record deal, people often think the artist has won the lottery and received a cheque for one million pounds to spend on whatever they like, but that's actually not the case. Advances are part of the recording fund. There is a recording budget for making the music, for the recording costs, and then any surplus goes into the pocket of the artist. The full recording fund is recoupable. It's important that management only commission on the personal advance, which is what's left over after the recording budget has been agreed.

Recouping a record deal ★ You'll often hear about how hard it can be to recoup a record deal. Some artists can go years and might still not have recouped what the record label spent on recording and marketing costs. And often when artists sign a record deal they don't always understand how it all works, but it's really important to know before entering a record deal all the ins and outs about it so you and your management/lawyer can negotiate the best deal possible and be across what costs are recoupable and non-recoupable. In major label deals the label gives you a personal advance payment and also has a recording and marketing budget so they can pay for your videos, social media teams, flights, producers, recording studios, photoshoots, etc. You name it they pay for it, but when you start releasing music all the money they've spent needs to be recouped first before you will make any money. And this is where it can get confusing. In a lot of major label deals they recoup at the rate of the deal. Meaning that if they spend 1 million dollars on you, when the money starts coming in every dollar is split at the rate of the deal, so they take their 70 cents on every dollar (70%) and your 30 cents (30%) on every dollar made goes towards the recoupment of that 1 million dollars that they spent. So the record label is earning revenue straight away plus getting the advance/recording costs paid off, but you as the artist don't receive any revenue until that 1 million dollars is totally paid off, and they can also keep spending, so they keep upping the expenses. So it can take a long time based on 30% of the money earned going towards the recoupment, and that's how artists can end up stuck, trapped and unrecouped. Back in the 1990s, when you'd see artists arriving at events in limousines or flying first class or in private jets that's all costs that the record label was paying for that needed to be recouped first before the bands would make any money, and often those artists would expect big pay cheques after their breakthrough hits and get a harsh dose of reality when they ended up with zero royalties when the money came in.

THE GOLDEN RECORD DEAL

Legendary record label executive and manager Chris Anokute has had a long successful career as an A&R. He found the song 'Pon de Replay' and got it to Rihanna, securing her first worldwide hit, and he was hugely important in Katy Perry's success, developing and being her A&R from her very first breakthrough album, and he continues to work with her to this day. He also managed Muni Long and was instrumental in the big breakthrough of her Grammy-winning song 'Hrs & Hrs', securing her a golden record deal, which he talks about here:

> *Stay independent as long as you can so you can basically write your own deal, and that deal should be where you have ownership and where you have a reversion on the license so you're doing an exclusive license with the record company and the rights revert back to you after ten to twelve years max. I also wouldn't do any more than a 70/30 split. With you, the artist, having at least 70%, preferably 80%, and the label having max 30%, preferably 20%, cos you want to give the label some skin in the game. I also want every dollar off the top, so if the record label spends 1 million dollars we're sharing that expense. So, if we make 10 million dollars that 1 million dollars that the label spent comes right off the top and of the 9-million-dollar profit it's 70% (6.3 million) to you as the artist and 30% (2.7 million) to the label, with no distribution fees.* **Chris Anokute**

Record deals have lots in them, make sure to hire a great music lawyer to negotiate the best deal possible for you and be very clear on all the points and terms so that you fully know what you are signing.

Record labels can be amazing vehicles to propel your music career to new heights, with substantial investment put into your music to help get your music seen and heard. But make sure you implement 'get-out' clauses in your deal to give you the flexibility to get out of it if it's not going well or goes downhill. You don't want to get shelved or trapped in a bad deal and neither does your music.

MANAGEMENT CONTRACTS

Okay, so we've talked about publishing and record deals, let's move on to another important contract which is a management contract. I've been with managers who don't do contracts because they believe in what they can do for you. They also believe it is a partnership, and if that partnership isn't working anymore for either party both manager and songwriter should have the flexibility to part ways amicably and honour the work that was done together but not have you stuck in a contract or partnership that isn't working.

On the other side, there are managers who have very airtight contracts and want everything on paper signed, sealed, delivered. My advice is, where you can, don't sign a management contract, or at least do a long trial with a manager before you do sign one, because once it's signed it can be hard to get out of. In the event that one is offered to you I'd like to talk you through the important points to look out for, negotiate and/or avoid.

There are three critical things in management agreements:

★ The term
★ The commission rate
★ Sunset clause

Let's break them down:

The term
This can be a fixed term with or without options. Most management deals will be a period of three years and no more than five years. Some management agreements include option periods similar to in a publishing deal but these options will depend on certain milestones being reached. Those milestones may be getting you a record deal, a publishing deal, a certain amount of money being earned, etc. and there should always be the option of terminating the agreement if the manager is not achieving various goals. Sometimes the contracts will be linked to an album cycle instead of a fixed number of years. Make sure you have flexibility to get out of the deal if it's not going well – do not get stuck with a bad manager.

The commission rate
A standard commission rate for management is 20%, which will be taken from your *gross* income. It's important to also note what aspects of your career your management will commission. Usually, a manager comes on board to manage your entire career, so that's every and any aspect of your brand. It's always good to make sure that if they are commissioning it, they are doing work to help each aspect of your career grow. Or you can try to carve out certain aspects of your career you want them to manage and ultimately commission.

For commissioning live shows, managers should typically take their commission on the net receipts. Gigs and touring can be costly for new artists and sometimes even generate a loss, and if you have an agreement to pay commission to a manager from the gross income of a tour you may end up having to pay out of your own pocket with money you do not have. Always make sure from a live gig and touring perspective that the commission to management is on the net receipts.

Non-commissionable
Any advances tied to recording costs, video costs, third-party producer advances or royalties, tour support should not be commissioned by management.

Sunset clause
This is a crucial part of the deal because it is the provision in place for when the deal ends. During the term, your management receives 20% commission of the royalties coming in from your songs. But because songs continue to generate royalties past the term, the 'sunset clause' is a gradual reduction of the management percentage. For example, when the contract is up, the 20% commission rate can be reduced to 10–15% the year after the contract has been terminated and then reduced again to 5–10% the second year and then

reduced to 0% the third year. This can be done at varying rates and varying lengths of time, but the principle is the same. The rate keeps reducing and eventually the commissions stop.

SONG DEALS

Now we've broken down publishing deals, record deals and managements contracts, but another very important deal in music is the song deal. This is basically a deal for the first mechanical usage of the song (so a song can be released into the world).

Say you've been in writing sessions for months, your songs are being pitched to find a home and you get what's called a '**bite**' on a song where effectively a label and/or artist wants to '**cut**' your song, which means recording it with a view to release the song. Or you've been in the room with an artist who loves the song you wrote together and the label want to release that song. Now is when the creatives of a song do a deal on that song with the label/artist.

It's very important as a songwriter/producer that you understand the song deal terms and that you negotiate what you feel is fair for what you contributed. Song deals used to be quite straightforward. Two writers in the room 50/50 split on a song... done. Now they can be very complicated and get quite messy because more and more people get publishing on songs and sometimes people who didn't even write the song get publishing... which is a whole other issue.

There are two main things to talk about with a song deal, the publishing and the master, and things are changing in this sphere so it's important to understand what was and what is now happening. Let's talk about the main points in a song deal.

The main three things in a song deal are:

★ **Song splits**
★ **Fees**
★ **Master points**

Now, let's break each of these down:

Song splits

The very first thing to agree on in a song deal and of utmost importance is the song splits. Remember, there are two sides of revenue for a song. The publishing side and the master side. The first thing to be agreed upon before a song is released is how much of the publishing you each receive. There is no legal amount you must all get.

The creative process varies, and songs are written in a lot of different ways so I'm going to give you a bunch of creative scenarios that happen in songwriting and how it would usually be split. Personally, I've spent my career always doing song splits in the fairest way possible. I believe in fairness, taking the split that is fairest to what I contributed to the song. So, this is my personal guide to how I would split the publishing in different scenarios.

SCENARIO 1: STARTING FROM SCRATCH

You're in a room with four people, a producer and three topliners, and you write a song. You start the song completely from scratch, all bouncing off each other, someone's coming up with chords, others coming with melodies and lyrics and it's a full team effort, a creative game of songwriting ping-pong, tennis, football, and before you know it, it's the end of the day and you have a great song recorded ready to find a home. In this scenario I would always do equal splits between everyone in the room. Therefore, it would be 25% each.

You go in with just you and another writer or you and another producer, you start a song from scratch together 50/50 split easy peasy. Starting from scratch basically for me means everyone is equal in the splits. And this is why when starting a song from scratch there should be no one else in the room, only the creatives who are all contributing. If someone is sitting mute in the corner and says nothing and does nothing, well, they don't get an equal split. This is why I don't like anyone in the room who is just a fly on the wall.

It's also important to remember that often in songwriting rooms, just how the song was written in terms of who came up with what lyric, what melody, etc. can vary in the minds of the creatives. Sometimes we all have a different memory of who came up with what and sometimes someone may have said the idea five minutes before, no one acknowledged it and then someone else may say it again five minutes later and it'll go in the song.

The origin of the ideas can come from anyone in the room at any time, writers can influence each other, guide each other to the winning idea, and that's why it is such a collaborative effort. Someone can start a melody that inspires me to sing the next piece of the melody or sing their melody and tweak it slightly and then that's the melody, so that's why there's no point when you start a song from scratch trying to negotiate the splits on the basis of, 'I wrote more lines then you', or 'I came up with all those melodies' or going tit for tat on exactly who did what. It all depends what role you're playing that day, but the song wouldn't be the same without all the players in the room that day. Always keep that in mind.

SCENARIO 2: ADDITIONAL WRITERS/ARTISTS ON A SONG

Now let's say after the song is written a label loves it and wants their artist to release it. That artist may want to rewrite the verses or change lyrics or tweak melodies to the song to make it more 'them', or they may bring in another writer(s) to do these changes and therefore they would then be part of the songwriting. But how much should they get? Well, it depends on how much of the song they change.

Chorus is king, so significant changes to the chorus can actually mean more publishing. In this scenario you look at how much they contributed, and go from there. For me, there have been times work has been done on a song and I'm asked to come in after the fact and be the song doctor and give my thoughts and make changes, or write a new verse, or write a new bridge, tweak the chorus etc. The absolute maximum. I would expect publishing-wise for a verse or a bridge of a song is a 12% song split. I would never expect equal publishing unless I re-wrote a new chorus plus made significant changes to the song as a whole. I would look at the piece I've contributed and take what is fair.

I think ultimate respect needs to be shown to the original writers on a song because without their original work that gets added to or tweaked, the song would not exist, and the added contribution would not exist, and that's important to remember. There is an unfair saying in this industry, 'change a word, get a third', and for me, I just would not feel right taking too much publishing away from writers who contributed more than me, and I feel good karma will come for you if you always approach song splits fairly. Greed might get you far in the short term, but you'll get a reputation, and it'll be a lonely road on the way down. No one is always writing hits, so treat your creative peers how you would want to be treated and sleep better at night.

Ali Tamposi and Andrew Watt

Andrew (Watt) had the business sensibility. And he just really took care of our songs. And he handled it all and transformed everything. He made 'Let Me Love You' happen because we had written that chorus. And we had verses to this folk song and DJ Snake heard it and had apparently said 'I'm gonna send these verses to every single songwriter in LA. So everyone can take a pass.' And Andrew caught wind of that and grabbed the reins. He knew

Justin (Bieber), from the days of him being Cody Simpson's guitar player and Cody Simpson opening up for Justin, he had that relationship, and said 'I'm gonna handle this the way it should be handled' and got the song to Justin and made it happen with us the original writers. **Ali Tamposi**

SCENARIO 3: ARTIST TAXES

The truth is some of the time an artist may not have been a part of the writing process at all, and often depending on how big an artist they are, they will want equal publishing or perhaps even more. This is a tough one because a big artist cut can be life-changing for your career and your bank balance.

Usually in the industry we call this 'Artist taxes', and it's worth noting there are lots of artists in the rooms actually writing their songs, but there are a lot of artists and DJs who don't write their songs and rely heavily on songwriters to write their songs for them, BUT then they want equal publishing.

This never used to be the case. Back in the day artists never got publishing unless they actually wrote the song. That has changed and often you can expect that when a big artist cuts your song, they will take a chunk of the publishing. It's never sat right with me because often the songs that songwriters write can be the reason their tour sells out or their pay packet goes up significantly, but we, as writers, don't get any part of tour revenue or merch revenue, we often have to even buy our own gold/platinum plaques!

Obviously, a songwriter's only form of revenue is the publishing, so it can be disheartening and disappointing to see our piece of the pie whittled down to a smaller percentage than we deserve, but it is just part of the industry. The bigger the songwriter you are, the more leverage you have to negotiate the artist taxes to a fairer place. As a new writer coming up, I would never advise you to lose a cut as it is part of the 'paying your dues' as a writer. We've all had to give publishing away that wasn't fair, but also as the saying goes, 'Having 5% of a hit song is much better than having 100% of a song that's a flop or that stays on your hard drive.' It's case-by-case and it's all about picking your battles in this industry and understanding it's a long game.

Try not to let it get you down, and know publishing splits aren't always the fairest, but a hit song can really change your life and sometimes the lower publishing split can be worth it in the long run because the more hits you have the bigger the rooms with the bigger artists you'll get in with.

SCENARIO 4: A SONG ALREADY WRITTEN

Now, what about the scenario where you write a song by yourself in your bedroom but you need it produced? So, you bring the song into a room fully written and you sit down and play it to a producer and the producer loves it and produces the music. Here's where it's important to remember what is **song composition** and what is **production**.

If you've written the melodies, lyrics and chords, the producer is not a writer on the song, he/she is the producer so you would keep 100% of the publishing and the producer would be paid their usual production fee plus they get points on the master for production. However, if the producer or another writer in the room changes chords, adds chords, tweaks melodies, adds lyrics, they then also become writers on the song. You will still have the lion's share of the publishing but you need to give some publishing to whoever else contributed to the song, whatever is fairest for their contribution.

I've done this many times and sometimes I even write full songs in my head but I don't always have the chords yet. I can hear the chords in my head and sometimes I'll do some, but I also like hearing where a producer/musician would take it. In that scenario, where a producer writes chords to my topline I would give them a publishing percentage. That will vary based on the scenario: if I feel the producer adds in a musical hook, or anything extra that can be sung as part of the composition, etc.

The same goes if I'm in a session and a writer comes in with a full chorus, already written lyrics and melody and we then write the rest of the song around their already written chorus, I would give that writer more publishing than me and vice versa.

SCENARIO 5: A PRE-EXISTING TRACK

Just like a pre-written topline can influence the chords and the music, the same can be said of a pre-existing track. There are times I'm sent backing tracks to write toplines — if it's just me writing to a pre-existing track, I would likely do a 50/50 split. However, each song split scenario is on a case-by-case basis. Be fair, stay true to the creative process and how the song was written.

Every creative process and scenario here is negotiable and valid and as creatives we are always serving the song and trying to write the best song we can that day. Being someone who is fair in song splits will really set you up for a long successful career, someone who has integrity and honesty — it's something I feel all creatives should strive to be. When one of us wins we all win and everyone should win together. Don't be the creative who is just out for him/herself.

FEES

Standard producer deals
A production deal is done with whoever is paying for the master recording of the song, so that is typically the record label, or if the artist is independent, the artist themselves. This is a separate deal to the song splits above which is negotiated with the songwriters of the song. Typically, after the song splits have been decided, the producer's management then liaise with the record label and agree on a production deal for the song. So a standard producer deal on a song is typically:

Production fee
A production fee is an upfront payment for producing the song. This is usually a recoupable fee against the master royalties, and it really varies depending how big a producer is. The bigger the producer, the larger his/her production fee will be.

Master points
What are master points? As I've stated a song is split into the master side and the publishing side and master points refer to the percentage of ownership in the master recording of a song. Each 1 point is equivalent to 1% of the revenue generated. For example, when we talk about an 80/20 record deal that means 80% (80 points) of the master revenue generated goes to the record label and 20% (20 points) of the master revenue goes to the artist. Producers and mix engineers get master points as well, and these usually come out of the artist's share of the master. Typically, producers will receive 3-4% (3-4 points) of master revenue and mix engineers receive 1-2% (1-2 points). As both come out of the artist's share, this brings the artist's points down to 14-15% (14-15 points). All of this is negotiable, and it's often case-by-case.

3–4% PPD* is the baseline for producer master points and they come out of the artist's share of the master.

*What is PPD? This stands for Published Price to Dealer, which means the producer is paid a percentage of the price that the record label sells the song for. This is much more beneficial than a net receipts deal where the producer is paid a percentage of the revenue that is left over after deducting expenses. Always try to do a PPD deal and try to avoid a net receipts deal.

Record one and recouping costs
Producer deals can be negotiated to look all different ways. Some producers may be paid from record one. This means the producer gets paid from the first record sold as soon as they have recouped the advance/upfront producer fee.

So if a producer gets an advance/upfront fee of £10,000 for producing the song, when the song is released that £10,000 has to be made back before the producer receives more revenue. This deal is not easy to get because most record labels will want producers to stand behind the costs of the record before they get paid. So most producer deals will be after the costs of the record are recouped and then the producers royalties will be negotiated on the net rate.

Independent producer deals

If you are an independent artist and doing a deal with a producer usually you will have less budget for their upfront fee. In this scenario, try to negotiate a deal where the producer perhaps gets more master points on the song to make up for the lack of upfront fees.

This means the producer is essentially a partner on the song – if it's successful you all win, they are taking a risk on the song with you. When you get paid they get paid. All the figures here are negotiable, so it's case-by-case but there is a deal that can be done where everyone feels accounted for and is fair.

New industry standard

Song deals usually consisted of the splits being negotiated on a song, and once approved that would be that. Some called this 'industry standard' but it is now the year 2025 and with it has begun a 'new industry standard' and with this new industry standard songwriters are slowly but surely asking and receiving "per diems" song fees and master points on songs being released. Already, we have seen certain record labels agree to a £50-75 per diem for any artist session a songwriter attends. This helps with expenses and is a great first step in the right direction for the career of a songwriter. In the next chapter I break down how songwriters make revenue and so that will explain why song fees and master points are more important than ever for songwriters in the streaming era. But in this chapter, I just want you to know what the new industry standard song deal is.

> *My take on this is there must be a real give, you don't just give your writing credit up because it is a celebrity singing your song, that is a 'no', and if they keep asking that means they really want the song and they will still want the song if you don't give them any writing. It's always a give and take. You should never just surrender your royalties that are yours to someone just because, so never do that, never. Find a trade-off, like trade some publishing for master points. Don't be afraid to ask and negotiate.* **Toby Gad**

Songwriter deals are being done on songs very similarly to a production deal. The fee varies case-by-case, the points vary case-by-case, but we hope to see it being implemented more and more by the industry as it is just the right thing to do.

These deals are completely separate from the song splits, completely separate from the production deals, they are negotiated directly with the record label or indie artist. And they consist of:

A song fee

This fee is an upfront payment for each songwriter once a song is going to be released for the songwriter's work on the song. This means whether the song is a hit or not you have received some payment for your time, skill and work on the song. The fee can and will vary depending on if it's a major label or indie label, new artist or A-list artist. The budgets vary for each project and therefore so will the song fee. It is very important to note that the song fee and points is not a buy-out of your rights. You still retain your publishing split.

Master points

Usually per songwriter a 1%–2% PPD master point on the song along with the song fee. At present this is coming from the artist's share, but we are trying to fight to have it come from the label's share of the master and maybe by the time this book is published we'll have made some progress on that.

A 'hold' fee

When it comes to songs, A&Rs at labels are collecting songs to be future singles, or album tracks, and this can mean release timelines can vary and change. So an artist records your song and the label are excited about it and say 'this will be our next single' or 'this will be the single that comes out with the album' or 'we need to find a feature for this song and then we'll release it.' There are a lot of different scenarios when it comes to song releases, and everything can change in the blink of an eye. This is where the '**hold**' fee comes in.

A 'hold' fee is a small fee that is basically a label or artist committing to a song in the way of 'holding' the song. They pay a fee to the songwriters, meaning their artist is holding the song for potential future release and you therefore don't pitch it out or find any other home for the song in the meantime. Usually a hold period can be anywhere from six months to one year or even as long as two to three years and it's usually case-by-case amount-wise between £1k-£2k per songwriter. What's good about the hold fee is that it at least gives the songwriters some commitment and protection. It means that no matter what, you have received a fee for your work.

If the label down the line decided the landscape of the music has changed or the song no longer fits the artist's trajectory or direction, they will let go of the song and you don't pay them the hold fee back, you keep the hold fee and you can then pitch the song and hopefully find it another home. Usually labels and artists pay a hold fee because they want to release the song so it's really giving you a good indication it will be released.

There are other instances where an artist and label will hold a song and refuse to give you a fee. If you wrote the song at a camp for the artist that the label paid for and covered your costs to be there, they technically own the masters of those songs and will try to hold those songs for as long as they want. This is not a nice scenario for a songwriter because if they don't end up using the song that they've held for two years it means essentially the song is wasted and you got no compensation, but, unfortunately, it's just 'the way it is'. Artists and labels will go on to release songs that will ultimately make them their investment back but a songwriter's investment, time and skill isn't always taken into consideration and this is a hard pill to swallow.

A label or artist can be so very excited about a song, tell you it's a hit, promise you 'oh, this is the big single' and then months or years later after you've been banking on that song for some revenue all of a sudden they just either ghost you or say 'we're now not using this song' and let the song go. For this reason alone, I always try to get a hold fee, and I believe no artist or label should hold a song without a hold fee for more than six months. Of course plans change, directions change, but creatives should be compensated for their work and skill and time.

First Mechanical Usage

The first mechanical usage is the first time a song is mechanically reproduced and distributed. When a songwriter writes a new song they have the exclusive right to decide who will be the first to record and release it. They can either release it themselves or grant a first-use mechanical license to another artist or label/company. This currently is the most leverage a songwriter has, and it can really help when trying to negotiate song fees and/or points for the initial release of the song.

Next, I want to talk about how you get paid as a songwriter, all the different revenue streams, how royalties are paid, how to read your statements and understand them, how to make extra revenue as a creative. So let's get into the next chapter...

CHAPTER 11

HOW DO WE GET PAID? MUSIC ROYALTIES EXPLAINED

"The fact is the system is unfair. Artists and writers are not remunerated properly or equally. They do not get their fair share of the pie. To fix this we need to have transparency and artists should be paid on a license, not a sale. Alongside this, songwriters should be getting a much bigger share as they are delivering the key ingredient. We don't even know what a stream is worth and there's no way you could even find out what a stream is worth, and that's not the basis for a satisfactory relationship."

NILE ROGERS

So we've talked through the deals, now it's vital we talk about how creatives in music actually get paid, where the revenue comes from. What music royalties actually are. Who pays them out and how it all works. How you can make the most of your deals and how you can make more money in this crazy music business where sometimes the money just seems to disappear. Of course you want to trust that your teams will be across all of this, but as someone who has been in the business for 20+ years you would be shocked at how much people can drop the ball. There are a lot of people in high positions in the music industry that do not understand how all of this works and it's time to empower ourselves as creatives and know everything about our business. Most songwriters don't have a clue how songs make money and how to read their statements; it's a huge area in music where a lot of us are uneducated. When I first started out it was never explained to me by anyone how it all worked.

Times are changing though, and it's more important than ever to have a handle on your own business and not just trust that the money will find its way to you. So as boring as this chapter may be to read, I feel it's vital to pass on what I've learned about this in simple, digestible terms and hopefully it'll help you understand how we get paid a lot better and how to get a little more bang for your buck. And if you aren't getting paid you'll know where to look. I also interviewed Helienne Lindvall to make sure we are giving you the most up to date accurate information. Helienne is an award-winning songwriter, musician and the President of the European Composers & Songwriters Alliance. She also chaired the Ivor Novello Awards and is the former Head of Business & Songwriter Relations for the song data management platform Auddly/Session, backed by Max Martin and ABBA's Björn Ulvaeus.

What are royalties?

A royalty is money paid to an asset owner for the right to use that asset. These royalties are generated when copyrighted songs and recordings get licensed and it's the main revenue stream for all music creatives.

What is a copyright?

A copyright is a type of intellectual property. It's the rights held by creatives over their original music. Music royalties are obtained from copyrights by way of a license. No one can legally use these copyrighted works without a license.

Songs have two copyrights:

The Publishing (Composition): The songwriting of the song: lyrics/melody/chords.

Owned by: The songwriters of the song.

The Master (Sound Recording): The actual recording of the song (what the listener hears).

Owned by: The master owner of the song, whoever paid for the recording of the song, i.e., the record label or the artist.

So the royalties generated by the sound recording are known as the **master rights** or recording rights and the composition royalties are known as the **publishing rights**.

And there are different uses of the song that generate the royalties:

Public performance royalties
When the music is played publicly it's known as performance royalty. So radio play, live performances, restaurants, gyms, bars, stadiums, TV and online.

Sync licensing
When the music is licensed for TV shows, movies, advertisements, video games, etc. These are known as sync royalties. These are usually a one-time payment between whoever owns the copyright and the company who want to use the music in this way.

Mechanical physical and mechanical digital – sales and streaming
When the music is sold, physically or digitally in any format, that generates royalties. These are known as reproduction royalties for the master sound recording copyright and mechanical royalties for the publishing composition copyright. Let's use 'Nice to Meet You' as an example.

The song: 'Nice to Meet You' – Niall Horan
Copyright: Master Sound Recording – recording of the song
Synch rights: Film/TV
Reproduction rights: When it's sold or streamed
Performance rights: Radio/Played publicly

Rights-holders of the master recording:
Performer: Niall Horan
Record Label: Capitol Records
Producer/Engineers: Julian Bunetta/Mark 'Spike' Stent

Copyright: Publishing Composition – songwriting of the song
Sync rights: Film/TV
Mechanical rights: When it's sold or streamed
Performance rights: Radio/Played publicly

Rights-holders of the publishing:
Songwriters: Niall Horan, RuthAnne Cunningham, Julian Bunetta, Tobias Jesso Jnr
Publishers: Universal Music Publishing, Reservoir Media Music, Warner Chappell Music, Downtown Music Publishing, Hipgnosis Songs Group

When royalties come in, they are split up and paid out to the rights holders. In the USA, standard mechanical rates are set by a panel of federal judges called the Copyright Royalty Board. In the UK and rest of the world, the streaming rates are negotiated and covered by non-disclosure agreements, so these rates are not public knowledge.

'*You have to remember you are running a business, you have your own business as a songwriter and as a creator, so always check your registrations and be educated so you can be empowered in your business.*' **Helienne Lindvall**

Who pays the royalties?
So now that we know the two different types of copyright and the different avenues of where royalties are generated from let's talk about who pays who and how creatives get paid. It's really important to know where the money comes from and to keep on top of your teams to make sure every avenue of revenue is properly registered for and coming in, so you are getting paid correctly what you are owed.

Who pays for the publishing composition side?
Public performance royalties:
These royalties are licensed and collected by Performance Rights Organisations (PROs). Songwriter's songs are registered with these organisations, and they collect the royalties due whenever a song is played in public, on radio, TV, live venue, streaming and pay these royalties directly to the songwriters. There are PROs all over the world including:

Three main PROs in the USA – **ASCAP, BMI & SESAC**

Main PRO in the UK – **PRS**
Main PRO in Ireland – **IMRO**
Main PRO in Germany – **GEMA**

When you sign to a PRO outside of the USA you will be asked which PRO you would like to collect your US royalties. Look into all the options and choose the best for you.

The PRO pays both the publisher share and the songwriter's share of the performance royalty they collect and it's a 50/50 split, and then the publisher will pay the songwriter their share of the publishing 50%, depending on what your deal split is with your publisher.

So if your publishing deal is a 75/25 split, the publisher would pay the songwriter 75% of their 50% share of the public performance royalties they receive.

For example:

★ Public performance royalties come in – £1,000
★ PRO pays songwriter – £500 (50%)
★ PRO pays publisher – £500 (50%)
★ The songwriter has a 75/25 split with the publisher so the publisher then pays £375 (75%) to the songwriter from the publisher share and publisher keeps £125 (25%)

If you are not signed with a publisher you are entitled to the publisher share and the songwriter share of the performance royalties as a self-published songwriter, so make sure you are registered properly to receive the correct amounts. It can get a bit confusing so read that a few times to really get your head around it.

Helienne said the following when it comes to registering with a PRO: 'Once you are registered with a PRO you will receive an IPI number (Interested Party Identification). This number is the equivalent of a National Insurance number for songwriters and it's important to have your identification numbers on your phone easily accessible because a song can't be registered without this IPI number. So when you do your writing splits and you're registering songs you need to have everyone's IPI numbers. Basically you're not gonna get paid unless you give everybody your IPI number and if you have pseudonyms then they will have a different IPI number but they will all lead back to your core name. Always check your registrations and make sure your songs have been registered correctly. Just because you have a publisher or manager doesn't mean it's been done correctly. I don't know a single songwriter that has not come across discrepancies with registrations.'

Who pays the mechanical physical royalties? Sales

These royalties are collected from the sale of music in physical form: a CD, cassette, vinyl etc. The retailer pays the record label – the label pays the music publisher – the publisher pays the songwriter.

Who pays the mechanical digital royalties? Streams

These royalties are collected from the sale of music in digital download form and interactive streams. Spotify, Apple Music, Amazon, Tidal, Deezer, etc.

The MLC – The Mechanical Licensing Collective administers licenses for streaming and download services. They collect and pay out the songwriters, composers, lyricists and music publishers owed. If you are self-published you can easily register through their website.

So how much are we actually getting paid from streaming? What is our piece of the pie? It's very important to be educated on this and know the breakdowns, especially when it comes to streaming services. These are approximate breakdowns for the simple reason that a lot of record labels have done private negotiations with digital service platforms, so we don't actually, as the creators of the music, even get to know the accurate amounts, but we have approximate numbers based on royalties received. It's also worth noting these amounts can change slightly year to year. I'm going to use approximate numbers to show you what this equates to.

Spotify percentage breakdown

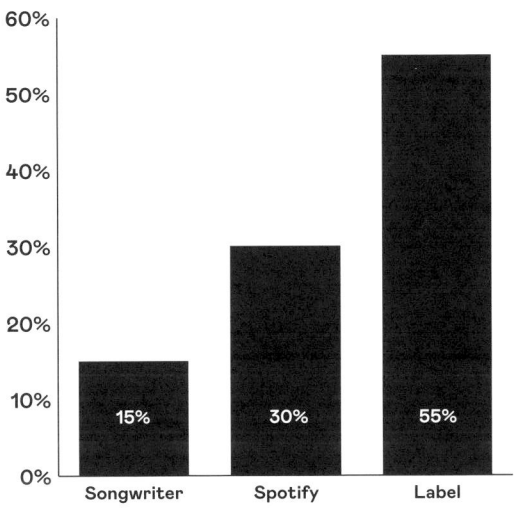

15% goes to songwriters
30% goes to Spotify
55% goes to record labels/master recording owners

1 million streams =
£400 approx. goes to the songwriters to split between them per their split agreements
£4,000 approx. goes to the record label/master owner

10 million streams =
£4,000 approx. to the songwriters and £40,000 approx. to the record label/master owners

100 million streams =
£40,000 approx. to the songwriters and a whopping £400,000 approx. to the record label/master owners

The pay gap is pretty astounding.

The President and CEO of NMPA (the National Music Publishers Association), David Israelite, recently posted the most up-to-date figures in dollars and said, 'The value of songwriters and music publishers from 1 million streams by service. None of these services would exist without songwriters.' He continues to fight hard to protect and advance the interests of music publishers and songwriters in matters relating to the domestic and global protection of music copyrights.

> *NMPA is essential for songwriters.* **Ross Golan**

Upon seeing these figures Steph Jones rightly said, 'This is absolutely, without question, undeniably, by definition… WRONG and this is also why no one should be acting shocked when songwriters ask for a master point. We deserve to have ownership in a song we WROTE.'

This illustration shows us that the copyright, which is made up of the publishers and authors, receives approx. €1.26 of a €9.99 approx. subscription… As you can see here the creators of the song receive the lowest amount… Even the VAT receives more than us, so the government gets more than we do… Pretty insane, right?

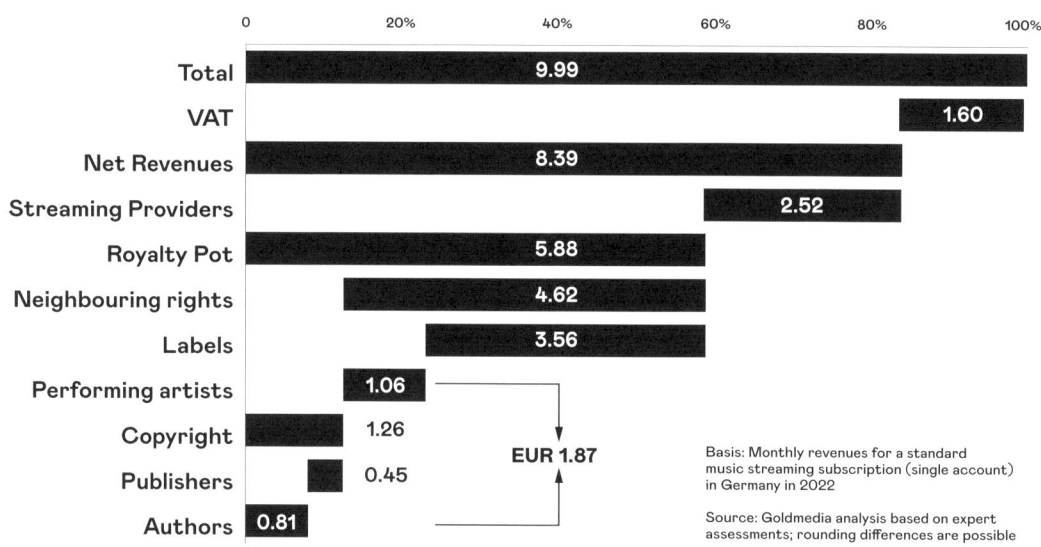

Sync license royalties

These royalties are paid out by advertisers, films and TV shows. Usually a one-off fee that is paid to the publisher, who then pays the songwriter or through direct licensing if self-published. Or you can also be hired as a composer to write original works for broadcast, which is usually paid by the buyer or agency contracting you, for compositions like soundtracks, scores, jingles, etc.

Other royalties paid to the publisher, who then pays the songwriter, are: lyrics display (lyrics displayed online, etc.), ringtones (this counts as a mechanical royalty and is paid to the songwriter directly via their publisher/admin or agencies like Harry Fox Agency), sheet music (your music in sheet music form generates a royalty paid to your publisher/admin and they pay the songwriter).

Okay, we've covered all the avenues of payment for the publishing side of the copyright, now let's talk about the master side of the copyright and who pays the royalties for that.

Who pays for the master sound recording?

Usually it is the record label/recording artist/producer and sound engineer who all have master points on the master recording and get paid these royalties. The record label, or whoever paid for the master recording (self-funded/independent artists, etc.), receives the revenue and pays out the royalties due to whoever participates in the master points (artist, producer, sound engineer). The royalties for the master sound recording copyright are paid out whenever the music is streamed or sold, performed publicly or licensed for film/TV.

Distribution royalties — Also known as reproduction royalties are due when the song is sold physically or digitally and for each use. These royalty rates are negotiated between the rights holders (record labels) and the retailers/service providers.

Digital performance royalties — These royalties are paid out by SoundExchange for Internet Radio such as Sirius XM/Pandora, etc. in the USA, by PPL in the UK, PPI in Ireland, and other societies across Europe.

Digital sales royalties — These royalties are from the sale of a permanent download, paid to the recording artist from the label or distributer (TuneCore, Band Camp, etc.).

Physical retail sale royalties — These royalties are from the sale of CDs, vinyl, cassette and are paid by the retailer to the recording label or third party services like Band Camp, CD Baby, etc., who then pay the master owners.

On-demand streaming — These royalties are paid when music is streamed on digital service platforms like Spotify, Apple Music, etc., and are paid to the label who then pay the master owners.

Sync licenses — This is a one-off fee for use of the master sound recording in film, TV shows, video games, advertisements, etc., paid to the record label or recording artist directly via a direct licensing deal.

Neighbouring rights revenue — The master recording owners are entitled to neighbouring rights revenue whenever your song is played in a foreign territory — radio play, TV or live performances to the public. So anyone who has a percentage of the master copyright, the artists and performers who have contributed to the recording. You have to make sure you are registered for the societies who collect this revenue. In the UK it's PPL, in Ireland it's PPI and there are 97 other current societies worldwide. If you register for your local society just check that they will be able to collect for you internationally.

In the USA neighbouring rights are currently called **digital performance royalties** for internet radio such as Sirius XM/Pandora, etc. This is the only neighbouring right generated in the US by law and it doesn't treat neighbouring rights the way the rest of the world does. This is currently under review and likely to change in the future. SoundExchange is the society in the USA that collects these royalties known as non-interactive royalties (satellite and digital radio), so make sure you are registered for SoundExchange for USA digital performance royalties.

USA-based songwriters and artists can still receive neighbouring rights royalties for any foreign performances of their songs outside of the USA so should still be registered with a neighbouring rights society to collect for them in Europe (e.g. PPL UK).

Songwriters, producers and musicians who are also the featured performers of the song are entitled to up to 50% artist performer royalties shared with the contracted feature performer, other featured performer and non-featured performer. This is another great revenue stream to keep in mind, so make sure it is contracted and registered properly.

Make sure you are registered correctly for all the societies that collect royalties because as you can see there are so many avenues of revenue to be collected for a song, so keep on top of it because it's very easy in the music industry to not be paid properly and for royalty money to be sitting there uncollected.

Whether you are a published or self-published creative always make sure you are registered with a **PRO – ASCAP, BMI, SESAC, PRS, IMRO, GEMA for performance royalties.**

And make sure you are registered with: **SoundExchange (USA), PPL (UK), PPI (Ireland) and/or your local society for neighbouring rights royalties.** (If you are registered for PPL in the UK they will collect from SoundExchange for you, so you wouldn't need to be registered for both.)

What is PPL? (Phonographic Performance Limited) – PPL is the UK's music licensing company that collects and distributes royalties for performers on a song (musicians, vocalists etc.) and recording rights holders (record labels, indie artists) whenever the song is used in public like on radio, TV, nightclubs, gyms etc. They collect the fees from those broadcasters and venues and pay the royalties to the performers and rights holders.

In Ireland, it is **PPI (Phonographic Performance Ireland)** and **RAAP (Recorded Artists**

Actors Performers Limited). Make sure you register for both.

Featured artist — Performed on the song and are credited as a primary artist.

These are lead singers, main instrumentalists, DJ/producers, if credited as artists and performed on the track.

Non featured artist — Performed on the song but are not named as a primary artist.

These include backing vocalists, string players, keyboardists, guitarists, drummers, orchestral players, choirs, programmers — anyone who contributed audible parts to the recorded performance.

Register — It's very important to register with PPL/PPI or the equivalent in your own country if you contribute to songs as a performer in any capacity.

Check your credits — When it comes to all of this stuff, PRS/ASCAP/BMI, PPL/PPI, SoundExchange, firstly, make sure you're registered and secondly, make sure that your credits are correct and if they are not, ensure you take the steps to fix the credits as soon as you can. All of these companies are the sources of revenue for creatives and every income stream is important to receive. You can make a performance claim stating your role and contribution and once it's approved by the rights holders you will receive royalties for your performance on a song.

Most performers miss out on these royalties because they never claim their tracks even if the label registered them correctly, so make sure you always make a performance claim. There is also the chance that the label/indie artist doesn't register the credits correctly and mistakes are made, so make sure you stay on top of checking your credits.

Self-published songwriters

If you are self-published there are also great options for you to make sure your royalties are being collected by way of a publishing administrator. There are several publishing administrators all over the world and Helienne had this to say about them: 'With publishing administrators like Sentric, Songtrust, etc. you can register your songs with them and you can do it on a song-by-song basis. They take a small admin deduction, and you receive no advance. What's great about this is if you get offered a publishing deal at whatever time you can take those songs back and include them in your publishing deal once you've given the administrators notice. So they collect your royalties for you, but they don't own your rights, they don't retain your rights, they just administer.'

Helienne also adds the most important piece of advice for self-published songwriters is: 'Make sure you are registered with MCPS in the UK or the MLC in the USA. You can only be with one of those. MCPS will collect from the MLC for you. A lot of writers assume that you are automatically registered with these societies, and in some Europeans countries like France you are, but not in the UK.'

If you are a USA self-published songwriter make sure you also register for: the MLC – Mechanical Licensing Collective. If you are a UK/Irish self-published songwriter make sure you also register for: MCPS – the Mechanical Copyright Protection Society.

Useful websites:

ASCAP
https://www.ascap.com/

BMI
https://www.bmi.com/

IMRO
https://imro.ie/

MCPS
https://mpaonline.org.uk

MLC
https://www.themlc.com/

PPI
https://www.ppimusic.ie/

PPL
https://www.ppluk.com/

PRS
https://www.prsformusic.com

SOUND EXCHANGE
https://www.soundexchange.com/

INTERLUDE 5

SONGWRITER STORIES

"The best songs come out of honesty. Write what you feel, not what you think will sell."

CAROLE KING

To conclude our songwriter stories we have a legendary songwriter/producer who I have collaborated with many times throughout my career, who told me the stories behind his biggest hit songs. The Grammy award-winning Toby Gad, who has written some absolutely HUGE global worldwide hits from the biggest artists in the world, his songs have amassed over 15 billion streams and these songs are certain to last the test of time.

Toby Gad and Fergie

'BIG GIRLS DON'T CRY' – FERGIE
Written by: Stacy Ferguson, Toby Gad
Produced by: Will.i.am, Ron Fair

I travelled to Los Angeles for a session and Jim Vellutato, who had worked at Sony, he connected me with Fergie, who at the time had just left a band she was in called White Orchid. And Fergie came in the studio in tears and I was wondering, why are you crying? And she said she just broke up with her long-distance boyfriend, whom she still loved a lot. And I suggested maybe write him a goodbye letter, maybe that will help us to get a song together. Then a few minutes later she hands me this piece of paper and I read it and it says 'the smell of your skin still lingers on me now you're probably on your flight back to your hometown, fairy tales don't always have a happy ending do they?' I got the chills and I brought my guitar out and thought wow, this is incredible, that should be the first verse, so then for the chorus I suggested some melodies and the words were just pouring out of her like 'I hope you know that this is nothing to do with you I have to figure myself out' and so on. And then for the end of that chorus I always have these notepads where I just write down hooks and titles and I had written down 'Big Girls Don't Cry' and I thought wow, this really might be a great bookend for this chorus. And then I went to the room next door and started putting a little track together with the guitar and a little drum beat. And then Fergie came in the room and had written the second verse.

And we laid that down and I had put down a few chord ideas for the bridge. And on this song, I mean, the words were just pouring out of her. It was so autobiographical for Fergie. So it was written really fast. Then that song just sat on the shelves for many, many years. I think it was 2002 when we wrote this song. And then Fergie joined the Black Eyed Peas and did two or three albums with them until finally it was her turn to do her solo album. And that song was almost not going to go on her album. Even a week before her album dropped, I was frantically scouring the internet for the track listing, and it wasn't on there and I was panicking. Eventually that song was on there, but it wasn't her first, second or third single. It was her fourth single of the album. And then it turned out to be her biggest song ever. It was the song that put me on the map. So from that point on, America knew me by a song which changed everything. I actually thought it was a nice song. I never thought it was a hit. But I recorded it with an artist on Columbia Records who then got dropped. And then eventually Fergie claimed the song back. And luckily... Thank God! **Toby Gad**

'IF I WERE A BOY' – BEYONCÉ
Written by: Toby Gad, BC Jean
Produced by: Toby Gad, Beyoncé

After 'Big Girls Don't Cry' was the song of the year and I felt now the world knows me by a song, I thought I really, really want to work with Beyoncé, and so I had meetings with her management, with her publishers, with her label, and played them all my latest songs and did that again and again. It took six months until I finally got the call that Beyoncé also wants to work with me. And then she booked me for six days at Jay-Z's studio in New York. I sat there in the studio waiting for her the first day, she didn't show up, and second day she didn't show up and third day she briefly came in and played me a few of the songs she had done and she played me 'Single Ladies' and I was like 'Wow, that's a really good song.' And then the next day she came in and says, 'Now I finally have time to write', so before we started I thought let's play her some songs that haven't been released yet and I played her 'If I Were a Boy', which I had just written with BC Jean, and she jumped up and says, 'I want to sing the song right now.' So I recorded her vocal right there and she was very professional. We did maybe six or seven takes and it was perfect, I mean, she's in great control of her voice. It was really amazing. When we got to the third chorus she asked me if I could suggest some runs or some variations and then I was just imagining all these endless runs she's done at Destiny's Child and I sang her some of those and she was like, 'Yeah, that's perfect.' **Toby Gad**

'If I Were A Boy' went on to become a massive song and then Toby went on to write the biggest song of his career, the grammy-winning, diamond-certified, fifth highest certified single in RIAA history and arguably the biggest wedding song of modern times...

John Legend and Toby Gad

'ALL OF ME' – JOHN LEGEND
Written by: John Legend, Toby Gad
Produced by: John Legend, Dave Tozer

I wanted to work with John for a long time. And my manager at the time was also John's manager. So John knew that I wanted to work with him for years and years but I thought he maybe he perceived me as a pop writer. John's music was very neo-soul, Philadelphia music, so I wasn't a natural fit for him. But after 'Big Girls Don't Cry' was the Song of the Year and after I had the song with Beyoncé ['If I Were a Boy'], John finally got in the room with me. I wrote a few songs with him, but I think 'All of Me' might have been our fifth song. Usually John's perception of chords and music always leans towards neo-soul and not the obvious pop chords, but that day he came in the room and he already had the idea, 'All of me loves all of you'. That was all he had. And he says, 'Toby, that's all I have. I'm not sure what to do next. Let's write this today.' And then I sat at the piano and I thought of my wife and her curves and edges. And so I continued that by 'love your curves and all your edges, perfect imperfections'. And then he went back on the piano and continued 'give my all to you' and so on. That's how we put the pieces together. And we were just trading places on the piano line by line. It went very quick. It was very organic. We had a lot of fun. We were just like two fools in love pouring our hearts out. So the song wasn't his first single. It actually took three years for the song to come out. It was the second single, but I remember like two years after we wrote the song, at a Grammy event Chrissy was running towards me and said, 'Toby, Toby, it's our wedding song. I love the song you guys wrote.' And that was when I felt, okay, the song now really means something to John. It was the second slowest climb in the history of Billboard to No. 1. It took six months to get to No. 1. You know how it goes. We write 180 songs a year and a thousand songs every five years, you have another thousand songs or so and, yeah, so you just keep going, and every day is another two sessions and it just adds up and you kind of forget these songs. But when Chrissy told me that that was their wedding song I felt oh my god, that's maybe a special song. And it came out as the second single and it went into the urban R&B radio chart and it stayed there. I remember it was Christmas and the song was No. 1 for like the third week in the R&B radio chart, but it would not cross over into any other charts. And then the Grammys came and John got to perform the song on the Grammys, and there is this camera angle where he was on a round stage in the middle of the people and the camera captured him looking at Chrissy in the audience while he was singing the song and I think that's what made the song cross over into mainstream radio. People suddenly felt this magic between the two of them. It became my second global No. 1 hit. And I didn't think it was going to be that big. I thought it was just a little love song. I'm still surprised that it's one of the biggest songs ever and it's certified Diamond, which is so hard to get. **Toby Gad**

Toby and I have written together throughout the years and I always love writing with him. We had an unlikely hit together, a song that upon release was a commercial flop but then years later went on to be a multi-platinum-selling hit. We talked together about the writing of the song and how it became a big song.

'LITTLE DO YOU KNOW'
Written by: Toby Gad, RuthAnne, Ali Tamposi, Sierra Deaton
Produced by: Toby Gad

RuthAnne: So, Toby, we had been working on the USA version of The X Factor and the winners were a duo called Alex and Sierra. You were working on the show as one of the music producers and I was one of the vocal coaches. After they won, Julian Bunetta hosted a writing camp for their album and we spent a week writing with them for it. So I had the title 'Little Do You Know' written down, and Sierra had told me a story about her and Alex and what their relationship had gone through in the past and I immediately thought the title was perfect. So I said it to Ali and she started singing the melody with that title. When I said it to her, I said 'Little do you know' meaning that she was still feeling insecure about the relationship. And you got on the keys and started singing the next part and we were going back and forth, and then we had that section, but then we took ages to get the next part, we couldn't figure out where to go. Do you remember that, Toby?

Toby: Yeah, and I remember debating because also on The Beatles 'Yesterday', for instance, the verse is the chorus and the chorus is the bridge. So we didn't know, do we need a chorus or not? And it's like a very strange structure, but it worked. And then we didn't question it, it just felt good. And what was really weird was it obviously came out as their third single and it was out a year too late, when everyone had forgotten who they were. And then some years later some TikTok kid found it and started posting with it and at some point my daughter came to me and was singing it to my wife, and sang 'little do you know'. And my wife said to her, 'Do you know that this is Daddy's song?' And she's like 'No way, this is a TikTok song.'

RuthAnne: That's amazing, Toby, and someone also sent me it cos there was loads of covers done of it as well. And there was a tribute made on YouTube for someone who had passed away and I think the song really started taking off there. And there were so many different versions and none of us even knew the song had picked up, it just all of a sudden picked up massively and now it's two times platinum in America and it's huge on TikTok and has almost a billion streams.

Toby: You know the songs will come out and they could find a whole new audience like five years later, the song never dies, the song is there. That one's just a really good example of people taking the song and embracing it and making it, because it definitely wasn't pushed by the label, it's one of those good examples where it's actually all power to the people. Someone liked it and it went viral because people like it and there are so many beautiful covers of it. And it means a lot to people, which is amazing.

Toby Gad and Sierra Deaton

RuthAnne, Sierra Deaton, Ali Tamposi

CHAPTER 12

THE BEST PIECE OF ADVICE I EVER GOT...

"The best piece of advice I ever got was from Peter Bunetta. He said, 'Take your work seriously but don't take yourself too seriously'. So work really hard but have fun, don't be too cool or don't be too serious, we're not performing brain surgery, we're just sitting around a piano trying to make something that feels good that connects with the heart."

JOHN RYAN

"Don't be an a**hole :)"

STEPH JONES

The best advice I always remind myself of is, Drew from The Chainsmokers, we were just having a chat before he went on stage and he was like, 'You've spent your whole life listening to music and knowing songs that you like and don't like and having taste in developing that, and you have great taste and that's a superpower. So if you can just have confidence in that when you're in a session, remember you're good' – which is so important to remember when you get a session and you're like, 'Oh, should I try that idea or do I even like what's happening.' Your instinct is everything, so just lock into that. Our taste is something we've developed and honed forever and it's such a good thing to remember. **Emily Warren**

In the early years of my career the best piece of advice was, 'It's not who you know it's who you avoid' – because the wrong person can derail your enthusiasm, your career, take advantage of your business. At the beginning it's not about knowing everybody, it's about avoiding the wrong people cos you can get sidetracked, you can develop bad habits. **Julian Bunetta**

As you go on in your career it's about knowing self-distance, distancing yourself from your work so you can judge it the way you judge other people's work. Because we all can put on a song for 10/15 seconds and say 'I don't like this', and for me to learn to have distance from my own music is the only way you can make it better. It's hard in the beginning because your ego and your pride are wrapped up in how good you make something, but now I'm not ashamed to say 'this part sucks' whether I wrote it or you wrote it. It's not about anyone's feelings it's about the song, so I say my opinion and if someone doesn't like it, I can also disagree with them. It's a practice, like meditating every day or exercising every day, you don't have to do it all the time but there need to be moments where you can step back and judge your own work.
Julian Bunetta

You don't have to be the best at everything. Don't beat yourself up for not being the best at writing every type of song. Trends in music change so often and sometimes it might not be your time and other times it will. Just keep concentrating on the things that make you unique and special and don't so get down about not being able to do all things. Play to your strengths and find the thing that makes you uniquely special and zone in on that and your time will come. **Simon Aldred**

Stargate once told me, 'You should always do whatever gets you the best results and don't feel bad about it.' **Autumn Rowe**

To quote John Mayer – 'Don't be afraid to walk like a one-man army in this business.'
Lauren Christy

Tom Vickers my old manager, said something I always pass on to songwriters, he said, 'Look after music and music will look after you' – meaning if you put a lot of time and effort and love into what you do you will be rewarded for it directly. What I've poured into songwriting I've got back. **Lauren Christy**

Take care of you, really take care of yourself and know that your worth is not dependent on your performance in the room that day. **Ali Tamposi**

Nile Rogers once said to me, 'Keep doing what you do. You are the special gift that brings this song to life. Every time you write remember you are the gift' – so now every time I write I have this confidence. **Kamille**

Someone who wasn't in the music industry gave me the best advice... Relationships are really important. Make sure that you're considerate and kind to everyone that you come across because that same receptionist or the runner or the person who works in the post room could end up being the biggest person running the labels. And I just think in general, in life, it's really important just to treat everybody equally. **Jin Jin**

Writing with Carole King was like the craziest masterclass I ever would have wanted to attend, she was very kind, spiky and funny. I learned two big lessons from her, a lesson of demeanour or grace because she definitely knew I was nervous because she was a legend and she knew what a big deal she was. I told her that I was a huge fan of her music and also that my mom was just over the moon about us doing this session, and Carol jokingly said, 'Well, thank you for making me feel old.' She knew I was nervous and she really really put me at ease.

The second thing I learned was she was always ready with another idea. For example, the song we ended up finishing, Semisonic recorded. I had a chorus that needed something and I didn't know what it was. I showed it to Carole – she was at her keyboard, her Casio, 48-key lucky keyboard. I sang her the chorus idea and she said, 'I love this, in reverse, like melodically with chords.' She sang a verse with a pattern in it that was a little bit like 'Closing Time' on the right hand of the piano. She was joking but she goes, 'The kids like this thing these days, don't they' and then she played something that was like 'Closing Time' but she wrote this verse and I was like, 'I don't know I'm not sure it sounds exactly right.' Carole, instead of saying why it was right and telling me that I was mistaken or advocating, she said, 'Okay, how about this' and she played a whole different verse, completely different, and it was great. I was blown away because being in a band and writing with people can be a constant argument about how your idea is better than their idea, it's constant pointless advocating. It was really, really instructive that this living legend was willing to say 'oh, not that, how about this instead' immediately, and the second thing she came up with on the fly as option b was incredibly great. **Dan Wilson**

The best piece of advice I ever got was from Ben from TMS, he said, 'There are 365 days in the year, if one of those days you're in a session and it's not going great, it doesn't matter cos you have 364 other days to write songs. We can just write one line today and it might turn into a hit or it might not and that's okay.' That takes all the pressure away and the great songs might not come every day but there's plenty of days that they will. **Plested**

The luckiest break was the first ever job I got at a music law firm, and that was sort of based on what one of my lecturers at university had said when I was just graduating. It was at the drinks reception and he was asking me, 'Do you know what you are going to go and do?' And I was like, 'You know, I really want to write and produce songs.' I may as well have said I want to go to the moon, you know. But he said, 'Well, what you've got to do is you've got to get yourself in and around the music business somehow. And you're going to have to maybe think innovatively about how you do that and don't be precious and you just need to be around people that can help get you to the next level.' And so that did turn out to be the job I actually ended up getting, which is more by luck than judgement because I kind of thought 'oh, this job's going to be really boring, I'll give it six months and then I'll try and go to a label or something', but actually I couldn't have been anywhere better than that place at that period in time because what you had coming through the door was every publisher, every manager, every producer. **Jon Shave**

Honestly, I don't think I ever asked for any advice. I didn't listen to a lot of people because I've had many of these 'that's never going to happen'. And then it's usually me saying, 'No, this is going to happen, I'm gonna prove you wrong...' **Toby Gad**

I feel like the best advice was the worst advice. And the worst advice was the stuff I had to learn, which became the best advice because I knew not to do it. Right, okay. So, most of the advice I got was really bad. It was like, don't go to that award show, you got to work, you got to do the session, pick the session. When I should have gone to the award show, I should have gone to the World Cup, I should have done all these things. But I was being advised, you got to work every day, you got to hustle, you got to hustle. And it was wrong, it was all wrong. I should have slowed down, but I couldn't understand it. Also, I don't even know if someone had told me if I would have taken it in. And I'll say that too. I wasn't ready to receive it. So it's really hard. And for your readers here, and your audible listeners, what I also hope they understand is even though when you read some of this advice from writers and Ruth and everyone here, you also have to be ready to receive this information. So often, you have to just live and earn your stripes and learn the hard way. But if you are ready to receive it and can learn, then good on you, because you can save yourself a good five, ten years of stress, of heartache. **Autumn Rowe**

My managers always tell me to put blinders on – when horses race they put blinders on them because if they don't they get distracted by the horse next to them and then they're not focusing on racing. They go off course cos they're too distracted. I think the same goes for us when we put blinders on, and we know that it's just about us and our own potential and our own creativity and you don't try to compete with anybody then you end up with the most honest results. **Ilsey Juber**

With Semisonic we experimented with a bunch of different types of music and most of it was pretty joyful and sort of uplifting, or at least kind of rowdy meets hopeful in the face of adversity. But I wrote this one song that was very, very dark and cynical and really ominous and it astounded me, and the band played it amazingly well. It was full of insightful lyrics but it was sort of scary. I played it for a friend of mine and he said, 'Dan, can I be honest?' and I said, 'Sure' and he goes, 'Okay, Dan, so this song is great, it's a dark and cynical and pessimistic song but that's not what we want from you. People who listen to your band don't want to hear you say that, that's not what we need from you, we need something else from you. So you could do this song and release it but it would be more of an ego trip just to prove to us that you could be scary but we don't need to know that about you.' And I was like 'wow'.

So in other words, I could write a bunch of really, really good songs but they may not be the kind of things to share with people because it's got to go with the resonance of me, it has to be connected and resonating with my resonance, and so maybe it was an early way of saying authenticity matters. I like the idea that there's something I have that people would need from me and I'm looking for that. Like 'Closing Time', which was written around the same time, it's loud, it's rowdy but it's optimistic, even though it's kind of melancholy sounding, there's a longing and a uplift and openness about it, and that's what people want from me. **Dan Wilson**

If it feels good keep it, and by that I mean, did it feel good? Did everyone feel good when that happened? Then keep it in the song. Don't try to be devil's advocate to something that's a no-brainer and felt good in the moment, because all it does it plant a seed of doubt in everyone's mind when two seconds ago everyone felt good. **Ed Drewett**

Amateurs copy, professionals steal, and by that I mean music is endless and there's been so many brilliant lyric writers and brilliant melodies, so don't copy, don't imitate, instead emulate, turn it into something new. Don't just take the thing and do the exact same thing. Take it, put it in a blender, flip it around and make something new. **John Ryan**

Really hone in your skills and try to be as good as you can in all areas of songwriting. Honing in on your skills completely so that you can be so sharp. **Ali Tamposi**

A poetry teacher I had in college once said to me, 'There's no such thing as "writer's block", there's only input and output periods, and your brain does a pretty decent job of telling you which one you're in.' I think hearing that so early on helped me because it freed me of a lot of anxiety around creating, and I think it's also a good reminder that to write great songs you need to live your life so you have moments to write about. **Amy Allen**

Don't hold it against people for what they bring to the writing room. It might sound weird but sometimes a writer not saying anything can be far more powerful then what they do say. **Jamie Hartman**

CHAPTER 13

WHAT'S NEXT? 10 STEPS TO SUCCESS

"There are thousands of songs that have never seen the light of day. I was known as the guy who came to New York and outworked everybody. So it's hard work. It doesn't just happen quickly."

TOBY GAD

So you've read this book and you're wondering, 'ok what next?' Whether you're just starting out, have never written a song or have written hundreds of songs but are still that one song away from the hit that'll change your life or maybe you've had hits and want some more, what *is* next?

Here are the next steps that I feel should be taken by any creative in the music industry today who wants to be successful in music and some of this might feel like a refresher as these tips are all over this book, but sometimes us creatives need the bottom line and so here it is…

You wanna have a successful, long career in music…

1. MASTER YOUR CRAFT

Write consistently ★ Do your 10,000 hours, work the songwriting muscle, learn what gets the best out of you and keep honing your skill and sharpening your pen and evolve as a creative.

Study the greats ★ Analyse lyrics, structures, melodies and hooks, be a student of song.

Learn basic music theory and production ★ I'm not saying you must be Beethoven, but having some knowledge and educating yourself on chord progressions, splice, vocal comping, playing some piano or guitar, drum programming, even the basics so you can write a song yourself and record a rough demo can really help your game. It is easier than ever to do this because of online free tutorials and music-making apps. Being as self-sufficient as possible and growing and learning more and more by utilising the tools at your fingertips will really be beneficial to your career in the long term.

2. COLLABORATE WITH OTHERS

Co-write with other creatives ★ The best way to get your music heard is by being out there, networking, finding people to collaborate with, other topliners, producers, artists. It's not only good for your songwriting but also for your mental health to find like-minded people who are going through the same things in the music industry that we all are. Collaboration can bring a whole other perspective to your songs and you can learn so much from other creatives.

Attend writing camps, open mics, online communities/groups ★ It's amazing to write 100% songs in your bedroom and you can still do that but it's no use having songs just sitting on a hard drive or in your head – get out there and get in amongst your peers. Post your music online, perform at open mics, go to music industry open events, talks or masterclasses. Go to writing camps. I've made so many amazing connections and friendships from going to writing camps even with some of the writers who I may not have written in the room with but from hanging at dinner after or breakfast before the camp starts each morning.

Find your people ★ Spend time collaborating and hone in on the people you have the best dynamic and chemistry with that get the best songs out of you, and keep writing with those people. Throughout your career you will have a variety of all sorts of different creatives that you will work with and mix it up! Just always make sure you're having fun and enjoying being with the people you're in writing rooms with because that's where the magic songs come from.

3. BUILD A NETWORK

Move in songwriter-friendly circles. There are cities where the music communities are really thriving like Nashville, London, Berlin, LA, Miami and Atlanta. Find your spot in a place where you can be in those circles and around creatives. Even if you don't live in these places, you can do writing trips or invite others to where you are based and get in and around the creative communities.

Join songwriter organisations like NMPA, Sona, Music Creators Collective, NSAI or The Ivors Academy.

Reach out to indie artists, producers, managers on social media platforms and shoot your shot, you have nothing to lose. If they don't write back it's their loss but if they do, it could be the beginning of a very fruitful life-changing collaboration. Connecting with your community is so important to build your foundations in the industry.

4. EMPOWER YOURSELF WITH KNOWLEDGE ABOUT THE BUSINESS

At present, it is more important than ever to really educate yourself about the business so that you can advocate for yourself and be strategic and smart with deals. Learning even the basics of publishing, copyright and royalties will be a huge asset to you and your business.

Each creative needs to remember that *you are your business* and you need to see yourself as a business no matter how big or small or successful. Empower yourself with the knowledge of the music industry so that you can make the smartest choices and make the most revenue you can. Register with a PRO like ASCAP, BMI, PRS, IMRO, SESAC etc. to ensure royalties are being paid to you.

5. GET PITCHING AND PROMOTING YOURSELF

Whether you're published or not, get pitching! Pitch songs far and wide to independent artists who are looking for new songs: artist managers and A&Rs, sync libraries/music supervisors for TV/film/advert placement.

Use platforms like Submithub Disco, Tracklib or Taxi Music. If you're signed to a publisher, have monthly or bi-monthly meetings to find out who needs songs and make folders of songs for artists who are looking so that your publisher can pitch on your behalf. If you're in with artists, play them songs or ideas and always have a main folder with your strongest songs ready for any moment.

Treat yourself like a business, not just a creative. Share your songs, your process, your story on social media. Even if you're not a performer and you're a lyricist or beat maker, find interesting ways to share your creativity. Build a simple website or electronic press kit (EPK) with your strongest song demos, a bio and contact info.

6. USE THE TOOLS TO YOUR ADVANTAGE

Back in the day, they recorded sounds onto tape, and it was a very lengthy process. There was no auto-tune, so singers and musicians had to record until they got it right. Nowadays, creating a track and recording vocals is a much faster process and that doesn't mean it's any less quality. Technology has advanced and is still advancing and it's good to lean in and use the tools and resources around you to create and have fun with it.

I always tell people that any sound can be a song; a foot stamp, a bottle opening, the sound of jiggling car keys, a certain synth patch on an old keyboard, digital sounds and all the plug-ins you can use to manipulate sounds and make something sound completely different, unique and fresh. Now is the time to lean in and use those tools. Splice is probably the most popular one and it really is a fantastic tool for every creative.

The future of AI ★ We of course must address the big elephant in the room. The truth is, AI tools are already here and a lot of songwriters and producers are already using tools like Suno, MuseNet, Chat GPT, LyricStudio, not to replace us as creatives but to inspire or assist. However, it's important that we are protected as creatives and compensated fairly, and that the use of AI is ethical and not infringing on copyright and intellectual property. I personally don't see a world where AI will ever replace the human experience, the human creation of music. Nor will it replace the human voice or the human emotion.

Is AI a threat to the music business? I think it depends on how it's used, who controls it, how the industry adapts to it and if the right boundaries and protections are put in place for creatives. Some companies are already using AI to create background music, stock music, and this could reduce demand for human written works in certain areas like ads, jingles etc. AI models trained on existing music may generate melodies and lyrics that are too close to a copyrighted work, blurring the line around originality and ownership. If music made by AI starts saturating the music market it could dilute the value and depth of songwriting done by real people and it could influence new up-and-coming writers trying to establish their name in a saturated AI market and create less opportunities. For now, I would use the AI tools ethically where you can but remember that it can never replace your own originality, emotion, storytelling and imperfection.

I think Rick Rubin summed it up perfectly,

> *If the AI has reason, then it won't be able to do what the human can do because we're not reasonable. All the breakthroughs come from what's not reasonable or what's not supposed to work. It's figuring out the thing that can't be done and allowing it to be done. The AI can't invent flight before the Wright brothers, it can only regurgitate what the Wright brothers did, and we do that not by knowing more, but by believing in something that can't be, it's something in magic that leap forward motion always.* **Rick Rubin**

7. THE 'NO' DOESN'T MEAN 'NO'

Music is subjective, I think one of the best things to remember in the music industry is that the word 'No' does not mean 'not good enough'. There are countless stories out there of label execs who said 'no' or passed on a song for their artist or said, 'that's not a hit' and then that song went on to become a big hit with another artist. Jon Bellion said the following, and as one of the biggest songwriters in the world right now it's really amazing advice:

> *The 'no' doesn't mean 'no'. Whoever needs to hear that, apply it to every aspect of songwriting. I hear 'no' 500 times a week. But that one 'yes' is very 'yes'. That one 'yes' is all you need. You hit the lottery. If you get a hit record it can change your life. People told me so many songs I played for them weren't good enough and then those songs ended up being big hits with big artists. And I knew when I made them, I had goosebumps.*

> *Anyone saying 'no', it's just not the plan right now. It does not mean 'not good enough'. It just means the timing didn't work out. For any songwriter just take this nugget: When someone says 'no' or passes in an email, it's not the right time. And that's okay. Keep going. They may not be right.* **Jon Bellion**

As creatives, we are sensitive, we pour our heart and soul into these songs and it can be hard and deflating to hear the word 'no' but just trust your own instincts. If you believe in the song, don't give up on it even if it's five years later. Keep it in your back pocket and with the right timing and the right artist who knows what could happen.

8. BREAK AN ARTIST

We talked about making your room the A-list room and I really wanna drill that in. So you might not be able to get in the room with Beyoncé or Dua Lipa yet ... but always keep in mind you could find and write with the next Beyoncé, the next Billie Eilish, or the next Ed Sheeran and that can be even more powerful and life changing and once you break an artist, watch ALL the big artists come your way knocking on your door. Don't count anybody out, write with the emerging talent, not just the big names. Search out breaking talent and bet on a new artist that you believe in. It can be a longer road but if you are part of writing songs that break artists, you really are showing the strength of your songs.

> *I was a big songwriter, I worked with Beyoncé, Rihanna, I worked with Miley Cyrus but it was Lizzo who changed my life. When Lizzo and I got together to write she wasn't 'Lizzo' (a big artist) yet. And it was 'in a minute imma need a sentimental man or woman to pump me up' ('About Damn Time') and that song took us from there to all the way up there. So do I need a Rihanna to take my song to number 1 or is my song so good it can take a 'Jane Doe' to number 1, and those are two different things.* **Theron Thomas**

9. HAVE GOALS AND CELEBRATE THE WINS

It's important to set goals — they can be long-term goals or short-term goals, and celebrate all the wins no matter how small or big along the way. From getting a writing session in the diary to a song of yours cut by an artist, to getting a sync placement, to getting your first number 1 or number 10 or a song in the top 40 or hot 100.

10. ALWAYS GO BACK TO YOUR 'WHY'

The music industry is tough. It's not easy for anyone, there is no such thing as overnight success and no one is always at the top all the time. It's a rollercoaster ride and there will be highs and lows and everything in between. Stay consistent and patient and when it gets tough, always go back to why you started in the first place. Go back to your passion. The making of the music will always be the purest part, the business will put you through your paces so remember to breathe and stay in it to win it. Most people who are successful in the business just did not give up and kept going with sheer determination, work ethic and perseverance.

CHAPTER 14

INSPIRATIONAL QUOTES

"You can never attribute success to one thing, it's a million little decisions that are made."

JULIAN BUNETTA

"It only takes one song to change your life – at 37 years old I wrote 'Thinking Out Loud' and it changed my life."

AMY WADGE

"You can't break into this industry by waiting for the door to open. Sometimes you have to build your own door."

DOLLY PARTON

"Being in the music industry is like surfing, you don't control the ocean. You just learn to ride the waves."

RICK RUBIN

I think songwriting is the ultimate form of being able to make anything that happens in your life productive. **Taylor Swift**

The only way you don't win the race is if you stop running, so just don't stop running. You might fall over a bit, you might get a few injuries, but if you just keep running then there's a real good chance you'll get somewhere, you'll get on the podium. For me it's been brutal, it's been all of the things, but in some ways it got too late to give up. I don't know how to do anything else so I've always just shifted and gone, 'Okay this bit hasn't worked, I'm gonna try this instead' and just by doing that and not giving up I got to the podium. **Amy Wadge**

Success in music is part talent, part timing, and a whole lot of persistence. **Quincy Jones**

If you quit then you really have no chance. If you're in the game, something's gonna happen, anybody can have a moment at any time. All it takes is one little spark, a moment of inspiration, and you never know who's gonna do it or where it's going to come from. It just falls out of the sky, you just kind of grab it, but if you quit, that's it. I've never wanted to quit, I don't think I could do anything else. **John Ryan**

You have to love it, it has to be your passion and you have to be able to do it without getting paid for the first however many years, and if you come out of the other end of that and you still love it, then this is for you. **Plested**

The reason I haven't stopped is because I just love it more than anything. The reason why I didn't stop when those doubts came in, is because I love to do it, so whether I've had years when I haven't had a lot of success and I've had years of 'where am I going?', I still get to do it, I get to wake up and sit in the room with friends and do what I love to do most. **Julian Bunetta**

A great songwriter is a person who has the guts to take the human experience and vocalise it and they're not afraid to share their emotions and their experiences. **Lauren Christy**

No idea is stupid, because they will all lead to something, and there is a connectivity that occurs. You know, in two years from now you could be in a session and you're going to go 'Oh, I have that lick from that song that I didn't use but I can put it in here now.' **John Shanks**

The music industry is a rollercoaster and there are highs and lows but in those lows it's about going further into your passion, into your craft. During those years of not having hits or people just aren't calling or answering the phone, in those moments I just tell myself that the very thing that made me have the success to start with is loving and focusing on your craft and finding new ways to be inspired. So instead of trying to go up against gravity just go deeper into what you love to do and get better at it and find new ways to be inspired. Then eventually you'll see a pinhole of light and you get yourself out of that low. **John Ryan**

I'm on my own path and if it's not working out on that path I just go in a different direction. **Lauren Christy**

My songs have never been trendy. They have always been just very personal. And so if they eventually resonate, then hopefully they become timeless. **Toby Gad**

It's peaks and valley, and ultimately, you're never gonna stay on top forever. And if you do this long enough, and you're good at it and you've practised enough and built your name up to a certain point you're never gonna stay on the bottom forever. The only way you stay on the bottom is if you give up. I just have to remember why I got into it and that I would be writing songs whether or not I was in it commercially or professionally. **Ilsey Juber**

Knowledge and Experience are my teammates. **Lauren Christy**

There is always time to write the best song you've ever written. **Amy Wadge**

Songs can be arrows through time if they come from the right place. They can fly higher and farther, last longer, hit harder. They can pierce the hardest armour of the human heart. **Bono**

It's most important to have something that lasts. **Toby Gad**

Sometimes you get it in your head that you know better and that is usually the most damaging thing you can bring to a room. You don't know better, you never know what's gonna happen, you don't know how the artist is feeling or what they're thinking about, so sometimes it's really important to take your ego, kick it out the door and just sit there and listen to what someone wants to do as an artist for their artistry because as a writer you serve the song and you serve the artist and I really learned that working with Celeste and trusting her vision. So always honour the song but also honour the artist who has the vision for their record because they're the ones who potentially have to sing these songs for the next 50 years. **Jamie Hartman**

The more honest you are in your writing, the more you believe it, then maybe other people will. Everybody just wants to be understood and everybody wants to be seen, and when you tell people how you're really feeling in a song people connect to that. **Ilsey Juber**

Not everything is going to reach the finish line, and some ideas are not good enough. But if you have a very strong feeling about something, it's worth trying really hard. **Toby Gad**

Stay as connected to the process as possible. **Ali Tamposi**

That's how I know that I've written a good song for myself – when I start crying. **Adele**

If you write great songs with meaning and emotion they will last forever because songs are the key to everything. Songs will outlast the artist and they will go on forever if they are good. **Elton John**

Stay true to yourself. People will come and go, but your authenticity will keep you grounded. **Taylor Swift**

GLOSSARY

"Music is art, but the music business is just that —
a business and you have to learn how
to protect your art inside it."

ALICIA KEYS

A&R (Artist and Repertoire): The person at the label who scouts talent and oversees music development. The A&R is the creative bridge between an artist and the record label.

Advance: Money given upfront by a label or publisher, paid back through royalties.

A cut: When a song you wrote is recorded by an artist.

Bridge: A musical passage that connects two sections of a song.

Chorus: The section of a song that is often repeated and embodies the overall lyrical message.

Comping a vocal: The process of selecting the best takes from multiple vocal recordings and combining them into a single vocal performance.

Copyright ©: Legal protection for your original music.

DAW – Digital audio workstation (Logic X, ProTools, Ableton, Cubase etc.): The software used to record, produce, edit, mix and master music or audio on a computer.

Demo: A rough recording of a song idea.

Drum bus chain: A series of audio effects applied to a single channel that all the individual drum tracks (kick, snare, hi-hat etc.) are routed to.

DSP: Digital service provider: These are online platforms where music is streamed, downloaded or sold. Examples: Spotify, Apple music, Amazon Music, YouTube etc.

EP (Extended play): This is a mini album significantly shorter than a full length album, usually between 3-6 songs.

Interpolation: Incorporates elements from a pre-existing song into a new composition, by re-recording.

LP (Long play): This is a full length album, usually 10-12 songs, total duration 40 minutes or longer.

Master points: The % of ownership in the master recording of a song.

Master recording: The recorded version of the song. Whoever owns the master owns the recording which is often the label or the artist.

Mechanical royalties: Earned from sales or streams of a song.

Middle 8: A section in a song that normally occurs around the middle of the song, and usually 8 bars long.

MIDI: short for Musical Instrument Digital Interface, is a digital language that allows electronic musical instruments, computers, and other devices to communicate with one another.

Mixing: Balancing and adjusting tracks into a cohesive song.

Mastering: Giving the final polish and loudness adjustment for distribution.

Music producer: Oversees the creation of a song or record, has the vision for the track, creating the track, arranging the track, directing the recording process and shaping the final sound.

Performance royalties: Earned from public plays (radio, live shows, streaming, TV).

Pitch song: A song that is written to pitch to other artists and/or artists teams (management/record label) for them to potentially record and release as part of their album, EP or as a single. Record labels will often send briefs to publishers and managers of what artists are looking for. Sometimes a pitch song is recorded by a few different artists and they can potentially pass on a song that ends up becoming huge with another act.

Plagiarism: Presenting other people's work as your own.

PPD: Published price to dealer

PRO – Performance rights organisation: (ASCAP, BMI, SESAC, PRS, IMRO, GEMA etc.): They collect and pay royalties to songwriters, composers and publishers when their music is publicly performed on radio, TV, streaming services, live performances and background music.

Recoupment: The proceeds of recovering an advance from the artists/songwriters future earnings.

Sample: A portion of a sound recording that is reused in another recording.

Song identifiers: Unique codes assigned to songs and recording that help music industry systems track, credit and pay the right people. It's the digital footprints for your music.

    IRSC – international standard recording code: this identifies the specific recording of a song.

    ISWC – International standard musical work code: This identifies the underlying song or composition, not the recording.

    IPI – Interested parties information number: A unique number assigned to songwriters and publishers.

    UPC – Universal Product code: The barcode used for an album or single release used by digital distributors and shops.

Song splits: The percentage of royalties each songwriter is entitled to of the song they've written.

Topliner: A songwriter who creates the melody and lyrics of a song.

Verse: Usually comes before the chorus, and is the story part of the song.

Writing camp: A collaborative event where multiple songwriters, producers and artists. come together usually on location to create songs typically for a specific artist or project.

Writing session: A songwriting session where songwriters and producers meet up in a studio and create new music

7 Rings
Words and Music by Richard Rodgers, Oscar Hammerstein II, Taylor Parks, Ariana Grande, Kimberley Krysiuk, Victoria McCants, Njomza Vitia, Thomas Brown, Charles Anderson and Michael Foster
© 2018 Warner Tamerlane Publishing Corp, BMG Platinum Songs US, BMG Gold Songs, Kobalt Music Copyrights Sarl, Universal Music Corp, Grandarimusic and Williamson Music Company
Warner Chappell North America Ltd, BMG Rights Management (UK) Ltd, Kobalt Music Publishing Ltd, Universal/MCA Music Ltd and Williamson Music Company
All Rights Reserved.
[This song contains a sample from "My Favourite Things" by Rodgers and Hammerstein © Williamson Music Company]

My Favourite Things
Lyrics by Oscar Hammerstein II
Music by Richard Rodgers
© 1959 Richard Rodgers and Oscar Hammerstein II
WILLIAMSON MUSIC owner of publication and allied rights throughout the world
All Rights Reserved.

Pastime Paradise
Words and Music by Stevie Wonder
© 1976 Black Bull Music/Jobete Music (UK) Ltd
EMI Music/Jobete Music
All Rights Reserved.

Gangsta's Paradise
Words and Music by Artis Ivey, Lawrence Sanders, Doug Rasheed and Stevie Wonder
© 1995 WC Music Corp, Boo Daddy Publishing, Large Variety Music, Madcastle Muzic, Universal Songs of PolyGram International Inc, Universal Music International Ltd, Black Bull Music Inc and Jobete Music Co Inc
Warner Chappell North America Ltd, Universal Music Publishing Ltd and EMI Music/Jobete Music
All Rights Reserved.
[This song contains a sample of "Pastime Paradise" by Wonder © Black Bull Music Inc & Jobete Music Co Inc]

Alibi
Words and Music by Douglas Rasheed, Artis Ivey, RuthAnne Cunningham, Ella Henderson, Stevie Wonder, John Morgan, William Lansley, Olivia Sebastianelli, Maegan Cottone and Larry Sanders
© 2024 Universal Songs of PolyGram International Inc, Madcastle Muzic, WC Music Corp, Boo Daddy Publishing, Reservoir 416, Sony Music Publishing (UK) Ltd, Black Bull Music Inc, Jobete Music Co Inc, B-Unique Music, Reservoir Media Music, Phrased Differently Music Ltd and Large Variety Music
Warner Chappell North America Ltd, EMI Music/Jobete Music, Kobalt Music Publishing Limited, Universal Music Publishing Ltd, EMI Music Publishing Ltd, Sony Music Publishing (UK) Ltd, Budde Music UK, Reservoir Media Management (UK) Ltd and Reservoir Media Management Inc
All Rights Reserved.
[This song contains a sample of "Gangsta's Paradise" by Ivey, Sanders, Rasheed and Wonder © WC Music Corp, Boo Daddy Publishing, Large Variety Music, Madcastle Muzic, Universal Songs of PolyGram International Inc, Universal Music International Ltd, Black Bull Music Inc & Jobete Music Co Inc]

As It Was
Words and Music by Harry Styles, Tyler Johnson and Thomas Hull
© 2022 HSA Publishing Limited, Universal Music Publishing Ltd and These Are Pulse Songs
Concord Music Publishing and
Universal Music Publishing Ltd
All Rights Reserved.

Big Yellow Taxi
Words and Music by Joni Mitchell
© 1970 Crazy Crow Music
Reservoir Media Management Inc
All Rights Reserved.

Bittersweet Symphony
Words by Richard Ashcroft
Music by Mick Jagger and Keith Richards
© 1997 ABKCO Music Inc
ABKCO Music Ltd
[This song contains a sample from "The Last Time" by Jagger/Richards © ABKCO Music Inc]
All Rights Reserved.

drivers license
Words and Music by Olivia Rodrigo and Daniel Nigro
© 2021 Sony/ATV Tunes LLC
Sony/ATV Music Publishing (UK) Ltd
All Rights Reserved.

Espresso
Words and Music by Amy Allen, Julian C Bunetta, Sabrina Carpenter and Stephanie Jones
© 2024 WC Music Corp, Songs of Universal Inc, Dragon Bunny, Music of Big Family, Sabalicious Songs and Smells Like Good Music
Warner Chappell North America Ltd, Peermusic (UK) Ltd, Universal/MCA Music Ltd and Reservoir Media Management Inc
All Rights Reserved.

Flowers
Words and Music by Miley Cyrus, Michael Pollack and Gregory Hein
© 2022 What Key Do You Want It In Music, Songs With A Pure Tone, Warner Tamerlane Publishing Co, These Are Pulse Songs, Wide Eyed Global, Songs By Gregory Hein, Concord Copyrights, Suga Bear Recordz Publishing and Sony/ATV Songs LLC
Warner Chappell North America Ltd, Concord Music Publishing and Sony/ATV Music Publishing (UK) Ltd
All Rights Reserved.

I Want It That Way
Words and Music by Martin Sandberg and Andreas Carlsson
© 1999 MXM Music AB and Maratone AB, Sweden
Kobalt Music Publishing Ltd
All Rights Reserved.

I Won't Back Down
Words and Music by Jeff Lynne and Tom Petty
© 1989 Gone Gator Music and EMI April Music Inc
Warner Chappell North America Ltd and EMI Music Publishing Ltd
All Rights Reserved.

Stay With Me
Words and Music by Jeff Lynne, Samuel Smith, James Napier, William Phillips and Tom Petty
© 2014 EMI April Music Inc, Sony/ATV Music Publishing LLC, Stellar Songs Ltd, Salli Isaak Music Publishing Ltd, Method Paperwork Ltd, Gone Gator Music, Wixen Music Publishing Inc and Naughty Words Limited
EMI Music Publishing Ltd, Universal Music Publishing Ltd, Wixen Music UK Ltd and Sony/ATV Music Publishing (UK) Ltd
All Rights Reserved.
[This song contains an interpolation of "I Won't Back Down" by Lynne/Petty © EMI April Music Inc and Gone Gator Music]

I'm Good (Blue)
Words and Music by Blete Rexha, David Guetta, Camille Purcell, Philip Plested, Maurizio Lobina, Massimo Gabutti and Gianfranco Randone
© 2022 Kiss Me If You Can, BMG Platinum Songs US, JackBack Publishing Ltd, Sony/ATV Allegro and Sony/ATV Music Publishing (UK) Ltd
Sony/ATV Allegro, BMG Rights Management (UK) Ltd, Sony/ATV Music Publishing (UK) Ltd, JackBack Publishing Ltd and Copyright Control
All Rights Reserved.

In The Name of Love
Words and Music by Martijn Garritsen, Chris Braide, Karen Poole, RuthAnne Cunningham, Stephen Philbin, Matthew Radosevich and Ilsey Juber
© 2016 Pulse Music Publishing, Universal Music Publishing BV and Sony/ATV Sounds LLC
BMG Rights Management (UK) Ltd, Universal Music Publishing Ltd and Sony/ATV Music Publishing (UK) Ltd
All Rights Reserved.

Levitating
Words and Music by Dua Lipa, Sarah Hudson, Clarence Coffee and Stephen Kozmeniuk
© 2020 Italians Do It Better, EMI Music Publishing Ltd, Tap Music Publishing Ltd and Prescription Songs
Warner Chappell Music Ltd, Warner Chappell North America Ltd, Kobalt Music Publishing Ltd and EMI Music Publishing Ltd
All Rights Reserved.

Ocean Eyes
Words and Music by Finneas O'Connell
© 2017 Last Frontier
Kobalt Music Publishing Limited
All Rights Reserved.

Paper Planes
Words and Music by Thomas Pentz, Joe Strummer, Topper Headon, Mick Jones, Mathangi Arulpragasm and Paul Simonon
© 2007 HiFi Music IP Issuer, L.P., Hifi Asset Acquisition Co Lp, I Like Turtles Music, Nineden Ltd and Zomba Music Publishers Ltd
Universal Music Publishing Ltd, Concord Copyrights and Copyright Control
All Rights Reserved.
[This song contains a sample from "Straight To Hell" by Strummer, Jones, Headon and Simonon © Nineden Ltd]

Rapper's Delight
Words and Music by Bernard Edwards and Nile Rodgers
© 1979 Bernard's Other Music and Sony/ATV Songs LLC
Warner Chappell North America Ltd and Sony/ATV Music Publishing (UK) Ltd
All Rights Reserved.
[This song contains a sample from "Good Times" by Rodgers & Edwards © Bernard's Other Music and Sony/ATV Songs LLC]

The Vow
Words and Music by Iyiola Babalola, Darren Lewis and RuthAnne Cunningham
© 2025 These Are Pulse Songs, The Family Pulse and Seeker From The Speaker Music
Concord Music Publishing and Downtown Music UK Limited
All Rights Reserved.

I firstly want to thank my incredible Management team, Caroline Trout and Matt Johnson from Redlight Management. When I mentioned I wanted to do a book, you just went a made it happen and I could not be more grateful for all the work and time you guys have put into this project alongside me, you are the best partners I could ask for. And to my whole team doing so much work behind the scenes, my publishers Reservoir, Donna, Russell, Jeremy, Amber, Ruth, Elspeth, Sabrina, Absolute, Jodie, Pippa and Emma, Joe, Laura and Jack. A special thanks to Lucy and the amazing team at Faber Music Publishing for believing in me, seeing my vision for this book and partnering with me to make this dream a reality. Lucy, you have been incredible to work with and I've learned so much from you and because of you I get to add Author to my repertoire. To all the amazing songwriters, producers, collaborators and friends who I interviewed for this book, for your time, your wisdom, stories and insights which were so invaluable, I love you all. Your contribution to the music we all love all around the world is so important and appreciated. To my husband Ollie who really took on the lion-share of most of the stuff in our house so I could write this book, thank you, I love you!! Thank you for believing in me and supporting me in every dream and being the best teammate I could ever ask for. Everything I do is for my two little girls Lily-Mae & Monroe, I hope one day you can both read this book and be proud of your Mama. To my Mummis and Papa Bear and sisters for all your support and encouragement over the years, you passed on your pure love of music to me and I would be nothing without you. To all my besties, my friends, my loved ones, you know who you are, thank you for being my sounding board through this process and thank you for being there for me all throughout my roller-coaster of a career. You are more than friends, you are family. To any and every creative who reads this book I really hope it helps, inspires and empowers you, and generations to come.

RuthAnne

Copyright © RuthAnne Cunningham, 2025
The right of RuthAnne Cunningham to be identified as the author of this work has been asserted in accordance with Section 77 of the Copyright, Designs and Patents Act, 1988.

Book design by Dominic Brookman
Edited by Lucy Holliday

© 2025 by Faber Music Ltd.
First published in 2025 by Faber Music Ltd.
Brownlow Yard
12 Roger Street
London WC1N 2JU

Printed and bound in Turkey by Imago
All rights reserved.

ISBN 10: 0-571-54319-7
EAN 13: 978-0-571-54319-9

Reproducing this book in any form is illegal and forbidden by the Copyright, Designs and Patents Act, 1988

To buy Faber Music publications or to find out about the full range of titles available please contact your local retailer or Faber Music sales enquiries:

Faber Music Limited, Burnt Mill, Elizabeth Way, Harlow, CM20 2HX, England
Tel: +44 (0) 1279 82 89 82
fabermusic.com